LAND REFORM AND DEVELOPMENT
IN THE MIDDLE EAST

LAND REFORM
AND DEVELOPMENT
IN THE MIDDLE EAST

A Study of Egypt, Syria, and Iraq

BY

DOREEN WARRINER

Second Edition

Issued under the auspices of the
Royal Institute of International Affairs

OXFORD UNIVERSITY PRESS

LONDON   NEW YORK   KARACHI

1962

Oxford University Press, Amen House, London E.C.4

GLASGOW NEW YORK TORONTO MELBOURNE WELLINGTON
BOMBAY CALCUTTA MADRAS KARACHI LAHORE DACCA
CAPE TOWN SALISBURY NAIROBI IBADAN ACCRA
KUALA LUMPUR HONG KONG

First edition 1957
Second edition 1962

PRINTED IN GREAT BRITAIN

CONTENTS

v

CONTENTS

TABLES

MAPS

PREFACE TO THE FIRST EDITION

IT was my intention to prepare a second edition of *Land and Poverty in the Middle East*, published in 1948 and long out of print. This, after I had visited the region again, seemed impossible.

The poverty is not out of date. But the original research and field work needed to establish its extent today could not be undertaken without much time and a knowledge of Arabic. The statistical material is much fuller than it was, and there is more monographic study, but these investigations do not as a rule get down to the bedrock of the rural standard of living.

Moreover, the perspective has changed. There has been development, far more than seemed possible ten years ago. Then it seemed necessary to justify the belief that poverty was a matter which should concern the Arab countries and the West. Today such justification is no longer needed. It now seems more important to stress the dynamics of change, as they affect the poor, rather than to study underdevelopment as a static condition, the only approach to the region which seemed possible in 1947.

The present study supplements the old, and carries its arguments a step farther by reviewing the results of the agrarian reform measures so far undertaken, and the relation of reform to development in the three countries where these are crucial questions. Except in a few short passages, nothing from the earlier book has been used, but I have taken the opportunity to correct mistakes in it, so far as I could ascertain where they lay. Throughout this book I have tried to emphasize what is uncertain, and hope that this may be useful to other students of the subject.

Thanks to a grant made by the Royal Institute of International Affairs, I was able to visit Syria and Iraq in the spring and winter of 1955, and Egypt early in 1956. An invitation to lecture in Cairo from the National Bank of Egypt enabled me to visit Egypt earlier in 1955.

PREFACE

My time was short. I used it to travel to see the new things in Dujaila, Tahrir, and the Jezira, and the old things changing in Amara and Upper Egypt. The accounts of these places are as full as I could make them in the time; though very incomplete, they may be useful to those who can undertake systematic studies.

During these visits, I had much help from many people, among them old friends, that speciality of the region. I cannot thank all who gave me help and hospitality, but would wish to express my sincere gratitude to those who enabled me to visit estates, villages, slums, and settlements, and whose views I have quoted and used freely. In Iraq, I must thank Mrs Bedia Afnan, Mr Hassan Mohammed Ali, Mr Abdul Jabbar Chelabi, Professor and Mrs Michael Critchley, Mr Haider al-Daif, Mayor of Amara, Professor A. A. Duri, Dr K. G. Fenelon, Mr Mohammed Hadeed, Dr Salih Haider, Mr Abdul al-Jawad of Mosul, Dr Jasim Khalaf, Professor and Mrs James Langley, Dr Salah al-Nahi, Mr Hassan Salman, Dr M. J. Ubousi, and Mr Mohyiddin Yusif. Mr K. Haseeb, at present of the London School of Economics, helped me very much by obtaining and interpreting statistics and documents. To Dr S. M. Salim, recently of University College, London, and now lecturer in anthropology at the Baghdad College of Arts and Sciences, I am greatly indebted for advice and guidance, and for his insight into the life of village communities.

In Syria, I must thank Mr George Faris, director of the Bureau des Documentations Syriennes et Arabes, Dr Jamil Mualla, Director-General of the Ministry of Agriculture, Mr Ahmed el-Kassem, Director of Rural Education, Mr Jacob Hannous of Kamishli, and Dr Amin Sharif. With Paul and Elizabeth Benson Booz, then of the American University of Beirut, I travelled through the Jezira to Mosul and Baghdad, and with Cecil Hourani and Yusif Ibish, also of the American University, I visited the Hauran, learning much from them. Professor Himadeh was, as ever, an invaluable adviser.

In Egypt Mr Sayed Marei, now Minister of State for Agrarian Reform, gave me every assistance. Mr Ali Gritli, Mr Nasmi, Mr Shalaby Sarofim and Dr Amin Niazi in Minia, and Mr Mohammed el-Misidy at Armant, gave me much information about the reform and different views of it. Most of all I am grateful to Mr Nikolai Koestner, who once made a revolutionary land reform in Estonia, and is now director of the Research Department of the National Bank of Egypt.

To the Royal Institute of International Affairs, and particularly to Miss Margaret Cleeve, I am indebted for their help in meeting the expenses of my visits to the region, and for steady encouragement at every stage of the work.

July 1956

PREFACE TO THE SECOND EDITION

SINCE the first edition of this book was published there have been fundamental changes in the political situation in Syria and Iraq. On 1 February 1958 Syria united with Egypt to form the United Arab Republic, and reform of the agrarian structure followed soon after the foundation of the new state. In Iraq the revolution of 14 July 1958 was followed by an agrarian reform law in October of the same year. Consequently there is less need to emphasize the necessity of agrarian reform. The important and interesting questions now concern the results of these reforms, and the methods of reform most likely to promote economic development.

Events have however not invalidated the generalizations about the relationship between land reform and economic development in the region, and the main argument concerning the three dynamics of change still holds good.

Egypt's régime has proved stable under attack, and continues to play its constructive role in the region. Naturally in five years the perspective has altered. The 1952 agrarian reform has receded in importance as a social revolutionary measure, though its significance as the act of commitment to a broad policy for the regeneration of rural Egypt has not diminished. Its economic success has provided the mainspring for a new direction in agrarian policy, adapting the system of supervised co-operation to the old co-operative societies. General economic development prospects still centre on the High Dam, now being built with Soviet aid. But that agrarian policy owes nothing to Communism is proved by the new land reform of 1961, representing a renewal of the principles of 1952 through more radical redistribution of property in land. The revolutionary dynamic remains original and genuine.

In Syria the three years' drought revealed the limitations of the private enterprise dynamic and only too drastically confirmed the view that the expansion in dry farming was so precarious that it necessitated stabilization of production through more irrigation and resettlement of farm people. This reorientation was being accomplished in conjunction with the agrarian reform, which together with the Five Year Plan held out the hope of more balanced growth in the future. But the coup of 28 September 1961 ended the reform and the plan as well as the union with Egypt, and so restored the old situation.

In Iraq the old régime was overthrown by a revolution of unforeseeable savagery. So far as can be judged from a distance, its results to date have been mainly negative. The oil revenues contribute less, not more, to the economic and social progress of the country. Agrarian reform policy has followed an uncertain course; at the moment of writing, its administration is in Communist hands. So the social vacuum persists.

Since the interpretation of the situation in early 1956 is still broadly relevant to the present situation, it has seemed advisable, in revising the book for a second edition, to retain the original chapters, with some minor corrections, and to bring them up to date by inserting references to a new chapter. The 'Postscript' on agrarian reform in the United Arab Republic supplements the first three chapters, and also discusses the question of the application of an Egyptian type of reform in a different setting. Material for this chapter was obtained during a visit to the United Arab Republic in January and February 1961, undertaken to prepare a study on land reform and community development in that country as a contribution to a United Nations report.

Unfortunately it has not proved possible to bring the chapter on Iraq up to date in the same way, because it was not practicable to visit the country. Since minor revisions based on secondhand information would be of little value, this chapter has been left unaltered, as an account of the pre-revolutionary situation.

During my recent visit to the United Arab Republic Mr Sayed Marei, then Central Minister of Agriculture and Agrarian Reform, gave me every possible assistance. To him and many others, particularly Mr Mohammed Mahdi in Aswan, Mr El Minchawi in Aleppo, and Mrs Eva Garzouzi in Cairo and Damascus, I am greatly indebted. My acknowledgements are also due to the Social Affairs Department of the United Nations for permission to include material collected while acting as consultant.

October 1961

INTRODUCTION: THE MEANING OF LAND REFORM

POVERTY still exists in the Middle Eastern countries. But its setting has changed. In Egypt there has been a political revolution and an agrarian reform. In Syria the prairie provinces have been opened up by mechanized farming. In Iraq, the poorest and most primitive of the three countries, new capital has been used to build the long needed flood-control and irrigation works on the Tigris and the Euphrates.

These are great changes, each in its way a revolution. They transform the situation of ten years ago, when the economy seemed static and the social structure paralysed. None of them wipe out rural poverty. But agrarian reform, capital, enterprise, and technical change can all contribute towards raising the general standard of living. Because these elements are now present, the abolition of poverty is within the bounds of possibility, as ten years ago it was not.

Each country has undergone a different type of change, with a different dynamic. Syria has deployed its enterprise, and owes the rapid increase in national income over recent years principally to new crops, new machines, and new risk-taking. In Iraq money floods the economic scene, and flows into long-term investment in capital construction. Only in Egypt is the dynamic conscious and purposive, making a direct attack on rural poverty through the redistribution of income.

It is not the purpose of this book to analyse these different mainsprings as if they offered comparable or even rival methods of vanquishing rural poverty. The discussion of the problems of 'underdevelopment'—i.e. of raising the general living standard in poor countries—has advanced beyond the point when any remedy could be advocated in terms of a single 'solution'. Nor is it intended to discuss the merits of political revolution, *laisser-faire*, or engineers' planning in the abstract. On the contrary, a case for each as the highest priority can be made in the context of the conditions of the country concerned. Egypt, already cultivated to capacity, needed agrarian reform most urgently, since redistribution of farm income was the only immediate way of raising the rural standard of living. Syria could not do much to raise rural living standards without raising output per head, and that could be done quickly only by cultivating more land. Without investment on a scale far beyond the rate of internal capital accumulation, Iraq could never have hoped to bring its extraordinarily difficult environment under control.

Now that these first necessities have been met, the priorities change. For Egypt political revolution was the *sine qua non*, and agrarian reform the end of the beginning. With a measure of income redistribution completed, the Government next turned its attention to the task of relieving unemployment and increasing the national income through the construction of the High Dam and through new industrialization. In Syria and Iraq, with increasing national incomes, the question of redistribution of income moves into the foreground, and agrarian reform acquires a new relevance in the changed conditions. A state agricultural policy also becomes more essential; now that the obstacles to expansion of the cultivated area have been removed by mechanization and water control in these two countries, it is time to think of better farming.

The aim of this book is to consider the need for agrarian reform as a means of raising the standard of living, in relation to the economic development of each of these countries. This necessitates a study of the relationships between different sets of conditions: the methods of farming and land use; the distribution of landownership and the legal and customary institutions of land tenure; rural social conditions, and the political forces which work for or against social change. Agrarian reform is not a single-track subject; it represents a point of intersection between economic development and social change, and it can therefore be treated only by taking cross-bearings between these different aspects of the life of each country.

But before turning to the study of the three countries, it seems necessary to relate this main topic to the new international 'climate of opinion' in favour of land reform. In recent years there have been agrarian reforms in many countries, and consequently there has been much discussion, in the United

Nations and elsewhere, of the relation between agrarian reform and the development of underdeveloped countries. There is so much variety in the conditions of 'underdevelopment' that broad general arguments about this relationship easily lose their force. They need more underpinning by investigations into the conditions of different countries. Global talk also tends to confuse issues, though it has its uses, and indeed has had some influence in the Middle Eastern countries which taught the world agriculture at a time when the advanced countries of today were very underdeveloped indeed. By examining the relationship between reform and development in the Middle East region, some light may be thrown on the general relationship, and also on the validity of the new conception of agrarian reform for a part of the world where until recently nothing at all had been done to improve the existing agrarian structure.

One result of the world debate is that there is now some confusion as to what 'land reform' really means. In ordinary usage, the term is generally understood to mean the redistribution of property in land for the benefit of small farmers and agricultural workers. Reforms of this kind may involve actual division of large estates into small holdings, as in Eastern Europe between the wars, or the transfer of ownership of the land from a large property holder to the tenant-cultivators of small holdings, as in many Asian countries. In the first case there is actual division of the land itself, and a change in the scale of farming operations. In the second case there is no change in the scale of farming, since the farm holdings were already small. In both cases the significant change is in the distribution of income; the aim is greater social equality.

In the past, land reforms were purely social in their aims. In Eastern Europe and in Mexico between the wars the peasants got the land only, without the means of working it, in the form of credit, marketing facilities, and technical guidance. Results varied: sometimes production increased, and sometimes it did not.[1]

Now a new conception of reform comes from America, which advocates reform as a comprehensive policy, including not only

---

[1] Some of these results have been reviewed briefly in my lectures *Land Reform and Economic Development*, published by the National Bank of Egypt, 1955.

'opportunity of ownership', but also a variety of other measures to assist farmers by means of greater security of tenure, better credit systems, better marketing facilities, agricultural advisory services and education, and so on. This conception flowered in the course of the cold war, as an answer to Communism. The United States first made advocacy of land reform part of its official foreign policy in 1950, when it supported a Polish resolution in favour of land reform in the General Assembly of the United Nations, and thereby challenged the Communist claim to leadership in the use of land reform as a political warfare weapon.

America's advocacy of reform is, however, much more than a tactical cold war move and has deeper roots. The ideal of the family farm springs from the anti-feudal tradition, and it embodies, by and large, the aims of land policy in the United States.[1] Family farming is regarded as an end in itself, the necessary base for free enterprise and political democracy. The American conception of reform is not merely a simple belief in the homespun values of family farming. Official statements drive home the need for the 'integrated approach', which means creating a framework in which the family farm can flourish, through the organized provision of credit, co-operative marketing, 'extension', and rural services of all kinds. The policy is, in fact, family farming by the Department of Agriculture out of the New Deal.

The essential difference between this new approach and the older and simpler conception is that reform is now regarded as an agricultural policy as well as a social policy. By contrast with the earlier reforms (and with recent Communist reforms) the aim is to give the farmers help, and so accompany the social change with a policy to increase productivity in agriculture.

As a result of this new conception the definition of 'land reform' is now somewhat confused. In their periodic surveys of progress in land reform, the United Nations reports include not only land redistribution, but also farm tenancy and labour legislation; land settlement; co-operation; farm credit; agricultural education and research; the registration of title;

[1] This does not mean that other types of structure, corporation farming for instance, are not important, or that the policy has always been consistent. American authorities do not claim a high degree of consistency. cf. V. W. Johnson and Raleigh Barlowe, *Land Problems and Policies* (New York, McGraw, 1954), p. 7.

4

methods of land taxation; and long-term policies for the control of land use. The use of the term 'land reform' to cover this all-inclusive catalogue represents the American conception, in accordance with the official American definition of land reform as 'the improvement of agricultural economic institutions'.[1] But although the American *conception* is a great advance on the older conception, a *definition* with so wide a connotation distorts the perspective. The redistribution of land, or rights in land, means a major social and political change, while the other measures lead to an improvement in the economic position of farmers and in agricultural production, without a change in their social position. In the following study it would seem inappropriate, for example, to say that Syria has carried out a land reform because it has started a system of agricultural education, or that Iraq has had a reform because large areas of state land have been registered in the name of large landowners.

For the sake of clarity and perspective, it is better to keep to the ordinary usage of the term and use 'land reform' to mean redistribution of land or rights in land. The term 'reform of the agrarian structure' may be used to include measures of this kind, together with other institutional reforms which affect the social structure, such as land settlement, the regulation of tenancy conditions, and labour legislation. Legal changes, such as registration of title, may affect the social structure, but are not, in the following chapters, included within the agrarian reform concept, for reasons which will be clear.

This distinction is not merely a matter of terminology. Particularly in regard to the Arab countries, it is important not to blunt the edge of the policy by widening it too much.

That the new emphasis on farm services is of great value, particularly in the countries of the Fertile Crescent, goes without saying. The international agencies have given it some practical effect; their experts in the field—contrary to the impression sometimes conveyed by their official publications—can really get down to the grass roots. In the following chapters several instances are quoted which show how constructive this influence has been. More important even than the new schools and new research institutes is the prestige which

[1] See UN, Dept. of Economic Affairs, *Progress in Land Reform* (New York, 1954), p. 49.

American influence accords to agriculture as a profession.

Yet so far as land reform itself is concerned, there is a certain danger in this wider conception for the Arab countries, and no doubt in other countries with similar land systems. Because the conception of land reform has broadened to include a variety of measures to improve land tenure and agricultural organization, the emphasis shifts from the foundation to the accessories, and the original—and still essential—aim of greater social and economic equality tends to be obscured. The integrated approach sometimes seems to offer everything except the land. This point has been well made by George Hakim.[1]

As generally used in international discussions, the term 'land reform' has come to refer to a wide gamut of problems of a legal, social, and economic character. This large conception does not give sufficient emphasis to the basic issue of the land tenure system. It was this that was mainly in the minds of those who originally raised the subject of agrarian reform in the United Nations and elsewhere. At the heart of the problem of land reform in underdeveloped countries is the question of who owns the land. This fundamental question has been confused and overshadowed by the attention paid to other factors, such as settlement of legal title to land, agricultural indebtedness, and land taxation, which, though undoubtedly related to the main problem, are not more than manifestations of this, the basic malady of the agrarian structure.[2]

The 'basic malady' in the three Arab countries here considered is the prevalence of institutional monopoly in landownership, linked with a monopolistic supply of capital to agriculture. There is nothing peculiar to Middle Eastern countries in this condition. On the contrary, it is a feature of the land systems of many countries in the three agricultural continents which are now conventionally described as 'underdeveloped'. In the sparsely populated countries of Latin America, landowners' monopoly is an outstanding feature of the latifundia system, in which great estates, worked by semi-serf peons, effectively prevent access to landownership for the farm labourers, keeping wages low and land use extensive. In densely populated Asian countries, large landholdings were generally not centrally managed farms, but were rented in small

[1] Formerly Minister of National Economy, Foreign Affairs, Finance, and Agriculture in Lebanon, now Lebanese Minister in Bonn.

[2] 'Land Tenure Reform', *Middle East Economic Papers*, 1954, Economic Research Institute, American University of Beirut.

holdings, usually through a series of intermediaries, to cultivators who paid high rents and had no security. In such systems, monopoly power is used to exact a high price for the use of land, and a high price for farm credit.

Landlordism in the Arab countries shares these characteristics. The great landholdings of south Iraq resemble the latifundia of Latin America in their broad social and economic effects. Egypt has a mixed system, combining highly organized capitalistic estates with tenancy in small units, on the Asian model. One useful result of the international discussions is that they bring out resemblances in the land systems of countries with very different histories and very different natural conditions.

Where the agrarian structure is a rigid institutional hangover from the past, the need for reform is generally twofold, a social need for a higher income for the cultivator, and an economic need for better farming through more investment and better methods. The general economic argument for reform of the agrarian structure in underdeveloped countries is that the existing land systems accentuate the shortage of capital and prevent investment, because they give rise to incomes which are not used to improve agricultural production or to invest in the land. Large landowners spend conspicuously; or purchase more land; or invest in urban house property (very noticeably in the Arab countries); or lend to impoverished cultivators at high rates of interest.

How far the land systems of Egypt, Syria, and Iraq are or were obstacles to economic development is considered in the following chapters. In all three countries the land system is the cause of social evils, keeping the rural population on a low level of income and status. But as obstacles to development the influence varies, as will be seen.

Obsolete monopolistic land systems can be reformed in various ways: by expropriation and redistribution of large properties; by settlement on new land; by giving tenants special credit facilities to purchase land; by legislation to reduce rents and prevent the eviction of tenants; and by labour legislation. These measures, or a combination of them, may be carried out simultaneously in a general agrarian reform policy, as in Egypt, or one or more of the other measures may be used as alternatives to land reform in the strict sense. The question of whether these other methods are real alternatives to redistribution in Syria and Iraq is considered in Chapters III and IV.

As to the type of agrarian structure which should replace the old, it does not do to be dogmatic, and it is not the object of this study to make recommendations. What can be done depends on what people want, and on what kind of farming is practised. New experiments in these directions are described in the following chapters; they do not provide a general formula. Obviously an elaborate organization suits Egypt, but from the standpoint of what the people want Dujaila,[1] in its own simple way, is just as good.

On this question, it should perhaps be emphasized that there is and can be no ideal standard. Because land reform is internationally discussed in the light of the cold war, the impression is created that there are ideal patterns, and that the choice lies between rival models, the American family farm and the Soviet collective. At the grass-roots level, complete individualism and total collectivism are not realistic alternatives. Most new experiments nowadays aim at some form of group farming organization, as a way of combining the satisfactions of independent farming with the economies of large-scale operation.

Moreover, transplanted into a different context, institutions tend to work differently. The 'integrated approach' to family farming does not necessarily produce family farms. The Italian land reform, for example, is extremely well organized; it is limited to uncultivated land which is reclaimed by the authorities and then settled by selected applicants, who receive ownership after payment of the purchase price in instalments spread over thirty years, during which period they are obliged to farm the land 'co-operatively', i.e. to use machinery and follow a common rotation. Some of the large settlements in the South are in reality, though not in law, extremely well-managed state farms with a degree of collective organization. This is an inevitable result of aiming at efficiency, and does not in the least detract from the social achievements of the reform, even though it does not establish independent farm units. If there are no services supplying credit and advisory experts, and no existing co-operative system, they must be set up specially to serve the new landholders. Where settlement on

[1] See below, pp. 162–9.

reclaimed land is involved, there must be costly large-scale investment as a preliminary. Consequently reforms on the 1950 model tend to be limited in scope, and managerially controlled, quite unlike the chaotic reforms in Mexico and Eastern Europe in the 1920's.

Now land reform has become respectable and fashionable. Efficiency has been won, and something has been lost. The older reforms had one merit: they gave people what they wanted. After a lengthy and expensive international seminar on land reform, 'I am afraid', said an Arab civil servant, 'that they make it all seem too difficult.' In the pomposities of international debate, it would be good if the old authentic note—of Zapata, for instance, or Stambulisky—could sometimes break through, so that it would not seem so difficult as experts like to make it.

Land reform in its initial and crucial stage is emphatically not a question for experts; it cannot be advised into existence, but must be based on an impetus arising within the country. Once that impetus is there, and recognized in a decision to legislate, experts can help in overcoming technical difficulties. The choice of the type of group farming appropriate for the country, as will be seen, is not a simple matter, and the experience of administrators who have themselves carried out reforms can be a useful guide. At this stage the integrated approach is relevant, though it is valid only when the economic sails are filled by a political wind. If there is no real drive for reform, experts can produce expensive little demonstration projects, but they will not be able to achieve any general and genuine improvement in the position of the cultivators.

This is obvious enough, but it needs saying, because there is a slightly morbid confidence in experts in the Arab world, even a belief that lack of experts is an obstacle to reform. Good farming, of course, does need experts and costs money, while bad farming costs the earth. But good laws cost nothing, and need no experts. Fortunately there are in the Arab world today politicians who can speak, and some who can even act, for the fellahin. Even the authentic note can be heard at times. In Egypt the impetus is obviously there; it certainly owes a little to the new 'climate of opinion', and so justifies the talk in the conference rooms in New York and Geneva.

I

THE AGRARIAN REFORM IN EGYPT

THE BACKGROUND

THE present Government of Egypt has ideals but no ideology, as revolutionaries nowadays are expected to have. No single intellectual influence has been predominant. It combines pure nationalists and revolutionaries, held together by Colonel Nasser in a tense union for action. Even at the outset it was not united, except on the issue of land reform.

Class interests do not play much part in its outlook. It is true that the Army Group is of middle-class origin,[1] and that its strong supporters are found in the sons of the farming middle class, well-to-do people with fifty acres in the Delta. Its left-wing adherents describe it as 'our bourgeois revolution'. But though the new régime commands respect from liberal opinion, it also encounters much criticism. Business men and professional people have come to terms, and so has the bureaucracy, without enthusiasm. The society over which the young Government rules is as old and sophisticated at the 'second level' as it was at the top. The bourgeoisie cannot produce an emotional response, even if it acknowledges the need for cutting out the dead wood. The aims of the Egyptian revolution are a long way ahead of middle-class opinion.

Confronted with a Government which seems to fit into no ordinary pattern, Western observers have sought for labels, such as 'Kemalist', which relate it to the past or to modern Europe's political categories. But it is they, and not the Government, who are out of date. The *ad hoc* policy which the Government has followed does not correspond to any dated political 'ism', but it does correspond to the new line of thinking about the economic development of underdeveloped countries, a line to which the United Nations report on *Measures for the Economic*

---

[1] As H. C. Ayrout points out, this class has produced most of Egypt's eminent men (*Fellahs d'Égypte*, 6th ed. (Cairo, Éditions du Sphynx, 1952), p. 47).

Development of Under-Developed Countries first gave international sanction, and which has since been elaborated.[1] This new line starts from a typical situation, or model, of 'underdevelopment', characterized by over-population, underemployment on the land, a low rate of capital accumulation, and an institutional structure inimical to investment. Egypt, on the whole, fits into this pattern, though its agriculture is too advanced to correspond to the usual projection. The rate of population growth exceeds the rate of increase of agricultural production; it has an enormous rural population surplus; and it cannot absorb this surplus, or check the fall in living standards, without public investment on a very large scale. Consequently the policies which fit Egypt's conditions are the policies recommended by the new line of thought: foreign loans for big multipurpose investment schemes, industrialization, and institutional reform, in a mixed economy.

The revolution is original in that it takes the economists' recommendations literally, and insists on their implementation, both on the national and the international level. It makes the new line of thought a line of action. The lack of a doctrinaire ideology has been an advantage, in that it has increased international bargaining power. The empirical approach allows quick decision and action, in the course of which ideas have emerged. 'À force d'y forger, on devient forgeron'.

The aim is to meet Egypt's needs: more equal income distribution, more land, and more industry. These needs are axiomatic, the stock in trade of the economics textbook; and they have long been recognized and discussed. But discussion never produced practical remedies. The problem of the rapid rate of population growth has been discussed by economists for the past thirty years; its gravity has never been denied. Projects for fuller utilization of the Nile waters have long been considered; but they remained under consideration. Land reform has long been recognized as a social necessity; but in thirty years of parliamentary government not one measure was passed for the benefit of the fellahin, on whom Egypt's economy

[1] UN, Dept. of Economic Affairs, *Measures for the Economic Development of Under-Developed Countries* (New York, 1951). Other important works on the same topic are Ragnar Nurkse, *Problems of Capital Formation in Underdeveloped Countries* (Oxford, 1953), J. Arthur Lewis, *Theory of Economic Growth* (London, 1955), and Gunnar Myrdal, *An International Economy* (1956).

depends. On two occasions, in 1945 and 1950, bills were introduced for the limitation of the size of holdings, but both were
overwhelmingly defeated.[1]

Land reform was the issue on which the Army Group decided to take power openly. At the time of the first coup d'état,
in July 1952, the decision to undertake land reform was announced; the main lines of the law had already been prepared.
But the law was not immediately put into force, and the Group
evidently believed that it could be enacted by politicians of the
old style. It is said—and there seems no reason to doubt the
assertion—that the Group then had no intention of taking over
the Government. But in the interval between the first and
second coups d'état, the usual pretexts for delaying action—
the need for research and the danger of haste—were well aired,
and seemed likely to succeed in preventing the reform law from
being enacted. When it became apparent that Ali Mahir, under
the pretext of 'studying the experience of other countries', was
in reality opposing the introduction of the law, the Army
Group evidently decided that the one sure lesson to be learnt
from the experience of other countries was the danger of land
reform on paper. On 7 September 1952 they decided to take
over the Government, and on the following day the Agrarian
Reform Law was put into force.

How and why reform became a central issue for the Army
Group is not self-evident. For reasons of humanity, land reform was needed, but until the Army Group came to power
there was no channel through which the need could be expressed. No political party and no group of intellectuals had
ever advocated land reform, though individuals had done so.
There had never been a fellahin movement, though in the years
since the war there had been outbreaks of violence on some
estates. Discontent was smouldering; but there was no ground-
swell of popular feeling. There was no obvious reason for a
group of young officers to concentrate on this question. An
officers' movement might be expected to devote itself to the
reform of the Army and the strengthening of Egypt's military
power; but it would not be expected to make a social-revolu-

---

[1] Charles Issawi, *Egypt at Mid-Century* (London, RIIA, 1954), p. 135. The 1945
bill proposed a 50-acre maximum, and so was more radical than the present law.

tionary measure a test of its power to enforce its convictions.

The motives behind the reform may be surmised to have been three. One was a sincere desire and determination to carry out reform for humanitarian reasons. The second was a revolutionary aim, to break the power of the old ruling oligarchy, with its roots in the big estates. This was the crucial issue which necessitated a show-down. The third reason was that in 1951–2 land reform was very much in the air internationally. America's advocacy of land reform was said to be a green light, and State Department influence certainly played a part in the preparation of the decree, probably strengthening the revolutionary element in the Group.

As there was no ideology at the start, and no political tradition to appeal to, the decree came out in a curious modern dress, combining the abolition of feudalism with Keynesian economics. The 'abolition of feudalism', the main theme of all official statements, is a more exact description of the reform than at first sight appears. The highly capitalized estates, with their big machinery and heavy expenditure on fertilizers and seed, their qualified managers and accountants, and their wretched tied villages are, in an economic sense, capitalistic in the extreme. Yet socially the term is a clear conception. When an Egyptian economist was asked what he meant by a feudal estate, he replied 'It means that the landowner keeps a private army to defend his house and his person; and that armed men stand guard over the crops'—a definition that could hardly be improved. Whatever the system is called, it ought to be abolished; and the use of the term 'feudal' makes political good sense.

The second aim, as stated in the preamble to the law, was to break the landowners' desire to hold wealth in the form of land, and so induce them to invest in industry. This was a muddled bit of thinking, brought in to satisfy the Minister of Finance, Dr Emery, who had been a member of Ali Mahir's Government, and whose support could be won only if reform seemed likely to stimulate investment. The Minister of Finance believed that this result could be achieved by making the land bonds negotiable, but fortunately this inflationary course has not been followed.

The fact that the law was a measure for the redistribution of income was too crude a truth to be told, and there was no way of expressing it. 'The land for the peasants' was not its meaning. The Mexican watchword of 'restitution' had no historical parallel, and 'bread and books' was too revolutionary also. The 'abolition of feudalism' was the safest approach and, in the political sense, that is what it has accomplished.

So far as its actual provisions are concerned, the redistribution enforced by the law is not apparently a revolutionary measure at all. It affects only about 10 per cent of the land area. It allows landowners to retain 300 acres, which in Egyptian conditions represents an annual net income of £5,000–£6,000 at least. Expropriated owners receive a reasonably high rate of compensation.

Consequently it seems surprising that revolutionary means were needed to carry out so moderate a measure. The shock which the law administered to Egyptian opinion was out of all proportion to the degree of change which it enforced. Violent opposition was expected; it appeared only in the case of Adli Lamlun, the scion of a family whose estates in Upper Egypt had been the scene of disturbances in the past. When the reform was announced Lamlun, with a band of retainers, attacked the prefecture at Maghagha, and was then arrested with some of his supporters, tried, and condemned to penal servitude for life.[1] After this sentence the submission of the landowners was secured, though their hostility is still very great.

The explanation of the paradox is simple. The reform was revolutionary in its political effects. It was a political measure directed against the royal family and a small number of very wealthy landowners. Of the total area to be expropriated, about one-third is the property of the 'Mohammed Ali dynasty', i.e. the King and members of his family. Prince Yusuf Kemal, for instance, held as much as 14,000 acres in one block, in the district of Nag Hamadi, in addition to his lands in other parts of Upper Egypt.

So far as the private landowners were concerned, the greater part of the land now in the course of expropriation was held by fifteen to twenty families, as for example the Badrawi family, with 18,000 acres, and Ahmed Abboud, the millionaire industrialist, who owned large sugar plantations in Upper Egypt. The effect of the reform has been far greater in Upper Egypt

[1] He has since been released.

than in the Delta, because these vast holdings monopolize the narrow valley. It was the expropriation of these very large holdings which was revolutionary, not the taking over of 100 or 200 acres from the landowner with 400 or 500. The intention of the reform was to remove the wealthy families from their dominating position in the life of the country—a position never previously challenged.

What the reform abolished, therefore, was a strong concentration of landed wealth, a citadel that first had to be taken by storm, even if it was later to be bought out in bonds bearing 3 per cent interest. This is the political significance of the reform. In economic terms, its significance is a considerable redistribution of income in favour of the fellahin. The reform is best regarded as a labour policy, in the interests of the tenant-cultivators. The law was intended to achieve a general reform of the agrarian structure, including the redistribution of property (land reform in the strict sense), the reduction of rents, and the raising of agricultural wages. Its primary aim is the redistribution of incomes, not agricultural development.

To see why agrarian reform must aim at raising rural living standards, and cannot aim at increasing employment in agriculture or at increasing agricultural production, it is necessary to look briefly at the economic background, in particular the demographic position.

The Demographic Position

The main feature in this background is the rapid rate of population growth on a small land area already cultivated to capacity, and rigidly limited. The typical conditions of underdevelopment exist in an extreme form: an excessively high density of population; rural underemployment on a large scale; and a rate of population increase which greatly exceeds the rate of increase in agricultural production.

So far as the density of population is concerned, Egypt is among the most densely populated countries in the world.[1] On a cultivated area of 6 million acres it has to support 22 million people, of whom about 8½ million are actively em-

---

[1] For comparable figures of population densities see UN, Dept. of Economic Affairs, *Land Reform; Defects in Agrarian Structure as Obstacles to Economic Development* (New York, 1951), Appendix.

ployed in agriculture and about 16 million dependent on it. Thus each acre of arable land must support $3\frac{1}{2}$ people, and there is only one-third of an acre per head of agricultural population.

The surplus population on the land is now estimated to be 5 million (including dependants), or 30 per cent of the total agricultural population.[1] Though estimates of surplus population are never exact, because there are no exact methods of measurement, it is certain that the surplus is large and that it is increasing.

The rate of population increase now outstrips the rate of increase of agricultural production. For the past fifty years the race between them has been neck and neck, but now the rate of population increase is certainly well in the lead. The land of Egypt is almost rainless, and cultivation depends on irrigation, so that the extension of the area cultivated depends on the expansion of water-storage capacity for the Nile waters provided by the barrages. Since the 1880's there has been a great expansion of the areas cultivated and cropped, through the construction of new irrigation works. But the increase over the last fifty years has not kept pace with population growth, as the following table shows.

TABLE I

Egypt: Expansion of the Cultivated Area in Relation to Population

Year	Cultivated area (million acres)	Crop area (million acres)	Population (millions)
1897	5·1	6·8	9·7
1907	5·4	7·6	11·2
1917	5·3	7·7	12·8
1927	5·5	8·7	14·2
1937	5·3	8·4	15·9
1947	5·8	9·2	19
1949	5·8	9·3	20

(SOURCE: *The Population Problem in Egypt*, p. 11.)

[1] Egypt, Permanent Council of Public Services, Economic Sub-Committee of the National Population Commission, *The Population Problem in Egypt* (Cairo, 1955), p. 22. (Hereafter referred to as *The Population Problem in Egypt*.)

According to these figures, the population doubled between 1897 and 1947, while the cultivated area increased by 14 per cent and the crop area by 37 per cent. There are no figures showing the increase in agricultural production over the whole period, during which yields per acre rose considerably. Between 1924–8 and 1950 the volume of agricultural production rose by 40 per cent, while population in the same period (1927–50) rose by 43 per cent, so that agricultural production barely kept pace. Charles Issawi holds that the volume of production did just keep pace, because he considers that the census figures exaggerate the rate of growth between 1937 and 1947, because the 1937 census underestimated the population, while the 1947 figure was probably inflated, and should be 18 instead of 19 million. This may well be so; the point is that it was a near thing and that the race is not yet over.[1]

During the 1930's the rate of increase of population was

TABLE 2

Population of Egypt

Year		Population (000)	Average annual increase (per cent)	Urban population* as per cent of total
Census of	1882	6,804	—	19
	1897	9,715	2·9	20
	1907	11,287	1·6	19
	1917	12,751	1·4	21
	1927	14,218	1·1	23
	1937	15,933	1·2	25
	1947	19,022	1·9	31
Mid-year estimate for	1948	19,494	2·2	31
	1949	19,888	2·1	31
	1950	20,393	2·5	31
	1951	20,872	2·3	32
	1952	21,473	2·9	32
	1953†	22,062	2·7	32
	1954†	22,651	2·7	32

* Urban comprises the Governorates of Cairo, Alexandria, Canal, Suez, Damietta, and the provincial capitals and district seats.　　　† Preliminary.

(SOURCE: *Statistical Pocket Year-book, 1954.*)

[1] *Egypt at Mid-Century*, pp. 54–5, 61, and 79–80. See 'Postscript', p. 199, for more recent data.

much lower than it had been in the 1890's, as a result of the decline in the birth rate, and the position therefore appeared less serious than it is now. There was, however, some controversy as to the extent by which the birth rate had actually fallen.[1] According to the official figures, the rate of increase during the 1930's was 1·2 per cent. The preceding table gives the official estimates of the rate of population growth for the years 1948–54, and shows that the rate of increase is now 2·7 per cent.

The rate of increase is higher because birth rates have risen slightly, while the death rate has fallen, chiefly as a result of the decrease in the infant mortality rate. The following table shows these changes.

TABLE 3

Egypt: Live Births and Deaths

Year	Births (000)	Crude birth rate per 000	Deaths (000)	Crude death rate per 000
1948	833	43	398	20
1949	831	42	411	21
1950	905	44	389	19
1951	934	45	402	19
1952	969	45	381	18

(SOURCE: *Statistical Pocket Year-book, 1954*, p. 14.)

The infant mortality rate has declined, from 165 per thousand in 1937 to 130 per thousand in 1950. This improvement is a result of better health conditions, and is likely to continue.

According to these figures, the population increased between 1937 and 1952 by 34 per cent, while agricultural production in 1952 was only 11 per cent over the pre-war level. During the war crop yields fell sharply owing to the shortage of fertilizers, but have since recovered. The following table shows the increase.

[1] According to A. E. Crouchley ('A Century of Economic Development in Egypt', *L'Égypte Contemporaine*, February–March 1939), the rate of increase during the 1930's was 1·0 per cent against 3·0 per cent during the 1890's. C. V. Kiser, however, holds that there was little evidence of a decline in the birth rate during the 1930's and considers that the true rate of natural increase was 1·25 per cent in 1937, when the true birth and death rates were 44·8 and 32·4 respectively ('Demographic Position in Egypt', in F. W. Notestein, ed., *Demographic Studies of Selected Areas of Rapid Growth*, New York, Millbank Memorial Fund, 1944).

TABLE 4

Index of Agricultural Production in Egypt[1]

(1935–9 = 100)

1949	109
1950	105
1951	101
1952	111
1953	104
1954	115

(SOURCE: *Statistical Pocket Year-book, 1954*, p. 36.)

Even if the official figures overestimate the rate of population growth, there can be no doubt that it is now faster than the rate of increase of agricultural production. It is therefore quite certain that in the period since the second world war population has outstripped agricultural production.[1]

There has been no new land since the 1930's. Land reclamation was stopped during the war and has only recently been resumed.

The existing land area is used with high efficiency. Agriculturally, Egypt is a pressure-cooker. The Nile valley holds the world's land productivity record; cropping rates are high: as Shakespeare said, the land 'shortly comes to harvest'. On four-fifths of the land (the area perennially irrigated) three crops a year can be harvested, though in fact the average cropping rate is five crops in two years. Yields are high, the cotton yield being the world's highest and the maize yield as high as the United States level, while wheat yields are comparatively low, though they exceed the European average.

The following figures show yields, in comparison with other countries.

TABLE 5

Crop Yields in Egypt and Other Countries

(Average 1948–50: 100 kg. per hectare)

	Cotton	Maize	Wheat
Egypt	5·5	24·9	18·0
U.S.A.	3·2	24·6	11·1
U.K.	—	—	26·8
Europe	1·5	14·3	14·5

(SOURCE: FAO, *Yearbook of Food and Agricultural Statistics*.)

This achievement is not solely the gift of the Nile, though it

[1] See 'Postscript', p. 199, for more recent data.

is the fertility-renewing Nile flood which has given Egypt its 5,000 years of agricultural continuity. The modern economy of Egypt multiplies the fertilizing effect of the Nile by three, through the system of perennial irrigation. Artificial fertilizers are heavily applied, chiefly in the form of nitrates, and maintain the high yields, which fall off sharply when applications diminish, as happened during the war when imports of nitrates were cut down. Capital, skill, and organizing ability have gone into the standardization and improvement of the varieties of cotton. Through the cotton crop the whole economy—and most of the population—is geared to the world market.

The high level of land productivity is accompanied by a very low productivity of labour. Gross and net output per acre are extremely high, while output per man is extremely low. Estimates of the Egyptian national income show that in 1953 the average gross agricultural output per acre amounted to £63, and the average net output per acre (i.e. gross output less estimated inputs of materials) to £45. Net income per head of active agricultural population amounted to £34. This figure does not, however, indicate the income actually received, as rent is not deducted; after deduction of rent net income per head would amount to only £25.[1] The contrast with Europe may be indicated by comparison with figures for a group of fourteen West European countries, which show average gross and net outputs of £28 and £24 per acre in 1950, and an average net income per head of active agricultural population of £190.[2] The figures are not strictly comparable, since the European figures are calculated in arable equivalent acres, and net output is calculated by deduction of purchased materials only; but the difference does not invalidate the contrast in levels of land and labour productivity. Broadly speaking, Egypt's land produces twice as much per acre as these European countries, while its labour earns only one-seventh as much, although the West European group includes some countries with very low rural standards of living.

Since the population on the land is now increasing faster

---

[1] Ministry of Finance and National Economy, *National Income of Egypt for 1953, Official Estimate* (Cairo, 1955) and National Bank of Egypt, *Economic Bulletin*, vol. 8, no. 2, 1955.

[2] UN, ECE, and FAO, *Output and Expenses of Agriculture in some European Countries*, First Report (Geneva, 1953), p. 16.

than production, incomes per head are certainly falling. It is therefore essential, if a further fall in the living standard is to be avoided, to increase agricultural production. But because the level of land productivity is already so high, there is not great scope for increasing agricultural production on the present land area. More fertilizers and better seed could raise yields, but the cost would be high. In the view of the Population Commission, the maximum possible increase in output per acre might be 25 per cent above the level of 1947–51.[1] Nor is there any prospect of a *large* increase in the areas cultivated and cropped, without more water. Official schemes provide for the reclamation of an area of 300,000 acres by the end of 1956. But the extent to which supplies can be diverted away without damage to land already cultivated is a controversial issue. The scope for increasing employment on the land is nil. The technical improvements which could be made would not increase the demand for labour, and might even reduce it.

These three conditions, extreme and growing congestion on the land, the limited land area, and the high level of land productivity, mean that the fall in the living standard can be checked only by increasing employment in industry and by greatly extending the area cultivated, which is impossible without a great increase in water-storage capacity.

These needs the Government is meeting by its industrial schemes, by an agricultural development and land reclamation programme, and intends to meet by the construction of the High Dam. The industrial schemes include the construction of two new power stations (one already in operation), the iron and steel plant at Helwan, a synthetic fertilizer plant and an electrical power installation at Aswan, the last two being under construction.[2]

Much larger sums, amounting to £40 million over the three years 1953–5, have been invested in agriculture, chiefly to convert land in Upper Egypt to perennial irrigation, by installing pumps, and for general improvement of irrigation and drainage. The four-year programme for reclaiming 300,000 acres by the end of 1956 includes conversion to perennial

---

[1] *The Population Problem in Egypt*, p. 20. See 'Postscript', p. 199.
[2] Both are now in operation.

irrigation in some districts of Upper Egypt, chiefly on the estates expropriated under the agrarian reform, and also on estates belonging to private landowners. The programme also includes land reclamation in sections of the Tahrir province, described below, and the reclamation work undertaken by the Egyptian-American Rural Improvement Service (EARIS), an organization jointly financed by Point Four and the Egyptian Government, and advised by American experts. This has completed the reclamation of 25,000 acres in the province of Buhaira, by means of forage crops, using no extra water, and is also active in the Fayyum. The land reclaimed is to be assigned to small farmers for purchase over thirty years.[1]

The High Dam above Aswan comprises the long-term programme for the expansion of the cultivated area, and for industrial expansion. Its object is to make fuller use of the Nile water, much of which is now wasted in the flood season. The scheme is still in the course of preparation, but some current estimates of its size and importance may be given. The reservoir behind the dam is intended to have a capacity of 130,000 million cubic metres, and will therefore be the largest in the world. The 25 per cent increase in water-supplies which this storage capacity would provide could add 1,300,000 acres of new land (in the Tahrir province) to the present area of 6 million acres, and would allow the conversion of 700,000 acres in Upper Egypt to perennial irrigation, and so double the cropped area on this land, which at present only carries one crop per annum. This should permit, according to official calculations, an increase in the total agricultural income of some 50 per cent, when the whole of the reclamation work is completed. In addition to the gain in water-supplies, there will also be a considerable gain from the flood-protection works in connexion with the dam.

The work is intended to be undertaken in two stages, the first ten-year period which will see the construction of the dam, reclamation of part of the additional land area, and partial use of the power capacity. The total power production at the site is estimated at 8,300 million kilowatt hours, of which half could be available at the end of the ten-year period in which the dam should be completed.

[1] See 'Postscript', p. 202.

The cost of the first stage is estimated at £209 million. This sum includes £68 million for the cost of the construction of the dam itself: the cost of constructing four power stations, flood-protection and navigation facilities, turbine and generator equipment, and the cost of reclaiming 400,000 acres and converting 700,000 acres to perennial irrigation.[1] By the time that the dam is completed, the total population of Egypt will have increased by between 5 and 6 million, so that the prospective increase in areas cultivated and cropped will provide only for the prospective increase in population.[2] Thus even with much fuller utilization of the Nile water, there is no prospect of relieving pressure on the land, so long as Egypt remains a mainly agricultural country. But the dam can none the less provide the way out of the demographic impasse, in that it will greatly increase Egypt's industrial capacity, and could raise the rural living standard through increased employment in industry. The full power potential of the dam will be considerably larger than the total which the Egyptian economy is likely to absorb for a number of years after construction is completed, and for this reason only half the energy available is to be harnessed in the ten-year period.

This vast project is rightly regarded by the Egyptian Government as a matter of life and death for the Egyptian economy. As has already been emphasized, Egypt is a test case for the ability of the international economy and its agencies to deal with the problems of underdevelopment. In January 1956 the International Bank for Reconstruction and Development had reached an agreement in principle with the Egyptian Government on a loan of $200 million, and the United States and the United Kingdom had pledged grants of $75 million towards the cost of the scheme. Had the needs of the Egyptian economy been better understood in the West, and had the Egyptian Government succeeded in convincing these Governments of its good faith, the dangers of going back on these undertakings might have been avoided. As it was, the international economy failed to pass the test, and the Western refusal to finance it makes this great undertaking a source of international crisis. Construc-

[1] For details see UN, *Economic Developments in the Middle East, 1954 to 1955,* pp. 116–17.
[2] *The Population Problem in Egypt,* p. 20. See also Gamal Abdel Nasser, 'The Egyptian Revolution', *Foreign Affairs,* January 1955.

tion of the High Dam began in 1959, with Soviet help. (See 'Postscript', p. 200.)

In the meantime, the main way in which the standard of living of the fellah can be improved is by redistribution of income from agriculture. Over-population does not diminish the need for reform; on the contrary, it increases the need, though it sets limits as to what can be accomplished. The growing pressure of population allows landowners to take a larger share in the national income by raising rents. As population increases, the inequality of incomes increases also. Land reform was needed, not only because the distribution of property was unequal, but also because it gave the landowners a vested interest in retrogression.

THE LAND SYSTEM

The distribution of property in land before the reform was extremely unequal, as the following table shows. Holdings are here identical with properties, not farms.

TABLE 6

Egypt: Agricultural Land by Size of Holdings, 1952 [1]

Size-group (*feddans*)*	Owners		Area		
	(*000*)	(*per cent*)	(*000 feddans*)	(*per cent*)	*Average area* (*feddans*)
1 and under	2,018·1	72·0	778	13·0	0·4
Over 1–under 5	623·8	22·2	1,344	22·5	2·1
,, 5– ,, 10	79·3	2·8	526	8·8	6·6
,, 10– ,, 20	46·8	1·8	638	10·7	13·6
,, 20– ,, 30	13·1	0·5	309	5·0	23·6
,, 30– ,, 50	9·2	0·3	344	5·7	37·4
,, 50– ,, 100	6·4	0·2	429	7·2	67·3
,, 100– ,, 200	3·2	0·1	437	7·3	137·2
,, 200	2·1	0·1	1,177	19·8	550·9
Total	2,802·0	100·0	5,982	100·0	2·1

* 1 feddan = 1·038 acres.

(SOURCE: *Statistical Pocket Year-book, 1953*, p. 33.)

From these figures it appears that of the total agricultural land area of nearly 6 million acres, 2 million or 34·3 per cent

[1] See 'Postscript', p. 195, for 1957 figures.

was held by proprietors with more than 50 acres; 1·8 million or 30·2 per cent was held by proprietors with between 5 and 50 acres; and 2·1 million or 35·5 per cent by proprietors with less than 5 acres. This was a more equal distribution than exists in Syria and Iraq, because there is in Egypt a fairly large class of medium-sized proprietors, numbering 150,000; this class is far less important in the other two countries. Nor are there the enormous properties of 200,000 acres, or more, which characterize the land systems of Syria and Iraq. It will be remembered, however, that cultivation is highly intensive. With a net income of £40 per acre, the income of a 2,500-acre holding in Egypt corresponds to the income of a 50,000-acre holding in Syria and Iraq, where only half the land is cultivated in each year, and yields are very low.

None the less, by any other standard the distribution of property in Egypt was highly unequal. Of the $2\frac{3}{4}$ million proprietors, 70 per cent had less than half an acre each, while 2,115 had over 200 acres, with an average of 550 acres each. Within the size-group over 200 acres, 188 proprietors owned holdings over 1,000 acres, with an average holding of 2,600 acres each.[1]

Nor does the distribution of ownership reflect the full extent of inequality. In addition to the $2\frac{3}{4}$ million proprietors, there is a large section of the farm population, numbering perhaps $1\frac{1}{2}$ million families, which owns no land at all, and lives by share-cropping on small areas of land or by casual labour.

On all properties except the smallest and the largest cultivation by tenants is general. In recent years the proportion of the land leased to tenants has greatly increased. According to estimates made by the Ministry of Agriculture, 60 per cent of the land was rented in 1949 against 17 per cent in 1939.[2] Formerly money rents were general, but it would appear that share-cropping tenancies are now more prevalent.

The increase in tenancy is a result of the growing pressure of population. The change from owner-operation to tenancy in a plantation economy is a retrogressive adjustment, offering em-

---

[1] According to figures showing distribution in size-groups above 200 acres, published by the National Bank of Egypt, *Economic Bulletin*, vol. 5, no. 3, 1952.

[2] Figures quoted by Mohammed Riad Ghonemy, *Resource Use and Income in Egyptian Agriculture before and after the Land Reform, with particular reference to Economic Development* (North Carolina State College, unpublished D. Phil. thesis, 1953), p. 45.

ployment on increasingly unfavourable terms. As population increases, the price of land rises more than the income derived from it. Official figures published by the Ministry of Agriculture show that the average net income per acre in 1947–8 was £17 5s.;[1] and the interest rate was 9–10 per cent. The capitalized value of an acre of land should therefore have been £185, but in fact the average price of land was £430. Rent rises more than the net output, so that the landowner could obtain a higher income per acre by leasing the land than he could by farming it himself. Dr Ghonemy quotes the example of the royal estate at Kafr el-Sheikh, in Fuadia province, with an area of 16,000 acres. The average net revenue per acre owned and operated by the estate was £5 in 1937 and £15 in 1949, while the cash rents per acre for land leased on the same estate were £8 and £36 respectively.[2] According to official figures quoted by Dr Ghonemy, the average net revenue per acre of owner-operated land in Egypt was £16–19 in 1946–7 and 1947–8, while the average cash rent per feddan was £22–3.[3]

A further cause of the increase in tenancy was the rise in cotton prices during the war, which enabled small owners to increase their demand for land.

The largest properties were managed partly as plantation estates, with central management and a large administrative staff, and partly leased to tenants. In the past they were run entirely under central management, with paid labour, but tenancy has increased in recent years. On two large estates visited part of the area had been leased before the reform, although these estates were highly capitalized and there had been a large administrative staff. Some large estates were entirely cultivated by small tenants, as, for example, the former royal estate at Faroukia, described below. But some smaller estates were entirely owner operated, as, for example, a property of 400 acres at Mansura, which employed 100 labourers permanently, paid by the grant of a small allotment of land, and 1,300 labourers seasonally, in gangs hired through contractors.

The distinction between owner-operation and share-cropping tenancy is not sharp, because the practice of share-

---

[1] The unit is the Egyptian pound, which is worth slightly less than the £ sterling, used for convenience throughout this chapter.
[2] *Resource Use and Income*, pp. 55–6.   [3] ibid. p. 57.

cropping is not a contract between landowner and tenant to divide the profits of the farm, but simply a method of reducing the costs of management and labour supervision and of cutting labour costs by reducing wages. When land is rented to a tenant-farmer with some capital, rent is payable in money, and the agreement may be of the nature of a leasehold contract. Share-cropping agreements had no legal status, and were usually not written. They run for a short period, sometimes only for one crop season. On big estates intermediaries were used: a portion of the land would be leased, in return for a fixed share of the crop, to large tenants, who would sub-let to small cultivators.

Different divisions of the gross product were used for different crops. A common arrangement was for the landowner to take all, or all but a small fraction, of the cotton crop, half or more of the wheat crop, leaving the maize and berseem for the cultivator and his buffalo. Blank agreements, with no division of the crop specified in advance, were sometimes made.

Working capital was usually provided by the landowner, in the form of seed and fertilizers for the cotton crop; the fixed capital, including the irrigation channels, is maintained by him. (The upkeep of the main canals is the responsibility of the Department of Irrigation.)

The status of the small tenant-cultivator on a holding of 2 or 3 acres was that of a labourer rather than that of a tenant. Formerly he had no security of tenure, and no incentive and no means to invest, since the landowner undertook this function, and his income barely covered his needs. His position was better than that of the casual labourer only in so far as he was more regularly employed. It is for this reason that the Agrarian Reform Law should be regarded, as has already been emphasized, primarily as a policy for agricultural labour. Although, as will be seen, it has not benefited the casual labourers, and has even caused some reduction in their employment, its most important and effective provisions are those which concern the tenant-cultivators, who form a majority of the farm population, and are landless or own small holdings of less than half an acre. Protection of the tenants by preventing eviction and reducing the rent level therefore means raising the income level and the status of a large section of the working population.

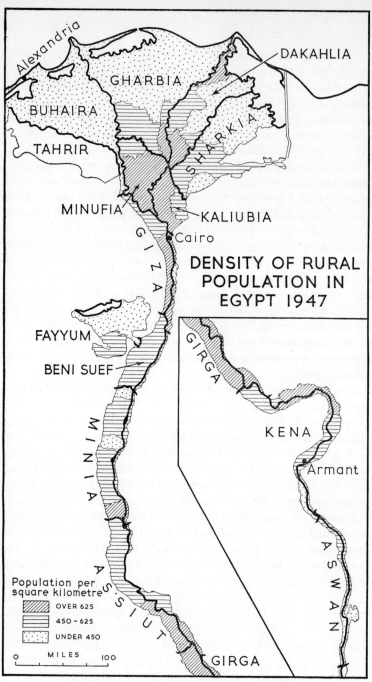

DENSITY OF RURAL POPULATION IN EGYPT 1947

Population per square kilometre

- OVER 625
- 450 - 625
- UNDER 450

0   MILES   100

Based on a map in National Bank of Egypt, *Economic Bulletin*, vol. 8, no. 3, 1955.

28

The average rent level before the reform was £30 per acre, equivalent to about 50 per cent of the gross produce and 75 per cent of the net produce (according to the figures given on p. 26 above). The level of rents in terms of money rose with the rise in cotton prices in 1950–1. The share of rent in the gross agricultural income, i.e. the proportion of rent to output, has increased with the increase in population.

The influence of population pressure on the standard of living is shown by the fact that the agricultural income per head of agricultural population varies with the density of the agricultural population per acre. The map on p. 28 shows the density of rural population per acre by provinces. Figures published by the National Bank of Egypt show that agricultural income per head in Buhaira and Gharbia, the less densely populated provinces of the Delta, is nearly twice as high as in Kena and Girga, the most densely populated provinces in Upper Egypt.[1] The level of income per head of agricultural population is shown by these figures to be negatively correlated with the density of the population, and positively correlated with the proportion of the cropped area under cotton.

The amount of rent per acre varies with the density of agricultural population and also, to a lesser extent, with the proportion of cropped area under cotton. Where the area of cultivated land per head is very small, as in Giza, Minufia, and Kaliubia, rents are higher than in provinces with lower population densities, as for example in Buhaira and the Fayyum,[2] although the proportion of land under cotton is less in the three former provinces than in the two latter.

Pressure of population also shows itself in the continuous downward trend of the size of the smaller holdings. These are subdivided on inheritance, while larger properties are not. The distribution of land as between small and large owners shows little change in the last fifty years, as Table 7 indicates.

The high price of land made it impossible for the small tenant-cultivator to purchase land. High rents and debts prevented him from accumulating the necessary capital. In 1947 a farmer would have needed to save £2,350 to purchase 5 acres

[1] National Bank of Egypt, *Economic Bulletin*, vol. 8, no. 3, 1955.
[2] Ghonemy, *Resource Use and Income*, p. 53.

TABLE 7

Egypt: Agricultural Land by Size of Holdings, 1900–52

Size-group (acres)		No. of owners (000)		Area (000 acres)		Average area (acres)	
		1900	1952	1900	1952	1900	1952
5 and under		761	2,642	1,113	2,122	1·5	0·8
Over 5–under 10		80	79	560	526	7·0	6·6
,, 10– ,, 20		40	47	551	638	13·8	13·6
,, 20– ,, 30		12	13	301	309	25·1	23·6
,, 30– ,, 50		9	9	345	344	38·3	37·4
,, 50		12	12	2,244	2,043	187·0	174·6
Total		914	2,802	5,114	5,982	5·6	2·1

NOTE: Original table in feddans.

(SOURCE: National Bank of Egypt.)

of land, together with the necessary capital equipment. For labourers with an agricultural wage of 94 millièmes per day (1*s.* 10*d.*) the purchase of land at this price is clearly out of the question.[1]

Consequently the outstanding feature of the land system before the reform was gross inequality, and also growing inequality. The growth of population on the land allowed landowners to use their monopoly power by charging a higher price for the use of land, in the form of ever more extortionate rents, while at the same time it increased inequality through the continuous subdivision of the smaller properties.

Among the landowners two types can be distinguished. One is the very large landowner, generally an absentee and always a lavish consumer, usually in Europe. Of him it has been said 'Il gaspille en une soirée ce qui ferait vivre ses fellahs une année, trouvant très naturels et leur misère et son luxe.'[2] The other is the landowner with 300 or 400 acres, living on his estate or in a provincial town. He may be a professional agriculturist, farming most efficiently, even carrying out scientific experiments with seed varieties, fertilizers, and irrigation dates; or he may leave the management to an agent, and neglect the estate. Among

[1] ibid. p. 61.   [2] Ayrout, *Fellahs d'Égypte*, p. 46.

the large estate owners few families did anything to improve the conditions of their workers, and then only by providing some medical service. Nor did the state do anything for the fellahin, except through the provision of health clinics in some villages; in the years after the war these had made considerable progress.

THE AGRARIAN REFORM OF 1952 AND ITS EFFECTS

Any real measure of agrarian reform is bound to be contentious. In Egypt the landowners have never previously experienced any encroachment on their interests, and paid only light taxes on their property. From their standpoint, any reform appears catastrophic. In 1952 it was said that reform was certain to reduce production. In 1954–5, this hope having failed, the commonly voiced criticisms were that the cultivators were no better off, and that labour had been displaced. There were also vague charges of waste and mismanagement on the part of the authorities. Some landowners have found new fields of activity, and are not overtly critical. Others are still hostile, and one even tearfully asserted that the reform was Communism, engineered by the Americans. More disinterested critics think that the peasants have only changed masters, and speak of collective farming. The students of Cairo University, on the other hand, expressed the view that the reform had not done enough, and wanted to go faster and farther than the Government has seen fit to do.

What follows is an attempt to assess, in the light of these criticisms, the results of the law, so far as these could be ascertained in visits to three estates and in conversation with the authorities, with some observers in a position to judge independently, and with a few landowners. One estate was seen on an official visit, the others visited independently of official guidance. Official statements have been checked where possible, since there is a natural tendency on the part of the authorities, in the face of so much criticism, to be over-optimistic. On one important point, the finance of the reform, no information is published, nor were balance sheets available at the estates. On the estates, officials and co-operative society secretaries gave information readily on agricultural questions and on farm incomes, but it was not possible to press inquiries about finance. The information is therefore not complete by any means. On the crucial question, the benefits to the fellahin, there is sufficient evidence to refute the criticism that they are no better off. Nor does the charge of mismanagement appear valid; on the contrary, the reform appears to have been carried through with a high degree of administrative competence. In this respect, it compares well with other countries, even with the highly efficient reform in Italy.

As has been stated, the Agrarian Reform Law had three aims: the redistribution of ownership; the reduction of rent; and the raising of agricultural wages. The provisions of the law, and their results in practice, may be considered under each of these headings.

1. *Expropriation and Redistribution.* The law, in Article 1, laid down that 'no person may own more than 200 acres of land'. Landowners may retain up to 300 acres, if they distribute 50 acres to each of two children. Land in excess of this maximum was to be requisitioned by the Government over a period of five years.

Land under reclamation was exempted from expropriation under Article 2, which allowed companies and private persons to own more than 200 acres of fallow or desert land under reclamation. Land owned by industrial companies is exempted for a period of twenty-five years, and also, under a later amendment, land belonging to agricultural, scientific, and industrial societies in existence before the decree was issued.

Owners of expropriated land receive compensation at the rate of ten times the rental value, assessed at seven times the basic land tax (i.e. at seventy times the basic land tax). Tax assessments were low, amounting to £2–£4 per acre, and the rental value fixed on this basis is therefore much lower than the real rental value. The legal rental value would range from £140 to £280 per acre, whereas land prices before the reform ranged from £400 to £600 per acre. To the sum payable in compensation for the land must be added the value of buildings, installed machinery (chiefly pumps), and trees. Compensation is payable in state bonds, bearing interest at 3 per cent, and redeemable in thirty years. The bonds are not negotiable, but may be used in payment for uncultivated land purchased from the Government for reclamation, or in payment of land tax and death duties.

The requisitioned land was to be distributed among small farmers and farm labourers, in holdings of not less than 2 acres and not more than 5 acres per family. In distributing land preference was to be given to those actually cultivating the land as tenants or labourers. Owners of more than 5 acres are not eligible to receive land. Orchards were to be distributed in lots not exceeding 20 acres among graduates of agricultural institutes, provided that they do not already own more than 10 acres of land.

The new owner was to pay, in instalments over a period of thirty years, the full purchase price of the land, assessed as above, plus interest at 3 per cent and 15 per cent for the costs of administration. Until the purchase price is fully paid, the holding may not be sold or otherwise disposed of. Since the purchase price is based on rental value based on land-tax assessment, the instalment payable annually is much less than the previous rent paid, usually by about 50 per cent.

The distribution of an expropriated estate is not made until its income, the number of persons dependent on it, and their resources outside it as owner and tenant, have been surveyed by the officials of the Higher Committee for Agrarian Reform, the department charged with the execution of the law. Great care is taken to ensure that the land is fairly distributed among all those who are entitled to benefit. The size of holding granted varies between 2 and 3 acres, according to the size of the family. The general rule is that all former tenants receive land, with the exception of those who own more than 5 acres (these are few). Permanent labourers usually receive a holding, but not all casual labourers can do so, since there is not sufficient land. As the new owners do not wish to employ labour, some displacement of labour results. How much is unknown: a figure of 5 per cent of the total number of tenants and labourers previously employed is officially given, and confirmed by observation.[1]

The scale of redistribution is not large. Of Egypt's total agricultural land area of 6 million acres, 1,177,000 acres, or

---

[1] See Sir Malcolm Darling, 'Land Reform in Italy and Egypt', in *Yearbook of Agricultural Co-operation, 1956* (Oxford, Blackwell).

20 per cent, was held in properties exceeding 200 acres. About half of this total was scheduled for expropriation and redistribution, so that land reform in the strict sense can affect at most only about 10 per cent of Egypt's land. The official figure for land liable to expropriation is 656,736 acres, requisitioned from 1,789 landowners. It is probable, however, that the total actually available for redistribution will be less than the area legally liable to expropriation, because many landowners escaped expropriation through private sales.

Under Article 4 of the law, landowners were permitted to sell land in excess of the legal maximum in lots not exceeding 5 acres, to farmers (not relatives) whose holding did not exceed 5 acres. This provision was included as a compromise, to satisfy the Minister of Finance, who believed in building up a peasant middle class. Very large areas of land were quickly sold, and the price of land fell by 50 per cent. The official figures[1] give 145,000 acres as the total sold privately; but it may well have been more. Landowners evaded the provision obliging them to sell to small farmers, and instead sold to larger farmers, commercial interests, and civil servants.[2] Had this provision continued in force, no land would have been available for distribution. Article 4 was therefore superseded, later in 1952, by a decree which prohibited private sales of land liable to expropriation after 31 October 1952.

The total land available for redistribution is therefore presumably not more than 500,000 acres, perhaps less. Up to the middle of 1955 a total of 320,000 acres had been expropriated, of which 120,000 were the property of the King and other members of the royal family.

The Agrarian Reform Law made no special provision concerning the estates of the royal family, which cover in all 178,000 acres. The law for the confiscation of the property of 'the Mohammed Ali dynasty', however, laid down that these estates should be expropriated in full, leaving no residual holding, and without compensation. Since the Higher Committee

---

[1] These may be found in the Higher Committee for Agrarian Reform's *Replies to the United Nations Questionnaires relating to Egyptian Agrarian Reform Measures* (Cairo, 1955; hereafter referred to as *Replies to United Nations Questionnaires*).

[2] An official publication of the Higher Committee for Agrarian Reform states that among such sales of land there were some in contravention of the law, which the Higher Committee intend to annul, in order to make the land subject to expropriation (Sayed Marei, *Two Years of Agrarian Reform*, 1954, p. 11).

receives payments of purchase instalments from the farmers in respect of their holdings, but need pay no compensation, the acquisition of these properties greatly facilitates the self-financing of the reform.

Up to the end of 1955, an area of 250,000 acres had been distributed to 69,000 families, comprising 415,000 persons, in holdings averaging 3½ acres.[1]

The recipients of land gain an immediate increase in income. During the first year after the estate is requisitioned, the new landholders pay rent to the state at the fixed rent maximum (i.e. seven times the basic land tax). This is about half the previous rent level. In the following year they receive provisional title to the holding, and thereafter pay the instalments of the purchase price. In addition to the instalment, the farmer also pays the co-operative society, of which he is a member, for seed, fertilizers, machine cultivation, and administrative expenses. The payment is effected by delivery of the whole of the cotton crop. The total sum payable annually works out at about five times the basic tax assessment. In addition, he pays land tax. His total expenses are therefore equal to six times the basic land tax. Assuming that the gross income remains the same, the net income increases by the difference between the previous rent level and the annual payment. Gross income per acre has remained the same, and on the expropriated estates has risen slightly, as a result of heavier use of fertilizers.

An example may illustrate the method by which the income redistribution is carried out. At Faroukia, in the province of Sharkia, an estate of 1,500 acres, formerly the property of King Farouk, has been distributed to 511 former tenants. (A few were excluded by reason of ownership outside the estate.) As tenants, they had formerly paid rent on a share-cropping basis, under which the landowner took all the cotton and half the wheat, leaving the tenant half the wheat for sale, the maize for his own consumption, and the berseem for the buffalo. This was a usual type of arrangement, and comparatively favourable: the landowner provided seed and fertilizer for the cotton crop, and got the labour free.

Under the new law the former tenants received holdings be-

[1] See 'Postscript', p. 193, for results to the end of 1960.

tween 2 and 3 acres, varying with the size of the family, and corresponding roughly to the acreage cultivated before. They deliver the whole of the cotton crop to the co-operative for sale, as they formerly delivered it to the estate manager, and the proceeds of the sale meet the cost of the instalment payment, land tax, the cost of the fertilizers and seed, and administrative expenses. The farmers retain their maize and berseem as before. The chief difference in their position is that the whole income from the wheat crop is their property, instead of half. The gain in money income is equivalent to £20 per holding, or £7 per acre, an increase of 50 per cent on the former net income. Figures for four provinces examined by Sir Malcolm Darling show that an increase of 50 per cent is general.[1]

There is no change in the type of farming or the scale of operation. The estate is still managed as one unit, and sales of the cash crops are handled by the management. Cotton finances the transfer of property, provides the working capital, and covers the costs of administration. In 1954 the proceeds of the sale of the cotton crop through the co-operative amounted to £27,000. This sum covered the annual instalments of the purchase price payable by the farmers (fixed at £12 per acre), land tax (£3 per acre), the cost of seed, fertilizers, and services provided through the co-operative, and the costs of administration. The total annual payment made per acre is £18; on the basis of the land-tax assessment the annual instalment of purchase price should be only £7 (i.e. the tax of £3 × 70 ÷ 30). It is, however, fixed at £12, which must be an arbitrary figure, since for former royal property no compensation is payable. In the absence of published accounts, it cannot be ascertained how much of the £18 paid by the farmer by delivery of the cotton crop is taken up by the costs of operation and working capital and how much is profit.

The requisitioned estates vary considerably in the amount of capital invested per acre, in gross output per acre, in the costs of operation, and in the level of rents charged before the reform. How much of the total income from the sale of the cash crops is to be allotted to new investment in fixed capital, or in additional working capital, and how much is to be distri-

[1] 'Land Reform in Italy and Egypt'.

buted, is a matter for the accountants to decide. In Upper Egypt the large estates were highly capitalized and extremely profitable (as, for example, the 5,000-acre estate at Armant, with a gross income of £235,000 from the sale of the sugar crop). On these estates rents were high and wages low: consequently the gain in the incomes of the new farmers is much greater than on the estates in Lower Egypt, where rents were lower. One estate visited, Bourgaya in Minia province (Upper Egypt), was exceptionally productive, with yields well above the average, and here, according to information given at the estate, farmers' net incomes had risen by nearly 100 per cent, to £39 per acre.

Since there are these local differences, the authorities have worked on the principle of levelling up incomes in Upper Egypt, and so allowing a larger increase in the farmers' net income than in Lower Egypt, where incomes were higher. The object is to guarantee a minimum income of £16 per member of the farmer's family.

Figures have been published by the Higher Committee for Agrarian Reform which show still greater increases in income, ranging between 100 and 200 per cent, on six estates, three in Lower and three in Upper Egypt, where the largest increases are shown.[1] These figures may not be representative of the average, though it is certainly true that redistribution has brought much greater gains in Upper Egypt, because rents were exceedingly high before the reform. On the basis of the figures analysed by Sir Malcolm Darling, and of direct observation, it is safe to conclude that cultivators' incomes have risen by about 50 per cent on estates expropriated in Lower Egypt, and that the income gain is greater in Upper Egypt, and may be as much as 100 per cent.

There can be no doubt that the farmers have gained a considerable increase in income. It is true that they have not become independent owners, and that the co-operatives are managed by state officials, in what is in effect a system of collective farming. Whether this form of organization is essential is considered later. None the less, there is a gain in status as well as in income, for the new farmers have economic security comparable to that of individual ownership.

[1] See *Replies to United Nations Questionnaires*, p. 156.

There can also be no doubt that the new landholders appreciate the change. Inquiries as to whether they are better off would naturally be answered affirmatively when officials are present. But the reply is often so lengthy and emphatic that its sincerity convinces, even though it is unintelligible. Sir Malcolm Darling[1] quotes examples:

The most enthusiastic of the new owners was the society's secretary. When asked whether he was better off, he touched the ground at his feet, flung his arms upwards to the ceiling and exclaimed—*that* is the difference between then and now', and still doubting whether we understood the magnitude of the change, he added almost in despair—'I cannot explain to you how much better off we are.'

On another estate, large enough to have 9 societies, members showed the same lively appreciation of the change. 'Before, we had to give up our crops at low valuation: we can now do what we like. We used to mix maize and wheat for our bread; now we eat more wheat, and meat twice a week instead of once. Our extra money we spend on soap, food and clothes, on four shirts instead of two. Ten of us have bought wirelesses at £20 to £25 each, but first of all we buy buffaloes. Twenty of us have recently married; we no longer have to wait four or five years to do this, but we still borrow or sell cattle to do it. Ten per cent have more than one wife, one has just taken a third.' Such was the burden of their talk, summed up in the parting remark, 'We all very happy'. Here the shops had increased from four to nine, and owing to the greater consumption of meat the butchers were killing several times a week instead of once or twice.

2. *The Reduction of Rents.* Article 33 of the law decreed that the rent of agricultural land may not exceed seven times the basic land tax. As has already been explained, this meant that the level fixed was much lower than the previous level of rent. In the case of share-cropping rents, the law decreed that the owners' share shall not exceed one-half, after deduction of all expenses. This provision also meant a large reduction in rent, since before the reform rent on an average represented one-half of the gross produce.

Agricultural land may be let only to a person who intends to farm it himself. Leases of land may not be concluded for less than three years, and must be in writing. In the absence of a written agreement, the rent shall be deemed to be based

---

[1] 'Land Reform in Italy and Egypt'.

on crop-sharing for a period of three years, during which the owner's share shall be one-half, after deduction of all expenses.

It is always extremely difficult to enforce legislation for the control and reduction of rents, and in a country where the demand for land steadily rises, as it does in Egypt, enforcement would appear impossible. All that can be said with certainty is that rent reduction did take place, and that in January 1955 rents had fallen by about 40 per cent. This fact was attested by many independent authorities, of whom the officials of the Crédit Foncier were the best qualified to hold an impartial opinion. Landowners were loud in criticism of the rent reduction.

Enforcement was possible because the reform alarmed landowners, and also because cotton prices fell. The price of land fell sharply in 1952–3 to about half its previous level, as a result of private sales of land. Without the threat of expropriation, enforcement of the rent reduction would certainly not have been possible. By the end of 1954 land prices were rising again, and possibly as the fear of expropriation recedes rents may rise in contravention of the law.

In the meantime the incomes of farm tenants have risen. An official statement puts the increase at 50 per cent, from an average net income of £19 per acre to £29 per acre. Four million farmers are estimated to benefit, and the aggregate increase in the income of farm tenants is therefore £40 million.[1] These figures possibly exaggerate the extent of the increase, but the numbers affected are presumably correct and an increase certainly took place. This improvement in income and legal status for a very large section of the farm population is by far the most valuable achievement of the reform. In 1961 this was no longer true, for the legal provisions fixing maximum rents are now generally evaded. The income gains through rent reduction therefore proved impermanent, though security of tenure has improved. (See 'Postscript', p. 196.)

3. *The Raising of Agricultural Wages.* The Agrarian Reform Law provided that the wages of agricultural workers should be fixed annually by an official committee, formed by the Minister

---

[1] *Replies to United Nations Questionnaires*, p. 8.

of Agriculture, with an official of the Ministry as President, and composed of six members chosen by the Minister, of whom three should represent owners and tenants of land, and three agricultural labourers. Agricultural workers were given the right to form trade unions. A subsequent decree laid down minimum wage rates, 18 piastres (3s. 6d.) per day for men and 10 piastres (2s.) a day for women.

These rates have not generally been enforceable. On expropriated estates, the former tenants become landholders. When estates were operated as a single unit, the majority of the former labourers acquire secure tenant status with a guaranteed minimum income. In neither case is additional employment created, and, as has already been said, there is usually some reduction in employment. In the Liberation province,[1] the minimum wage rates are paid, to about 14,000 labourers employed on land reclamation and building; to this extent wages have risen. The reduction in employment resulting from redistribution has been more than offset by this scheme, and by the land reclamation and industrial construction work undertaken in the last three years.

The Effects on Production and Investment

At the time that the Land Reform decree was issued, its opponents argued that the distribution of the land would certainly reduce production. It was then assumed that the reform would mean division into very small farms in place of the large estates. Since Egyptian agriculture is so highly geared to intensive cropping and high cropping rates, the danger was real. Some of the very large estates—not all—were extremely well farmed and well equipped with capital, which the tenant-cultivators did not possess.

As it is, these forebodings have not been realized, because there has been no transition to small farming. On the three estates visited in 1955 yields were slightly higher than before, as a result of the good harvests and also because more fertilizers were used. This was the case even when yields had previously been exceptionally high, as on the sugar plantations at Armant. Since 1952 yields per acre for all crops have risen and the production of all crops, except cotton, has increased. The area

[1] See below, p. 49.

under cotton has declined as a result of the fall in prices. The overall production results cannot, however, be attributed to the redistribution, which up to the present has affected only a small proportion of the land. But the reduction of rents, which affects a very large proportion of the land, has been accompanied by heavier use of fertilizers, so that the reform has certainly contributed to the increase in production.

The reform is sometimes held responsible for the decline in the quality of cotton since 1952, for the higher grades are not coming forward to the same extent. The true explanation of this decline is that the Government, in fixing cotton-seed prices, mistakenly priced the top grades at a higher level than the low-quality seed. Another supposed effect of the reform, the 'black spot', which concerns Liverpool, is caused by packing cotton in nitrate bags.

The reform was intended to increase investment in industry, by breaking the landowners' desire to hold wealth in the form of land, thus increasing the amount of new investment. It was the original intention to make the land bonds negotiable, to achieve this result. However, as the bonds are not negotiable (except for the purchase of land for reclamation), the payment of compensation cannot cause the landowners to reinvest. Indirectly, the reform probably has caused some transfer of capital into industry, commerce, and building, since the proceeds of the private sales of land were probably reinvested in urban building, possibly also in industry. Prices of land have now risen again, for the demand is insatiable, so that the transfer is not continuing. There may have been a net increase in investment, in so far as 'good Pashas' who have been expropriated now have a finger in many financial pies, and prudence dictates that they should invest more and consume less.

Investment in agriculture and land reclamation has certainly increased. On the large estates which have been expropriated new pumps are being installed, and more fertilizers are used. Some expropriated landowners are active in land reclamation. Foreign companies are still engaged in land reclamation, and are not affected by the law, since, as has been stated, land under reclamation is exempt from redistribution.[1]

---

[1] See 'Postscript', p. 193.

LAND REFORM AND DEVELOPMENT
STATE OR CO-OPERATIVE FARMING

The view that reform means collective farming is partially right. Article 4 of the law describes the new landholder as 'the proprietor'. But he does not acquire ownership for thirty years, and in the meantime is not free to sell or sub-let or to farm independently. It was the intention of the law that the functions of the former landowner in distributing seed and fertilizer, and in marketing, should be taken over by a co-operative society, membership of which is obligatory for all grantees of land. The society should carry out these tasks through its Board of Management, composed of eleven members elected by the farmers. The law gave the co-operatives wide powers. They are to provide loans to their members, and to organize the supply of seed, fertilizers, livestock, and agricultural machinery, and the storage and transport of crops—all of which might, of course, be undertaken on behalf of independent farmers by a co-operative society of the ordinary supply and marketing type. But the functions of the co-operative are also to include 'organizing the cultivation and exploitation of the land in the most efficient manner, including seed selection, varieties of crops, pest control and digging of canals and drains.' They are also to sell the principal crops on behalf of the members, 'after deducting the price of the land, government taxes and agricultural and other loans'. They are required to render all agricultural and social services on behalf of their members. Societies are to be officially controlled, and must exercise their duties under the supervision of officials chosen by the Ministry of Social Affairs, since 1956 by the Ministry of Agrarian Reform.

In practice, the management is taken over by the official manager appointed by the Higher Committee. He is highly trained and experienced, sometimes a former estate manager, and has under his control an administrative staff comprising accountants, agronomists, mechanics, store-keepers, and foremen. He is not a member of the Board, but can refer decisions of which he disapproves to the Higher Committee. In practice, disagreement probably does not arise. At Faroukia the members of the Board held a meeting, but the manager had prepared the agenda. They listened impassively while the man from the Ministry explained the arrangements for seed purchase, and approved. The topic of breeding rabbits roused sudden interest, but the manager introduced two girl experts from the Ministry of Agriculture who explained the programme for the distribution of breeding stock, and again the Board acquiesced. They raised points concerning the organization of labour, and it was evident that they were really a Works Council, which can voice grievances and give advice, but does not and cannot control operations.

This is hardly surprising: it could not be expected that the peasants, so long accustomed to acquiescence, could immediately develop the power to manage their own affairs. There are some real co-operative societies in existence, as, for example, the star example of Zafaran; but the newly created ones are artificial. Sir Malcolm Darling believes that a strong educational effort could create a co-operative spirit, for which the Egyptian village is good ground, by reason of its informal mutual-help arrangements, and its family network. In the meantime, the aim of substituting the co-operative society for the landlord is not realized;

for the time being, the State must take his place, with the infant societies led paternally by the hand until they can learn to walk by themselves. The teacher is therefore all-important, and if not properly taught himself, paternal may never develop into co-operative control, may even harden into bureaucratic.[1]

Sir Malcolm doubts whether co-operative societies of this size—with 1,500 members or more—could function as genuine co-operatives.

Even if the co-operative societies should gain the power to manage their own affairs, they would still be obliged to farm collectively. The way in which the land is laid out obliges all farmers to follow a common rotation. The area of the estate is large—2,000, 5,000, even 10,000 acres. The whole area is divided into blocks, and in each block the land is divided into three or more large fields, each under a single crop. The farmers receive a piece of land in each field, so that their total holding is divided into three. In each harvest season of the year each field is under one crop, and each holding is under three different crops. The pieces composing the holding may be contiguous, stretching crosswise across the lengthwise field division. This was the case at Faroukia, where the field plan resembles that

---

[1] 'Land Reform in Italy and Egypt'.

used in the new settlements in South Italy—perhaps a result of advice given by Professor Bandini. The general field plan resembles that of the old open-field system in Europe.

The field layout facilitates deep ploughing (otherwise impeded in the Delta by permanent drains) and farming operations in general, as, for example, the co-operative picking of the cotton crop. In Sir Malcolm Darling's view the compulsory rotation is the most productive feature of the reform. There has been no change to small-scale farming. On the contrary, in so far as estates were rented to tenants, as even the largest were in part, the scale of operation is larger. Tractor-cultivation is being introduced, wherever it was not used before, which should allow the cultivator to reduce his working livestock and produce more meat and milk. It used to be said that Egypt is a country of large properties and small farms. So far as the requisitioned land is concerned, the reverse is true, for it is now held by small proprietors and farmed in large units.

Income from the land, however, is distributed in accordance with the output from each holding, and not, as in fully collective farming, in accordance with labour. The cash crops are sold to the co-operative for marketing, and the proceeds are credited to each member, after deduction of the annual instalment of the purchase price, the land tax, and the cost of fertilizers, seed, machine use, and any other services provided by the co-operative. Subsistence and fodder crops are retained by the cultivator. Livestock are owned by the farmers individually, but the estate dairy herds are owned by the co-operative.

On estates of the type so far requisitioned, it would not have been economic to divide the land into independent units. Official control was needed to maintain and add to the fixed capital; on the three estates visited there had been considerable new investment, since the reform, in pumps, wells, and machinery.

Management on estates of this kind is a professional job. There is nothing simple or medieval—as the open-field rotation may suggest—about an Egyptian estate. It combines a variety of complex routines. Lavish use of machinery is combined with lavish use of labour. At Bourgaya, in Minia province, a former private estate of 2,000 acres, previously partly directly farmed and partly leased, and extremely productive, had been

44

divided among 800 families. It used steam ploughing, on the so-called Fowler system, by which two cumbrous 45-h.p. steam engines (fuelled by Diesel oil or cotton stalks) uncoil a cable driving a plough which can cultivate as much as 20 acres a day. The whole area is under perennial irrigation, the fields divided into patches 6 feet square by shallow ridged ditches, which are ploughed over after every harvest and must be re-dug for every crop, so that labour requirements are enormous. Technical methods are as old as history and as new as science can make them. New pumps are being installed, while Archimedes screws are carried swiftly about on donkeys. Camels in the great court-yard load quarter-tons of nitrates; but the vines are fertilized by the manure supplied by 15,000 pairs of pigeons, housed in the fantastic white dovecote. Machine spraying with bulk oil is used in the superb orange grove, still awaiting the 'agri-cultural graduates', who, according to the law, should farm it co-operatively in units of 10 acres. Orange crates are made at lightning speed from date-palm stalks, held in the craftsman's toes. All this intricacy needs expert supervision. The co-opera-tive board met in an optimistic mood (net income per acre is unusually high) and the Chairman spoke powerfully in favour of the revolution.

The great estates of Upper Egypt are more highly capitalized and mechanized than most estates in Lower Egypt. The low cost of labour is not, as is often believed, the reason for the lack of mechanization, but the permanent drains which in the Delta impede tractor ploughing. In Upper Egypt the drains are not permanent, and although wages are much lower than in the Delta, big estates use more machinery. The sugar-cane plan-tations in Kena province are very highly capitalized indeed, equipped with railways to move the crop, caterpillar tractors for rooting up the cane, and pump irrigation.

The question of the right form of organization on the plan-tation estates was difficult. Most of the land is under sugar, which remains in the ground for three years on good land and two years on medium-quality land, and consequently the land cannot be divided into holdings to provide subsistence crops. The Higher Committee at first intended to run these planta-tions with employed labour. Before the reform these estates were centrally managed as to pump irrigation and heavy machinery, but the land was leased to large tenants who cropped it with gangs of low-paid labourers. The Higher Committee decided that this system was inconsistent with the aim of raising the income of the cultivator, and therefore decided to retain the land in state ownership, leasing it to a large number of share-croppers with secure tenure and a minimum share income.[1]

At Armant, across the Nile twenty miles south of Luxor, an estate of 5,000 acres, formerly the property of Ahmed Abboud, has been reorganized on this basis. Of its total area, 2,250 acres are under sugar-cane, 1,000 under cotton, and the remainder under wheat, vegetables, and berseem. The greater part of the land is under perennial irrigation, supplied by two Diesel pump installations, with five pumps totalling 850 h.p. A new pump is being installed, to convert the basin land to perennial irrigation. The gross income from the sugar-cane alone on this estate amounted to £235,000 per annum. Cane yields average 50 tons to the acre, 20 per cent above the national average.

The estate has now been allotted, under permanent share-cropping agreements, to 1,700 families. The land is divided according to its quality into three areas: the best land, which grows sugar-cane for three years in succession and is then re-planted with cane; the second quality, which grows cane for two years followed by one year under another crop before being replanted; and the third quality, not good enough for cane, which grows cotton, wheat, and berseem. Each family receives two pieces of land, a holding of 2–5 acres comprising either one piece of the first quality and one piece of the third, or two pieces of the second quality, so that in any one year half the holding is under cane and half under other crops.

Formerly the land was leased to 100 contractors who employed labour at the wage of £3 per month. The net income now earned by the share-cropping farmers (according to information given at Armant in 1955) is now £6 per month for a holding of 2 acres, £9 for a holding of 3 acres. This corresponds to net income per acre of £36 per annum; gross output per acre for the whole estate averages £100. Costs of management,

---

[1] It is interesting that a somewhat similar type of organization has been introduced in Puerto Rico on the Proportionate Profit Farms. See UN, Dept. of Economic Affairs, *Progress in Land Reform*, p. 86.

irrigation, machinery, seed, and fertilizers therefore account for £64 per acre.

Harvesting needs more labour than the family can provide, and is carried out in groups of four families working together on each other's holdings, the men cutting and loading the cane on to camels, women stripping the leaves for fodder and loading them on to donkeys. The cane is carried to trucks on the estate railway for transport to the sugar factory and weight is recorded in the tenant's name by a tarbushed overseer. Across the river from Luxor there is a very similar scene in the mortuary chapel of Prince Menna, manager of the royal granaries and director of the cadastral survey, depicted as he checked the output of the harvest fields 3,000 years ago.

The dark side at Armant is seen in the two *esbahs* (the landowners' tied villages) on the borders of the estate. The estate employs five villages, three of which are prosperous, and two very poor. In these villages huts are only six feet high, without windows or doors, and their inhabitants were obviously destitute. Only a few had acquired a holding and the rest lived by casual labour. Earnings were said to be higher, but were evidently still very low. Probably the equalization of incomes results in concentrating employment among the families of the share-croppers, reducing the employment for the labourers. So far no houses have been built for the fellahin, though areas of land have been reserved for the purpose. The contrast between this level of living and the immensely high productivity of the land and its splendid equipment is a grim reminder of the gravity of Egypt's land problem.

The reform in practice is very managerial. The idea of creating a strong small-peasant class, which influenced liberal opinion when the law was passed, has disappeared completely. So far as the very large estates are concerned, it is difficult to see how this course could have been avoided. Up to the middle of 1955, only the very large estates had been taken over. Expropriation of the smaller estates had begun. Presumably the same methods of management will be used here also, though it will be costly to maintain such a large administrative staff on farms of 100–200 acres. On estates where tenancy has been the rule there is no technical reason why farmers should not become independent. Most of Egypt's cotton comes off the small and medium-sized farms, and distribution of seed and fertilizers creates no problems, though doubtless it could be improved. But independence, in a country so densely populated, could only be a short-term condition. Ownership of land does not provide income stability, because of the continuous pressure to subdivide and sub-let which reduces farms to uneconomic sizes, and renders them very weak risk-bearers. The experience of other over-populated countries, for example India, shows that one of the main problems of reform is to make ownership stick. The co-operative form of organization gives greater income stability. What the farmer gains is not economic independence, but a higher income with a guaranteed minimum; he can consume the income gain, since the management looks after investment. Overall financial control has been used to build up a stabilization fund to maintain farm incomes in years of bad harvests or low prices—a wise and very necessary precaution in an economy so dependent on one crop. The lack of independence is the price of greater social and economic security.

In practice, though not in theory, the redistribution of property means that the land is nationalized. Nationalization of the land is nothing new in Egypt's long history; one successful measure, linked with grain stabilization, is described in Genesis, and since then there have been other occasions. The control of Egypt's water is so highly centralized by the Nile itself that to any strong government the step to state ownership of the land seems easy. What is new is the idea of a fair deal for the fellahin, or at any rate a fairer deal. The real change is that the cultivator has a recognized legal status; that, in itself, is an immense change for the better, outweighing any criticism. If the reform can maintain this position, that is the greatest measure of success. The Government has done as much as was practicable, and far more than might have been expected.

It is true that the reform does not benefit the casual labourers, the poorest class. It means a real gain for the majority of the fellahin, either by giving them protection as tenants, or by giving them secure status as co-operative farmers. But it does not benefit the entire farm population. This is inevitable. No reform, even if it went much farther than the present measure, could provide land for all in this congested country, or could increase employment in agriculture. That the reform has not benefited the casual labourers is a result, not of a weakness in reform policy, but of population pressure. The Government can do no more than press on with its plans for more land and more industry.

It might be expected, none the less, that the difference in benefits would create jealousy, as between tenants and new owners, and as between these beneficiaries and the landless. Rent-paying tenants might demand the expropriation of all landowners, and the landless might demand land. On this point, the attitude of the fellahin, no outside observer can venture an opinion. Some authorities think that the situation is unstable, and that there is unrest, while officials of the Higher Committee believe that, so long as redistribution is carried out equitably between the claimants, no new antagonisms are created. Whether that is the case or not, the need for more land and more industry is increased, rather than diminished, by the greater degree of security which the reform provides for the majority of the farm population.

THE LIBERATION PROVINCE

The Liberation (Tahrir) province is a community creation, in the desert west of the Delta and south of Alexandria. Work first began on it eighteen months after the revolution, in December 1953. The area covered by the province is 1,200,000 acres; it is to include twelve districts, each to contain eleven villages. In fifteen years' time, when the additional water from the High Dam is available, there should be 800,000 acres of reclaimed land. At present there are 10,000 acres in process of reclamation, of which 5,000 acres are already under cultivation, water being supplied by pumps from the Rashid branch of the Nile.

'What exists now is only a bridgehead', said Major Mohammed Magdi Hassanein, the manager and moving spirit of the Tahrir province. Its objects are 'to accustom our people to the desert, to make the young intellectuals practically active in reclamation, and to give more work'. 'Humanity is to be the keynote', he said, and referred to the traditions of ancient Egypt as the inspiration. Sport and music are to be the influences in this new liberated life, not technical education, for that the inhabitants will acquire in the course of their work. No foreign experts are to be employed. The women are to participate fully, even to the extent of taking up sport—a revolution indeed. The province thus embodies the hopes of the Government for the new Egypt, an idea which action has created.

The new national spirit is evident in the names of the new settlements. The capital is Nasr, meaning victory, the secret password on the day of the revolution. The four villages which are being completed are named Omar Shahin, after a victim of the Canal fighting, Umm Sabr, after a woman victim, Omar Makram, a popular hero in the time of Mohammed Ali, and Ahmed Arabi, after Arabi Pasha. Each village is to have 230 houses, with 1,500 acres of land, of which 12,000 will be cultivated. So far they are not inhabited; the selected settlers are still being trained.

Land reclamation is not to be the only economic base of the province; it will include new industries. Those which supply the needs of the settlement are already in operation; a machine-repair shop, a furniture factory, and the cement brick works. An ammunition factory is under construction.

Fourteen thousand workers are at present employed in reclamation and construction. They come from Upper Egypt, and also from the adjacent provinces of Minufia and Dakahlia. Workers are paid at the rate of £12 per month,[1] a very high wage by comparison with existing rates, which in Upper Egypt would average only £3 per month. (Its immediate economic effect is a rise in wages for these low-paid workers.)

The land reclamation, the factories, and the building are directed by a large professional staff; it has evidently been possible to attract well-qualified engineers, scientists, and managers. The scheme has found a good architect. Community development schemes are rarely attractive, but the public buildings, the school, and the small mosque are simply and well built in clear pale colours which are in harmony with the desert landscape.

The settlers who are to populate the new villages are selected by Major Gamal Zaki, director of the Social Affairs Department, who 'majored' in the United States in community de-

[1] This official figure was confirmed in private conversations with the workmen.

velopment, and is terrifyingly adept in the jargon of the new subject. Settlers, he said, are selected scientifically on social, medical, and psychological tests. As social qualifications applicants must possess only one wife, no dependants other than children, and no property; they must have been only once married and must have finished their military service. Of 1,100 applicants so far, all had the right social qualifications, but only 382 families were accepted medically, because while most of the men were healthy enough, the women and children fell far short of the standard. Only 180 families survived the psychological tests (on 'special criteria developed by the Psychological Board'). Of these, 132 are now undergoing the six months' training, which includes a three-month probation period. 'We consider both people and land to be under reclamation.' When trained in the central village, they will be moved out to other villages as nuclei for the future settlements.

The training includes primary education, vocational individual training, and combined training as a group. The men's day begins with a pep talk at 5 a.m. followed by a news commentary and breakfast, followed by a full day's work in the fields with a packed lunch, till 5 p.m., followed by rest and dinner at 6 p.m., followed by two hours of social activity. The women do no field work and are excused the social activity; they work at dairy farming and receive instruction in child and house care, cooking, knitting, and sewing; they sing and play volley-ball. The children attend school in the afternoon, and rest collectively, away from their mothers under the supervision of teachers. Each family has an independent house, with water and electricity, a double roof to reduce heat, and a tiny garden.

Women school teachers supervise the women's care of the new houses and report on their standard. The teachers work an eighteen-hour day, with these and other additional duties. Everything is disciplined, standardized, new. The livestock are kept collectively and do not share the new house. Baking is done collectively, the only cooking arrangement in the house being a small oil stove. Even dress is standardized, the boys in blue boiler suits and pale green shirts; the women in short cotton dresses, white socks, and rubber shoes; the teachers in grey.

Still, some care is taken not to force the pace too fast. The doctor, for instance, in giving the women instruction in hygiene, alluded to birth-control, but the men, on returning from the fields, said that he had no right to interfere in such matters, and the subject was not pursued.

The nutritional level is very good, with an average calorie intake of 3,600 per day, including three ounces of animal protein. The impressive visible result is that the children are magnificently healthy, as a result of sufficient food. The babies are splendid, the boys and girls energetic, with no sign of eye diseases. The women, primly tending the model house, seem slightly dazed.

The new settlers will receive ownership of the house and the little garden, but will not receive ownership of land. All farming will be mechanized, in large units, managed co-operatively, in fact collectively, though, said the Director, 'we must keep the word collective out of our vocabulary'. The co-operatives are to be under the management of a council of eleven members, composed of the village mayor and five appointed persons, including the preacher, doctor, school teacher, and five selected representatives of the village. For the first three years they are to be kept under control by giving the mayor a casting vote— 'so you may say a dictatorship'. The co-operative members will purchase all equipment jointly, including tractors and livestock, over a period of thirty years, with the exception of the services normally provided by the Government out of taxes, i.e. roads and irrigation.

As to the economic side, it is difficult to form any idea of the prospects. The scheme is financed from the proceeds of the sale of the royal properties (which are alleged to have realized £70 million), so that sufficient funds are available. The cost of reclamation is low, much lower than in European countries. It amounts to £38 per acre for the reclamation of the land alone, £250 per acre if the costs of cement-lined canals, drainage, and housing are included. These figures are compared with £800 per acre in Italy and £4,000 in Holland. No figures were given covering the costs of the entire scheme, but the cost of the factories must be considerable, and there are some items as, for instance, the imported Friesian cattle, which seem extravagant. The reclamation work is expected to be self-financing, as it is calculated that when 250,000 acres have been reclaimed the resulting income will pay for the reclamation of the remainder of the 800,000 acres. Since the output per acre will certainly be high, the economic success of the land reclamation as such seems a reasonable hope.

The crops now grown are chiefly beans and berseem as reclamation crops; but for melons and strawberries Tahrir already has a reputation. It is intended to concentrate on fruit and vegetables, and to centralize marketing so that exports can be directed to the best markets. In recent years there has been a great improvement in the quality of citrus and other fruit in Egypt, but there is still room to improve. Success really depends on whether Egyptians can do with these new crops what they have been able to do with cotton over the last half-century.

The completion of this scheme and the reclamation of the whole area of the province will depend on the additional water which will be provided by the High Dam. But this must take many years to complete. In the meantime the land depends on water which is diverted from existing supplies. The new Liberation Canal is now almost completed, and will serve larger areas. How far existing supplies of water can be utilized without depriving areas which are already under cultivation is a matter of dispute. The supporters of the Tahrir scheme claim that there can be a larger diversion of water, because the present area of the Delta is over-watered. They rightly point out that in the years before the war reclamation was continuous, though it came to a standstill during the war, so that it can be resumed on a larger scale without damage. The construction of the new canal did not, however, pass without protest from neighbouring districts.

The aim of creating a new society as well as new land is ambitious. Many foreign influences have played an acknowledged part in the conception, for community development is a composite product, derived from the experience of many countries. Yugoslavia in the first flush of the Youth Railway also comes to mind: the notice-board photographs of the preacher, for instance, transformed from a pious delicate scholar into a robust 'outgiver' who retains only the long sheikh's coat as a sign of his profession. As in Yugoslavia, among the young teachers there is devotion to an undefined future.

But there is also originality. It is new for Egyptians to find practical inspiration in the fifty centuries of Egyptian history.

It is new to undertake community building with a wider horizon than the rather tedious new insistence on literacy and technology. Egypt has been, and still is, too great in agriculture to find inspiration in better farming as a way of life: but art and sport are missing in its over-professionalized life, and it is wise to emphasize them. The ideal of turning the young intellectuals to practical work is original also, and, if it is realized, Egypt will have solved a major social problem of the whole region.

About all such conscious human conditioning there must remain a faint sense of misgiving.[1] Perhaps there is too much sense of pulling out of the hideous poverty of the old villages and turning away from the accumulated debris of the past. In the other-worldly light of the Alexandria sky, Tahrir seems a little like Akhnaton's City of the Horizon. Yet it must be remembered that more land and more water is the main condition for leverage of the living standard of the country as a whole.

The contrast with Iraq is complete. There money for the dams is available and to spare, and foreign firms are doing the work which will bring the new water-supplies forward. But unless things change, the water and land will be used to grow poor barley crops with half-starved labour; there is no prospect that the resources will be used to serve the people. Egypt, on the other hand, has set its human values first, and gets the men and women and the land ready for the water, while raising funds and the whirlwind by playing Great Power politics. If the pitch seems rather too high, and the expenditure rather too lavish, that is probably the only way in which anything can be achieved in this very old country.

[1] See 'Postscript', pp. 200–1.

54

II

SOCIAL STRUCTURE AND
TECHNICAL CHANGE IN THE CRESCENT

THE Egyptian revolution had immediate repercussions throughout the Crescent: the 'rose-water revolution' in Lebanon,
stormy meetings of fellahin in Aleppo, and riots in Amara. The
repercussions continue. The Egyptian reform is so far the only
serious attack on rural poverty in the Arab world, and the
hopes which it raises outside Egypt are inevitably as important
as its achievements inside the country. Socially, the Arab world
has one main problem—the low status and low standard of the
fellahin.

Economically, however, the position in the Crescent is different. Agrarian reform came first in Egypt because it is more
advanced than Syria and Iraq, which are developing rapidly
but are not, as Egypt is, in a state of agricultural overdevelop-
ment. The economy of Egypt is fully capitalistic, and on the
existing land area cultivation cannot go much further in in-
tensity. The social structure is correspondingly more highly
evolved and stratified, with an agrarian hierarchy resembling
that of some European countries, present-day Italy for example,
or Hungary in the years between the wars. There is a rich landowner class, which has accumulated and invested capital, a
farming middle class, small peasant owners, and a large land
proletariat.

In Syria and Iraq, by contrast, land areas are expanding,
yields are low and variable, and agriculture is extensive, still
in part soil mining rather than farming. The social structure is
looser and less stratified. Large landowners include merchant
money-lenders, old-established *rentiers*, and tribal sheikhs; the
investing commercial magnate is a new phenomenon. Peasant
farmers exist, but do not form a distinct social stratum, as in
Egypt: they are localized in high rainfall districts, as for instance the Kurdish hills and the Jebel Druze, where peasant

55

life recalls Macedonia and Dalmatia. Middle-class farmers can be found in the Jezira, but they too are localized and do not form a separate class. Throughout the Crescent there is much local specialization, in village crafts and domestic industries which still supply the market of the poor.

This variety, the result of a less capitalistic level, and a less integrated national life, means that class antagonisms are less acute. Villages are isolated from each other and from the towns by great distances, often by stretches of uncultivable desert. The relationship between town and country is different. In Egypt the whole economy depends on the cotton crop, through layer upon layer of technical expertise, from the Alexandria cotton broker to the fellah with ten acres who collects the crop from his village and delivers it to the ginnery. In Syria and Iraq the villages are a world apart, a neglected hinterland which supplies food to the cities and gets nothing in return.

Because agriculture is one-sided and unstable, and was until recently primitive, the setting of reform in these countries is a different one. The aim, as in Egypt, is to give a better living standard and a social status to the fellah. But this aim can be realized only through a better system of farming. Grain farming with the horse- or ox-drawn plough is too unproductive and too unstable to provide a sound basis for small ownership. Reform in the Crescent must therefore be an agricultural as well as a social policy, and must be related either to irrigation, which is the only basis for productive farming in small units, or to extensive mechanized farming, in large units.

Today the arch of the Crescent, from Aleppo to Mosul and beyond, has gone over to mechanized farming. The tractor in these countries is not merely a useful technical improvement. It brings a technical revolution which removes old obstacles to the expansion of cultivation. It means the end of the long struggle between the nomad and the cultivator—the crucial conflict which Ibn Khaldun regarded as the meaning of history, as indeed in this region it has been. It completes the disintegration of tribal society, already undermined by motor transport in the inter-war years. The whole cultivable area can now be brought under cultivation. All the conditions which formerly checked the expansion of cultivation are removed.

In the past climate, primitive methods, and political insecurity combined to prevent the extension of cultivation and the improvement of farming. Although cultivation in this region is as old as agriculture itself, most of the land now cultivated has been brought under the plough only in quite recent times.[1] In the early 1950's, agricultural production in the Crescent and Turkey had increased by 50–70 per cent over the pre-war level, and most of this expansion has been achieved by bringing more land under tractor cultivation.

Climatic conditions make the Crescent a region of prairie farming. In the irrigation zone of south Iraq the control of water could enable more intensive farming, by double cropping and better practices to ensure higher yields. But without irrigation, extensive grain cultivation is the only possible type of agriculture in most of the rainfall zone. Except on the coast and in the mountains, rainfall is too low for more intensive land use. The Fertile Crescent is only fertile by comparison with the desert which it surrounds. It is a semi-circle of cultivable land, defined by the 8-inch rainfall line. In the desert steppe belt, between the 4-inch and 8-inch rainfall line, crops can be grown but they are poor and uncertain. The precise position of the rainfall belts on the inner rim of the Crescent is not known: they are indicated, approximately, on the map on p. 85.

Throughout the dry-farming regions, wheat and barley are the main crops; cotton can be grown as a dry crop only in the regions of higher rainfall. For wheat and barley the fallow system, with fallow every second year or even for two years out of three, is the general rotation. Yields vary round the average to a far greater extent than they do in Europe, owing to the irregularity of rainfall. In the Syrian Jezira, for instance, wheat gives a tenfold return in a good year, sevenfold in a normal year, while in a bad year it will only give back the equivalent of the seed.

So long as ploughing depended on the horse or ox, costs were

[1] For the history of settlement for permanent cultivation in Syria see Norman Lewis, 'The Frontier of Settlement in Syria, 1800–1950', in *International Affairs*, January 1955, a most valuable article which is the prelude to a book on the subject. An impression of how recent the change has been can be gained from Gertrude Bell's description, in *The Desert and the Sown* (1907), of her journey from Jerusalem to Amman, Homs, Hama, and Antioch, through regions which were evidently then still mainly nomadic. Dr Salih Haider in *Land Problems of Iraq* (London University Ph.D. thesis, 1942; unpublished) gives figures which show how little land was cultivated in Iraq in the late nineteenth century.

too high in relation to the return. The low yield in the inland plains meant that the cultivator could not cultivate enough land to produce a surplus above his own needs and the needs of his working livestock. The irregularity of rainfall meant that the margin of advantage over nomadic life was narrow and variable, for though grazing offered a poor return, capital could be accumulated in livestock herds, while grain cultivation offered too unsteady a livelihood to allow the normal way of agricultural growth through investment in livestock.

The economic instability of cultivation, and the lack of political security, explain the long survival of communal forms of land use and cultivation. In Syria and Palestine the *musha'a* custom, a periodical reallotment of unequal holdings,[1] was still prevalent in the 1930's, though it was then disappearing. In southern Iraq tribal ownership of land, with customary rights of individual ownership to plots of land within the tribal area, was prevalent in the early years of the present century.

Whether as cause or effect of the difficult natural conditions, the political institutions of the past did not provide a framework for stability or expansion. Communal tenures survived even when the economic basis of communal land use, grazing with intermittent cropping, was giving place to permanent cultivation. In Ottoman times no systematic registration of title was undertaken, and large landholders, either the tribal sheikhs or city merchant money-lenders, profited by the Government's failure to settle title to communal land on the basis of individual ownership. The uncertainty of yields meant that agriculture was permanently short of capital. Many large properties in Syria and in northern Iraq originated through money-lending to impoverished villagers. How little such city landowners interested themselves in agriculture can be seen by the fact that the *musha'a* custom of periodic reallotment often continued in their villages. The city landowner's function was to receive rents and advance loans, not to put money into cultivation. Now their function is changing. Tractor farming transforms the role of the city merchants into that of a technical 'carrier group', and in northern Syria has already transformed the agrarian structure.

---

[1] It resembled the Russian 'repartitional commune', of which the origin is controversial.

Share-cropping, i.e. the division of the crop between the landowner and the cultivator in a fixed proportion, is still the main form of tenure. It is a customary form, without any contractual legal basis or any legal protection for the cultivator. The proportion taken by the landowner varies in dry farming with the density of population, being high in the neighbourhood of towns, and low on the desert rim. In dry farming the landowner's share is generally pure rent, i.e. is payment for the use of a scarce factor of production, and not payment in respect of productive services. If these are provided, the share taken is higher. For irrigation farming the landowner provides water (for cotton seed is always provided), and the share taken is higher.

The system is, of course, a bad one, in so far as the landowner is a pure rent receiver and does not invest in the land. The cultivators, on a low subsistence margin, have neither the means nor the incentive to invest: they are labourers, rather than tenants, who work for a variable return, and cannot increase it by working harder or farming better.

This system is not peculiar to the countries of the Crescent. It exists through Asia, from Persia to the Philippines, in many local variants, and under different names. There is no generic name to describe what is probably the most widespread form of economic organization in the world. English writers often describe it as 'absentee landlordism', by analogy with nineteenth-century Ireland. But this term is inexact, for it implies that the landowner neglects his functions—the maintenance of soil fertility and fixed capital—by reason of absence. The evil of the system is not absenteeism as such, but the lack of any investing or managerial function. The object of the system is to avoid the costs of management and investment. It has a superficial resemblance to *métayage* in southern Europe, but the resemblance is only superficial, for *métayage* is a method of dividing the profits of the farm on the basis of a contract, whereas the share-cropping relationship in the Fertile Crescent is a simple division of the produce between labour and landownership, with no contract, and with no investment except in the bare necessities of seed and working livestock.

The system exists most generally in over-populated countries, and appears to be symptomatic of a static or retrogressive condition, in which the landowner can obtain a higher return by renting land than by farming it himself. In the Crescent it appears to be a function of landlords' monopoly allied with insecurity. On estates which were formerly tribal property, the practice of share-cropping originated in the sheikh's claim to a portion of the crop as revenue to provide for his political and judicial functions, and continues as rent after these functions cease to be exercised. On estates acquired by city merchants and notables, the share-cropping system originated in payment for debts or protection.

Most of the large properties now in existence in the Crescent appear to be recent in origin, because settlement for permanent cultivation is recent. The land system of the Crescent is often described as feudal, but in the historical sense the description is not accurate. If feudalism is understood to mean tenure in fief, the grant of land in return for military service, then the system cannot properly be so described, for the large properties which now exist did not, in the main, originate in this way. There has been no period of feudal order, and its absence explains much that is puzzling in prevalent social attitudes.

In European countries the pivot of feudal society was the identification of private rights over land and labour with public function. The grant of land in fief, in return for military service, conferred political privilege and function; the right to tax, to administer justice, to exact labour service or produce rents, from the serfs. Politically, it was an instrument for delegating power when the central government was weak—'le désordre érigé en système'. Economically it provided a framework for expansion. 'Nul terre sans seigneur' was a development policy, as well as a crude system of political security and a social hierarchy. In old feudal societies characteristic social attitudes survive the dissolution of the system itself: a sense of political responsibility, or 'noblesse oblige' on the part of the aristocracy; prestige attaching to landownership and strong incentives, on the part of the peasants, to hoard to acquire land.

In the Fertile Crescent these attitudes are lacking. Weulersse has emphasized the paradox, monstrous in Western eyes, of 'peasant populations devoid of peasant atavism, landowners without a feeling for land or respect for it, cultivators who despise cultivation, labourers who hate the plough and villagers who renounce the village to remain true to the tribe.'[1] For the landlord land is a convenient way of holding wealth; for the fellah it is a miserable means of subsistence. Though city patriotism is strong, there is no attachment to a country place among landowners, and no sense of political obligation or social responsibility attaching to landownership, except in so far as tribal loyalties survive. 'Il n'y a pas de noblesse terrienne en Islam, il n'y a pas de "Monsieur de . . ." ', says Weulersse. He considers that the lack of 'sens terrien' makes Arab civilization exceptional, and perhaps unique, because it is a civilization without a basis in land.[2] Other writers take the same view. Ayrout quotes from Ibn Khaldun a saying of Mohammed, that the plough never enters a house without bringing degradation.[3]

If the land is not loved, as it is in Europe, it is doubtless because it is not responsive. Water, the real staff of life, is treasured and fought for and celebrated in literature. There is no need to look for deeper roots for contempt for agriculture than the natural conditions of the desert. The wonderful artifact of Egyptian agriculture proves that this contempt does not hold good when nature favours easier control.

Because natural conditions were adverse for farming and favourable for trade and tribal life, the Fertile Crescent, by contrast with Europe, did not experience a long period of slow growth from tribal society to an urban trading economy through settled agriculture expanding on a land base. The three forms of economic life existed side by side, with agriculture dependent on the town, and threatened by the tribe. The elements from which feudal society evolved in Europe were present in the tribal sheikhs, but Ottoman rule did not rely on them, or attempt to incorporate them into a political system, imposing instead a centralized administration in which military officials were given rights which corresponded to feudal status in Europe. This system was abolished in 1839, and revenue was collected through tax-collectors, usually local notables, or heads of tribes and villages. In 1858 the Ottoman Land Code attempted to replace this system by establishing

---

[1] Jacques Weulersse, *Paysans de Syrie et du Proche Orient* (Paris, Gallimard, 1946), p. 66.
[2] ibid. pp. 70–1.   [3] *Fellahs d'Égypte*, p. 134.

registration of title to land, but without success. Apart from some grants of land made to influential politicians and collaborators, Turkish rule was hostile to large landowners, as rival sources of power. Consequently landownership was based not on military power and political obligation, but on money-lending, tax-collecting, or tribal authority—functions which were not tied in with political responsibility.

Today the landowners of the Crescent are extremely heterogeneous in function and origin. They do not, in any sense, form an aristocracy. There are true aristocrats who hold their properties by the tradition of military power over a community, as, for example, Kemal Jumblatt, a leader of the Druzes in Lebanon, who from the stronghold at Mukhtara has distributed land to his peasants. He now leads the Socialist Party, inspired by the principles of Asian leaders. Centuries divide this last stage of feudal power from the great sheikh landowners of the southern marshes of Iraq, tribal leaders in the process of becoming an aristocracy. The big grain farmers of northern Syria are commercial farmers, speculators and investors, and show more public spirit, as will be seen, than the old-established landowners or the sheikhs. The country-gentleman ethos is lacking, though individuals can generate it for themselves—as for example Hussein Ibish in Syria, and another Kurdish landowner on the Iraq–Syria border—when they undertake real farming.

Yet though the relation between the landowner and the state cannot properly be described as feudal, the relations between the landowner and the cultivators are of a feudal character, since they are determined by a social stratification which is rigid, even though its origin is recent. The extreme case is found in southern Iraq, where the cultivators are serfs entirely dependent on the landowner and subservient to him, and bound to the land in law. In the older regions of Syria, locally and more correctly described as 'seigniorial', a similar though less oppressive relationship exists on large estates.

Reform of the land system therefore involves the abolition of feudal relations, in this sense. But in other respects the social structure is not feudal, and as a label applied to the land systems of the Arab world the term can be grossly misleading, because it obscures the great differences between the countries. Egypt of the Pashas was an Edwardian society, with its sharp contrasts of surfeit and starvation, its luxury and vulgarity. Modern Syria is in a mid-Victorian expansion, with new capitalists and a rising working class. Iraq is a tribal society in the throes of a disembodied industrial revolution. The setting of the land reform problem therefore differs, and the methods of solution will differ also. Egypt's reform is social, Syria's will be political, and Iraq needs reform for reasons which are political, social, and economic.

As a result of the coming of the tractor, the land system itself is now beginning to change. Some of its results are observed in the following chapters: the rise of the merchant-tractorists, the substitution of paid skilled labour for the unskilled sharecropper, the displacement of labour, and the new extension of cultivation. These changes are only now beginning, but they will continue, bringing greater fluidity in social relations.

Because the impetus to reform must come from political forces, and because the serf-seigniorial relationship cannot be altered without political change, it is impossible to forecast the types of reform which will be carried out, or to make proposals, in the abstract, for any specific type of reform.

But whatever kind of reform is undertaken, it must take the technical change into account. There is no need, in countries which have sufficient land in relation to their population, to think in terms of maximum farm sizes in accordance with the area which can be worked by the farm family with draught livestock.[1] For irrigation farming tractors are needed to supplement cultivation by animals,[2] and in dry farming should be the only form of draught power. The tractor can, of course, raise yields, because it can speed work at the best seasons, which in the Crescent is vitally important. But it can very well endanger soil fertility, as in the Jezira it probably does. The remedy is not a return to the horse or the camel or the ox, but better rotations, and other measures to prevent erosion.

Even with better crop rotations, tractor-farming is not likely

---

[1] As, for example, the International Bank Mission did in recommending that 'Fundamentally the allotment should not be bigger than that which can be managed by the average farm family without outside assistance' (*The Economic Development of Iraq* (Baltimore, Johns Hopkins Press, 1952), p. 269).

[2] See, for example, the recommendations of the Soil Survey report on the Dujaila Settlement, quoted on p. 168 below.

to bring about much improvement in output per acre. Though yields in Syria and Iraq are low, the average wheat yield in Syria is only some 20 per cent lower than the average yield in the United States and Canada, as the following table shows.

TABLE 8

Grain Yields in the Crescent and in Other Countries
1948–50 Average

	100 kg. per hectare		cwt. per acre	
	Wheat	Barley	Wheat	Barley
Syria	9·2	9·3	7·3	7·4
Iraq	5·8	7·2	4·0	5·7
United States	11·1	14·0	8·8	11·1
Canada	10·4	12·6	8·2	10·0
United Kingdom	26·8	24·9	21·2	19·7
Europe	14·5	16·6	11·5	13·2

(SOURCE: FAO, *Yearbook of Food and Agricultural Statistics, 1954.*)

The most that could be achieved by better methods in dry farming would probably be an increase of some 10 or 20 per cent above the present level. Nor, of course, will tractor-farming stabilize yields. But the improvement in labour productivity ought to allow some saving in agriculture, to form a reserve against bad years, so that farm incomes could be stabilized, though the variations in output will remain. Tractor-farming is therefore not likely to raise the level of land productivity to any great extent. It does, however, raise the level of labour productivity, and so must play an essential part in any measure of reform which aims at raising the income of the cultivators.

Because reform must be linked with technical change, its methods must necessarily differ from the Egyptian. So far as the size of farm holdings is concerned, the Egyptian reform is not a good model, since tiny holdings of 2–3 acres would not provide a subsistence minimum in the Crescent. It is a good model, however, in so far as the unit of management and operation is large. Egyptian 'co-operative farming' could serve as a model for irrigation settlements, provided that the farm holdings granted are large enough not only to give a good standard for the farm family, but also to allow for a rising standard, and a higher rate of production to satisfy the demands of the growing town population. For dry farming the minimum new holding should be based on the area which a tractor can cultivate. Independent farming in family units should be feasible, provided that tractor repair and maintenance services are organized. (See 'Postscript', pp. 216–21, on the adaptation of the Egyptian model to Syrian conditions.)

The aim of reform in Syria and Iraq should therefore be not a minimum standard, but the best possible standard of living in expanding economies. In its essential aim, better standards and the guaranteed status, the Egyptian reform represents the right starting-point; and in the countries of the Crescent, with their new deployment of enterprise and money, it needs to be worked out in the context of the new farming methods. The realization of the Egyptian aim, in their conditions, could raise the rural living standard well above its wretchedly low level, and so sustain general economic progress. Social reform has had to wait on technical change, for without the tractor the low level of output per man would remain a permanent feature of the agriculture of the Crescent.

A NOTE ON STATE LAND AND THE LEGAL CATEGORIES
OF LAND

In the following chapters it will be seen that proposals for reform both in Syria and Iraq concern the distribution of state land to cultivators. It appears necessary, therefore, to give some explanation of the meaning of state land in Moslem law. The conception of state land is confusing to Westerners, who are prone to assume that the state's claim to ownership of the land means a form of public ownership analogous to that which exists in Western countries, in which the state owns the land as a juridical person, and controls its use and disposal. The conception of state ownership in Moslem law is quite different: in theory, the state claims ownership of all land, except in so far as this has been assigned in *mulk* and *waqf* tenure to individuals.

The legal categories of land are based on Moslem sacred law:

le droit coranique, extrêmement riche, complexe et touffu, mais dont la richesse même n'exclut pas un défaut de précision fondamental en ce qui concerne les questions foncières. De là une opposition flagrante avec les principes intransigeants du droit romain, source de nos conceptions juridiques.[1]

Though these categories today have little importance, because they have been superseded by a Western conception of ownership, some explanation of their meaning may be helpful.

Until the 1930's, when the legal basis of ownership was changed by new legislation both in Syria and in Iraq, land law was based on the Ottoman Land Code of 1858. This was an attempt to introduce order into a confused mass of earlier legislation. It recognized five categories of land, as follows.

1. *Mulk land:* land held in absolute freehold ownership. It is governed by the provisions of sacred law and not by those of the civil statute law. Landownership comprises two rights: the *raqaba*, or right of absolute ownership, and the *tasarruf*, or right to the usufruct of land. In *mulk* tenure both rights belong to the individual.

2. *Miri land:* land of which the *raqaba* or absolute ownership belongs to the state, but the usufruct or *tasarruf* to the individual. It is a form of heritable leasehold ownership in which the state leases land to the individual.

3. *Waqf land:* land dedicated to some pious purpose; except in Egypt, it is no longer important.

4. *Matruka land:* land reserved for some public purpose as, for example, village threshing floors; also very small in extent.

5. *Mawat land:* dead or unreclaimed land.

The significance of these categories can be understood by reference to the conception of ownership which existed at the time of the Moslem conquest.[2] The important distinction lay between the first two categories, *mulk* and *miri. Mulk* tenure confers absolute ownership; and at the time of the Moslem conquest was confined to land and houses in towns, the only goods which the Moslem conquerors recognized as the property of individuals. All other land was *miri* (from *emiriye*, princely), i.e. belonged to the state as the spoils of war and therefore as the property of the Moslem community. But the rulers did not wish to cultivate this land, and left it in the possession of its effective owners. Thus there arose the conception of two rights of owner-

[1] Weulersse, *Paysans de Syrie et du Proche Orient*, pp. 90–1.   [2] ibid. pp. 90–6.

ship over land, the absolute ownership, or *raqaba*, always vested in the state, and the right of usufructuary possession, the *tasarruf*, held by the existing occupiers. The state's right of ownership in practice meant the right to tax the occupiers of land or to exact labour from them; it did not imply any control over the use of land, or any degree of responsibility for its cultivation.

The three other categories are of lesser importance. The third category, *waqf*, is a peculiarity of Moslem law. It is a permanent endowment of land or buildings for religious or pious purposes, such as a mosque, school, or hospital. The endowment is irrevocable and inalienable, and in Ottoman times came under Moslem sacred law. *Waqf* properties were then administered by a special Ministry, which was one of the more important posts in the Empire. The institution was subject to abuse by means of legal subterfuges which diverted the income to private or political ends. A special form of *waqf* allowed individuals to dedicate property to a pious purpose in the future, after their family had died out. This form of permanent entail allowed large proprietors to maintain their property intact against spoliation by the Government and thus helped to promote concentration of ownership in the past. It has now been abolished in Egypt, Syria, and Iraq.

Matruka ('left-over') land was land reserved for public use, and corresponds to the Western conception of public property; it includes roads, rivers, public buildings, market places, or village threshing floors.

Mawat or *mubah* lands were desert or empty lands, the property of the state. Those who brought them into cultivation could acquire *miri* ownership, i.e. the right of usufructuary possession, by proving cultivation over a fixed period.

These minor categories overlap the major categories, *waqf* being a form of *mulk*, while *mawat* land is included within the category *miri*.

How far these legal distinctions had practical influence on the system of tenure is a question that cannot be answered without research. The greater security of urban property in contrast to property in land might be held to explain the strong tendency, still very evident, for landowners to invest in urban house property and to live in towns. But against this view, it appears that even in Ottoman times the distinction between *mulk* and *miri* had ceased to have practical importance, because in the course of time legislation gave security to *miri* landholders, and ownership of the *tasarruf* became equivalent to full ownership in that it conferred right of sale, inheritance, and mortgage.[1] The only conditional feature which remained was the state's right to resume ownership of *miri* land left uncultivated.

While the categories in themselves may not have had much importance, the absence of an effective system for the settlement of title in the late Ottoman period probably did represent an obstacle to settlement for permanent cultivation. There was no legal mould into which the existing communal tenures could dissolve, and consequently tax-collectors, sheikhs, and city merchants could acquire landownership more easily than they might have done had the Ottoman attempt to settle title on the basis of individual ownership been successful.

The Ottoman Land Code of 1858 was intended to introduce a general system of individual ownership; its main purpose was to introduce compulsory registration of title to all *miri* land, as the necessary basis for a reform of the tax system. From 1839, when the military fiefs were abolished, taxes were collected by tax-farmers, whose methods were arbitrary and produced little revenue. The object of the Land Code was to reform the system of taxation by establishing direct contact between the actual cultivators and the state. In order to tax every piece of land, it was necessary to establish its ownership, by means of registration of title, through the *senet tapu*, the grant of title.

At the time that the Code was promulgated, most of the land of the Ottoman Empire was *miri*, and was occupied by customary landholders, without legal title to land. These included settled village communities, practising semi-communal forms of cultivation, tribes exercising customary rights of ownership over large areas, and large landowners who had received grants of land from the Sultan in return for their services. The aim of the Ottoman Government was to grant title directly to the cultivator, and to prevent any intermediary interest in land between the Government and cultivating occupiers of land. Hence the theory that the legal ownership of *miri* land belonged to the state, and that title could be granted only to the usufruct

---

[1] Weulersse, *Paysans de Syrie et du Proche Orient*, p. 92.

of land, could be used as a weapon in the hands of the Government, serving to establish individual ownership as against the tribal sheikhs, and against the tax-collectors and other intermediaries. The Turks wanted to create a strong central administration over a large number of small cultivators, in order to be able to extract the maximum revenue, and at the same time to weaken all rival sources of power.

The Code was primarily a fiscal and political measure; but it would also have been a measure of land reform, in favour of individual small ownership, if it had been effectively carried out; and it would have introduced a Western idea of ownership, even though the old conception of the two rights was nominally maintained. In fact, the titles which were granted did not correspond to the rights of ownership recognized by custom, nor did they correspond to the areas actually held. Grants generally tended to strengthen the large landowners. The Code explicitly prohibited the recognition of any form of collective ownership, which was general at the time it was promulgated, either in the form of the semi-collective *musha'a* system, or in the form of tribal ownership. Article 8 of the Land Code states that 'The whole land of a village or of a town cannot be granted in its entirety to all of the inhabitants nor to one or two persons chosen from amongst them. Separate pieces are granted to each inhabitant and a title is given to each showing this right of possession.' In actual fact this provision was evaded, owing to the failure of the administration to register land title systematically.

No general registration was ever carried out. (In southern Iraq the Code was not applied even in theory.) The villagers, fearing that the registration was a preliminary to call up for military service, or for taxation purposes, falsified the returns, registering the property either in the name of the head of the tribe, or in the name of a member of the family who could not be liable for military service, or in the name of a city notable. In practice they disregarded the titles which were granted (known as the *senet tapu*) and continued to farm in various semi-tribal ways. Thus complete confusion resulted, since there arose one situation established by law under which certain owners held titles to divided land, and a situation existing in fact, in which the persons cultivating the land had claims recognized by custom or prescriptive right, which were enforceable by law to an uncertain extent.

In the years between the wars, registration of title and survey was carried out on a large part of the cultivated land in Syria and Iraq. This hastened the disintegration of the communal forms of cultivation and communal rights over land, and has given legal security to individual ownership. Since it did not, at the same time, give economic security to the cultivators, it has not affected their position: on the contrary, registration usually consolidated the property of the large landholders.

Today the only important remaining feature of the Moslem conception is that the state still has a formal claim to the possession of unregistered land. The legal status of state land differs in Syria and Iraq, and is considered below in the chapters dealing with each country. It should be noted, however, that the policy of assigning state land to cultivators is in no sense a new policy, and should not be regarded as representing a new direction. In Ottoman times colonization of state lands was carried on in Syria, and under the mandate this policy was continued, though on a small scale. It is only because the procedure of land settlement (i.e. the registration of title) has so generally favoured large landowners at the expense of the cultivators that the assignment of state land to small cultivators now appears to represent a change in the agrarian structure.

III

PRIVATE ENTERPRISE IN SYRIA

THE BACKGROUND

FEW underdeveloped countries in the past ten years have made such rapid progress in agriculture and industry as Syria. This point must be emphasized, because it can easily be overlooked. To the outside world, Egypt has a revolution and Iraq has money, but Syria has nothing to show but frequent coups d'état, 'feudal' landowners, and a marked aversion to foreign assistance.[1] It might be concluded that the economic life of the country was stagnant.

A glance at the agricultural production figures should suffice to dispel this impression. As compared with 1934–8, the area cultivated has doubled; grain production has increased by 64 per cent, and cotton production is now eight times its pre-war average. This is a strikingly rapid rate of expansion, even in the Middle East, where the rate of increase in agricultural production has been higher in recent years than in any part of the world except North America and Africa.[2]

The expansion in the cultivated area and in grain production is mainly the result of the cultivation of new land. Since the war the boundaries of cultivation have been pushed out very rapidly in the north along the Turkish frontier in the rainfed cultivation belt which forms the arch of the Fertile Crescent. The zone of new cultivation extends east from the neighbourhood of Aleppo up to the Iraq border, across the provinces of the Euphrates and the Jezira, chiefly in the 8–12 inch rainfall belt, shown on the map on p. 85. These regions now produce two-thirds of the country's grain output and the greater part of the country's exports.

The recent expansion in cotton has taken place in Aleppo

[1] The Government has refused to reach an agreement with Point Four (the US Technical Assistance Administration). It had not, up to the end of 1955, received any loans from the International Bank.
[2] FAO, *State of Food and Agriculture in 1955* (Rome, 1955), p. 76.

and Latakia provinces and also in the Homs–Hama plain, where cotton is grown on land brought under flow irrigation by the canalization of the Orontes. In the newly opened-up provinces of the north cotton is grown on new plantations on the Khabur and the Euphrates.

Cotton is not a new crop in Syria, for in the surroundings of Aleppo it has been cultivated since the eighteenth century. But cultivation on the present scale is new. Large-scale cultivation first began in 1924, and then increased quickly till the depression brought a decline, followed by recovery to the pre-war peak of 40,000 hectares. Expansion began again in response to high world prices in 1949, and reached its post-war peak of 217,000 hectares in 1951. The fall in prices and diseases of the crop led to some contraction.[1] The area under cultivation is

TABLE 9

Syria: Area and Production of Main Crops, 1950–5

Area
(000 hectares) *

	Average 1934–8	1950	1951	1952	1953	1954	Average 1950–4	1955†
Wheat	473	992	1,037	1,167	1,314	1,347	1,171	690
Barley	275	416	344	394	439	543	427	400
Total grain	748	1,408	1,381	1,561	1,753	1,890	1,598	1,090
Cotton	30	78	217	185	128	187	159	249

Production
(000 metric tons)

	Average 1934–8	1950	1951	1952	1953	1954	Average 1950–4	1955†
Wheat	459	830	510	900	870	965	815	600
Barley	290	322	155	467	472	635	410	150
Total grain	749	1,152	665	1,367	1,342	1,600	1,225	750
Cotton	5	35	49	45	47	80	51	85

* 1 hectare = 2·47 acres. † Preliminary estimates.

(SOURCES: FAO, *Yearbook of Food and Agricultural Statistics*, and UN, *Economic Developments in the Middle East, 1945 to 1954*, p. 183.)

[1] UN, *Economic Developments in the Middle East, 1945 to 1954* (New York, 1955), p. 182.

now about 180,000 hectares, and annual production averages 50,000 tons, most of which is exported. The preceding table shows the increase in areas and production of the main crops. (See 'Postscript', p. 220, for 1955–60 figures.)

The total area now utilized for agriculture is 3·9 million hectares (9½ million acres). Three and a half million hectares are used for dry farming, with half the land kept fallow each year, so that the area utilized for agriculture is twice as large as the area sown. About half a million hectares are under irrigation. How much land is still available for a further expansion of irrigation and of dry farming is not known.[1]

Agricultural production has increased more rapidly than population. In the years 1943–53 grain production doubled, while population increased by about 33 per cent, from 2·9 million to 3·9 million.[2] Thus output per head of population has risen. In this respect Syria's economic development has been much more favourable than that of Egypt, where output per head of population has fallen over the last ten years, and also than that of Iraq, where per capita output has increased, but to a lesser extent. The level of output per head in agriculture, measured in the main crops, is now much higher than it is in Egypt and Iraq. An agricultural population of between 1½ and 1¾ million[3] produces 1·3 million tons of grain and 50,000 tons of cotton. In Egypt an agricultural population of about 16 million produces 4½ million tons of grain and 350,000 tons of cotton, while in Iraq an agricultural population of 2½–3 million produces 1½ million tons of grain and 5,000 tons of cotton. In the absence of occupation statistics, no precise comparisons of output per head are possible; but it is clear that Syria's position is more favourable. As compared with Egypt it has twenty times as much arable land per head of agricultural

[1] Various estimates of the potentially cultivable areas have been made, but they are of no value since they do not distinguish clearly between the land which is potentially cultivable by dry farming, and land which must be reclaimed and irrigated before it can be cultivated. Since estimates of this sort are apt to take on a life of their own and become respectable with repeated quotation, it is better to omit them.

[2] The figure of 3·9 million is an estimate quoted by the Minister of Finance in his speech on the budget of 1955.

[3] Rural population was estimated to be 2·1 million in 1943 and 2·9 million in 1953. The agricultural population (i.e. the total number dependent on agriculture) was estimated to be 1·3 million in 1943, and assuming that the agricultural population has increased at the same rate as the rural population, it would number 1·7 million in 1953. It may be less than this, since industrial employment has grown.

population, and as compared with Iraq, it has made a far greater advance in intensive cultivation.

Mechanization has been the chief method of expansion. FAO estimates the number of tractors at 1,454 in 1954 and 2,000 in 1955. In the Jezira province and the northern regions of the Euphrates province almost all the grain crop is cultivated by tractors and harvested by combines, and farming is as fully mechanized as in any country in the world. Mechanization has also advanced in central Syria. Even in conservative Hama, disc-harrows come back into the town at night drawn by John Deeres and Fergusons among the camels and donkeys. Tubular blue neon lights outline advertisements of caterpillar tractors on the road into Aleppo, where the *souk* of the smiths has been turned into a row of machine shops, using electrical power.

The expansion in agriculture, judged by the inertia prevailing ten years ago, is surprising. It completely confutes some current doctrines. It is now fashionable to believe that the economic development of underdeveloped countries needs foreign capital, foreign experts, good public services, long-term planning, agrarian reform, plus, for good measure, a revolution. But Syria has had none of these things, and in the north, where progress has been so fast, every one of these conditions is lacking. Transport is expensive, roads are bad, labour is scarce, credit dear, and land tenure confused and insecure. Revolutions of course Syria has had, but they have been self-destroying seizures of power, without much effect on economic policy, and none on social structure.

Syrian governments have done almost nothing to promote agricultural development. The only important and highly beneficial economic measure was the foundation of the Cotton Bureau, staffed by experts from Egypt and with advice from FAO. This was set up under the Shishakli régime in 1952, when the rapid expansion in cotton had been checked by falling prices, crop diseases, and over-cultivation. The Bureau sells improved seed and controls and selects varieties. Cotton cultivation is now restricted to suitable areas by a system of licensing, and other control measures, such as the destruction of the plants after harvest, are also enforced. These measures were taken when experience showed them to be needed, and not as a matter of policy.

Otherwise, Syrian governments have pursued a policy of *laisser-faire*. No railways have been built since Ottoman times, though the Hejaz Railway, forty years after its destruction, is now being rebuilt. The new northern regions are without roads. Though great progress has been made in education since the mandate ended, little has been done, until very recently, to assist research or education in agriculture.[1] Far from undertaking land reform, the post-mandatory governments did not even continue the system of land registration introduced by the French.

But one essential factor in development Syria has had, the fourth factor of enterprise, so unaccountable and so often forgotten. The merchant class of Syria, and chiefly of Aleppo, famous as traders in other countries, has turned its business acumen back into its own country, and has used its capital to mechanize agriculture. The expansion in cotton has been financed almost entirely from commercial capital.[2] All the new expansion in grain in the province of the Jezira has been financed in the same way, and some mechanization in grain growing in the older settled regions also. The city, which formerly took everything from the village and gave nothing back, not even security, is now putting big money into cultivation. The improvement of the land itself does not get much attention. There is, however, some new investment by private enterprise in long-term improvement of the land in irrigation for cotton cultivation.

This is a great and certainly a healthy change, and one which is long overdue. The Ottoman Empire conspicuously failed to accomplish it. Its institutions were unfavourable to agriculture. How recently the land of Syria has been brought under cultivation, can be seen in the map on p. 76.[3] The struggle between the desert and the sown has been long protracted, and it has not been won for settled cultivation until today. Nomadic

---

[1] According to the International Bank Mission, in 1953 there was only one trained research agronomist (*Economic Development of Syria*, p. 302).

[2] 'In 1951, it was estimated that some £S200 to £S300 million had been required to finance the planting and moving of the cotton crop, of which all but £S50 million came from outside agriculture' (UN, *Economic Developments in the Middle East, 1945 to 1954*, p. 184).

[3] See Norman Lewis in *International Affairs*, January 1955. A. Granott, *The Land System in Palestine* (London, 1952), pp. 34-7, quotes observations by nineteenth-century travellers on the extent of cultivation.

grazing still continues, but has been pushed back almost entirely on to the uncultivable land.

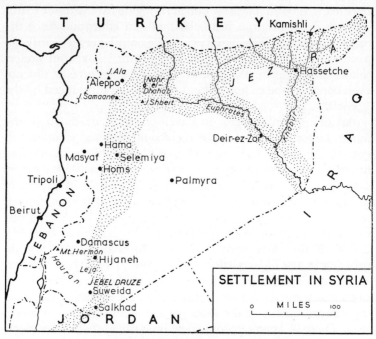

The areas stippled represent territory in which there were few or no permanent inhabitants in 1800, and which is now cultivated and inhabited by a sedentary population. The map is based on one accompanying an article by Norman Lewis, 'The Frontier of Settlement in Syria', in *International Affairs*, January 1955.

In this expansion there are obvious weaknesses—no improvement in soil fertility or in grain yields, a risk of soil erosion, and no stability. Yet it is an essential stage in the development of a country to get all its land cultivated, and not only for economic reasons. Politically this energizing drive was needed to draw together the diverse interests of the different groups and communities and classes of which the country is composed. Europe did not advance much until all its land was cultivated; nor did the United States. In Europe the expansion of the cultivated area was a long process, extending over centuries, and was achieved by the integrating principle of feudal organization. In the United States expansion was rapid, and the process was speculative and wasteful. Different countries have used a different dynamic, and Syria is unusual in that its merchant class has played the preponderant role.

It is possible that mechanization at this rate will turn the Jezira into a dust bowl; there is certainly a danger of wind erosion. In the view of the International Bank Mission, soil fertility may be endangered.

During the last two decades huge tracts have been opened up, especially in the Jezireh. This land has been idle for centuries and its reserve of chemical compounds caused by decomposition of the natural vegetation is considerable. Though very good soils do exist, particularly in the northeastern parts, the magnitude of the stored elements has generally been overestimated. The reserves, particularly of nitrogen, are not inexhaustible. The virgin soil of the Jezireh has often been compared with virgin soil types in Russia, the United States and Europe but it must be remembered that in Syria the humus has not been so abundant as in humid climates, so that the nitrogen reserve is very limited. When that reserve falls below a certain level soil productivity decreases rapidly even if other elements are in plentiful supply. In Syria continuous exploitation under a monocultural system has resulted in decreased yields in certain areas, notably the Jezireh, where the danger is not yet fully recognized. Even artificial fertilizers cannot replace organic enrichment and the fallow system in its present form is far from sufficient to maintain fertility. New farm techniques, a changed rotation system and increased use of green manuring and fertilizers are urgent needs.[1]

The dry-farming expansion is inevitably precarious and speculative, as is shown by the production figures quoted in Table 9 on p. 72. The spring drought of 1955 brought a harvest failure in the new regions and in most of the country. Banks had to call a moratorium, and the Government had to distribute seed. Great as the achievement of free enterprise has been, it cannot enable Syria to dispense with a policy for soil conservation and agricultural development.

Such a policy must aim at higher crop yields and greater stability, aims which can be attained only by more irrigation. Soil conservation requires afforestation. Research on methods of farming and a system of technical education could also do much. Until very recently the state had done little in any of

[1] *The Economic Development of Syria*, p. 300.

these directions, though the new entrepreneurs have undertaken irrigation and afforestation, and have employed technical experts.

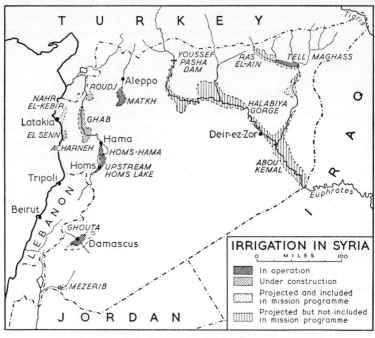

Based on a map in International Bank for Reconstruction and Development, *The Economic Development of Syria.*

The area under irrigation (in 1954 estimated to be 508,958 hectares) could certainly be increased, though the potential expansion cannot be estimated.[1] The location of the irrigated areas is shown on the above map; the areas are very approximate and possibly exaggerate the extent. The greater part of the land now irrigated has been brought under pump or flow irrigation by private enterprise. More than half of the area lies in the provinces of the Jezira and the Euphrates, and is partly new irrigation.[2]

[1] The International Bank Mission considers that the present area might be doubled (ibid. p. 41).

[2] Great uncertainty attaches to any estimates of areas irrigated because the Euphrates irrigation has not been surveyed. But the area irrigated certainly has increased. The Cadastral Survey Office figures give a total of 323,650 hectares irrigated in 1945.

State-operated schemes cover only 48,000 hectares. These are: the Homs–Hama irrigation system (21,600 hectares), the Mezerib in the Hauran (2,200 hectares), the Khabur at Tell Maghass (4,200 hectares), the Kuwaik river near Aleppo (15,000 hectares), and the Sinn river near Latakia (5,000 hectares).[1] The largest of these schemes is the canal-irrigation system on the Orontes in the Homs–Hama region, started by the French authorities and completed by the Syrian Government. It benefits chiefly the large landowners of the plain between Homs and Hama. The only other large scheme is that on the Kuwaik river south of Aleppo, which is said to be inadequate.[2] The state irrigation scheme at Tell Maghass on the Khabur is still not complete, though it has been under construction for ten years.[3] The remaining schemes are small. Thus the achievement to date has not been impressive.[4]

One large state land reclamation scheme (first considered in 1927) is now under construction. This is the reclamation of the Ghab valley on the Orontes, a large area of marsh at present largely uncultivable. The scheme is being undertaken in three stages. The first stage consisted in lowering the outflow of the river, which was blocked at the mouth of the valley by a basalt sill. This stage was carried out by a Yugoslav firm; in the spring of 1955 it was being undertaken by gangs of Alawis and marsh-dwellers working day and night in shifts and on 'norms' under the direction of a ruthlessly energetic Yugoslav engineer, determined to finish the job by the scheduled date, August 1955. The second stage is the construction of canals in the valley itself, now being undertaken by a German firm. When this stage is completed, it is estimated that an area of 26,000 hectares of waterlogged land can be reclaimed. The third stage is to be the construction of two reservoirs, to store water for the irrigation of the valley and also for the Acharneh plain upstream of the valley. It is estimated that a total area of 65,000 hectares will be supplied. In 1955 this section of the work had not been put in hand.

[1] Figures quoted in the Budget Speech by the Minister of Finance, January 1955.
[2] According to the report of the International Bank Mission (*The Economic Development of Syria*, p. 41).
[3] ibid. p. 43.
[4] For details of the seven-year investment programme, see UN, *Economic Developments in the Middle East, 1954–5*, pp. 129–30.

At present the cultivated land in the Ghab valley is held chiefly by large owners. The land which is at present uncultivable is State Domain, i.e. the state has the right of disposal, and consequently the question of the distribution of the new land has to be decided. The Ghab valley scheme is administered by a special Board, which has considered proposals for distributing the new land to small farmers. In 1955 no decision had been reached as to the principles on which the land was to be distributed. (See 'Postscript', p. 226.)

So far as afforestation is concerned, much greater progress has been made. It is, of course, one of Syria's great necessities. As long ago as 1872 Sir Richard Burton, who otherwise rejoiced in the absence of scientific farming in Syria, said that 'It wants only a Brigham Young to order the planting of a round million of trees.'[1] Recently the Government has embarked on an energetic programme for the distribution of saplings through the tree schools (the *pépinières agricoles*). In the three years 1953–5, 3 million saplings were distributed for planting. Private enterprise has a good record here also: one of the big entrepreneurs has planted 1 million poplars in his new plantations.

As a result of the recommendations of the International Bank Mission, funds for forestry, agricultural education and research were greatly increased in the 1955 budget, from £S450,000 to £S800,000.[2]

Agricultural primary schools now number 150. They are directed by Ahmed Kassem, formerly the Director of Agricultural Education in Palestine, where such schools gave a real stimulus to technical improvement through inter-school competition and village rivalry. Until recently there was only one agricultural secondary school, established at Selemiya near Hama in 1910. Four agricultural secondary schools and an agricultural high school have recently been established. The number of experimental stations has been increased; there are now thirteen, of which the oldest is the station at Homs, set up by the French. The two research stations at Homs and Ezra'a in 1955 were directed by young Palestinians. Shortage of staff is a great obstacle.

[1] Richard Burton and F. Tyrwhitt Drake, *Unexplored Syria* (London, 1872), vol. 1, p. 91.
[2] The currency unit is the Syrian pound, which is equivalent to one-tenth of the pound sterling.

It is against this background of expanding agriculture and the beginnings of a state agricultural policy that the problem of land reform must be considered.

So far as the new regions are concerned, it cannot be argued that land reform is a condition of development. In spite of the almost total lack of security of tenure, private enterprise has not been deterred from expansion. In the new regions entrepreneurs, large and small, complain of the lack of security, as they complain of shortage of credit and lack of roads. Yet it is arguable that the easy availability of land at low rents has facilitated expansion, by allowing new farmers to put all their capital into the purchase of seed and machinery.

It is none the less true that the old land system was an obstacle to development. The old *rentier* landowners and poor share-croppers could not have undertaken it. Ten years ago the possibility of development in the Jezira was well known, but seemed to exist only on paper, and at that time it was 'not easy to see where in fact the motive power is to come from'.[1] The motive power has come from outside the old agrarian structure, from the city merchants who are primarily risk-takers, gamblers in grain and investors in irrigation.

In the old settled regions there is a need for reform, as a labour policy to raise earnings. The spectacular expansion in the far north has meant a shift in Syria's economic centre of gravity, away from the old grain-producing regions of the south and centre.[2] But this shift has not drawn much labour away from the old regions into more productive employment in the north. Since grain production is completely mechanized, the demand for labour has not increased in proportion to the increase in production. Some of the old regions, notably the Hauran and the Jebel Druze, feel the competition of the Jezira, and their economic position is weaker. Consequently the expansion of cultivation in the new regions does not raise the rural living standard in the old regions to any noticeable extent, nor does it cause any improvement in the land-tenure system. Cotton cultivation has led to a great improvement in the incomes of the cultivators where they are small owners.

[1] *Land and Poverty in the Middle East* (London, RIIA, 1948), p. 97.
[2] A trend reinforced by the termination of the customs union with Lebanon in 1950, when the use of the port of Latakia was made compulsory.

But the majority of the rural population, the share-croppers and labourers on large estates, have not shared in the economic advance of the country, by reason of their small share in the produce of the land and their low wages.

CHANGES IN THE AGRARIAN STRUCTURE

There are no recent figures available showing the distribution of ownership by size of holding. The Cadastral Survey Office has published figures showing the distribution of ownership in 1951. These figures are presumably based on estimates, since cadastral survey and registration of properties was carried out in the mandatory period only in certain provinces. The figures for these provinces, Damascus, Aleppo, Latakia, Homs, and Hama, may give some indication of the distribution of ownership as it was recorded by the survey, though since the records were not maintained after 1943 the information given is presumably outdated. In other provinces, however, including the newly developed regions, no survey and registration was undertaken, so that the estimates for the provinces of the Jezira, the Euphrates, the Hauran, and the Jebel Druze cannot be based on any accurate record. In the newly developed regions, there is no precise record of areas owned, and there is much variation in areas cultivated. Nor is the area of State Domain land known, except in so far as it was surveyed and registered in the mandatory period in some regions. However, as the figures for the provinces surveyed and registered must bear some relation to existing conditions, and since they indicate regional contrasts which can be confirmed by direct observation, the figures may be quoted.

It will be seen that the figures show the distribution of ownership on a total area of 7·9 million hectares, an area twice as large as the area utilized for agriculture (3·9 million hectares, including fallow). They therefore include uncultivated and uncultivable land, and this ambiguity in the land areas diminishes their value as a guide to the distribution of property.

The figures show a preponderance of small and medium-sized properties in the provinces of the Hauran, Jebel Druze, and Latakia, where there is certainly a larger proportion of small and medium-sized holdings than elsewhere. The importance of large properties in the Aleppo province also corresponds to the results of observation. For the Jezira and Euphrates provinces the figures bear little relation to reality, since the scale of operation and of ownership is certainly very

TABLE 10

Landownership by Size of Holdings in Syria
(hectares)

Province	Private property			State Domain	Total area
	Small (under 10)	Medium (10–100)	Large (over 100)		
Damascus	178,000	413,345	347,700	24,500	963,545
Aleppo	264,800	732,500	831,848	462,800	2,291,948
Homs	37,500	284,708	157,000	720,000	1,199,208
Hama	8,350	195,200	259,435	269,200	732,185
Latakia	175,000	164,161	207,000	8,000	554,161
Euphrates	74,041	236,300	196,300	2,000	508,641
Jezira	55,600	463,300	277,500	95,600	892,000
Hauran	194,100	188,000	27,000	10,900	420,000
Jebel Druze	110,100	214,900	45,000	—	370,000
Total	1,097,491	2,892,414	2,348,783	1,593,000	7,931,688

(SOURCE: Bureau des Documentations Syriennes et Arabes, *Étude sur l'Agriculture Syrienne* (Damascus, 1955), p. 24.)

large; small and medium properties exist chiefly in the riverain tracts along the Euphrates river.

The most striking feature in Syria's agrarian structure today is the contrast in population densities between the new regions and the old. The newly developed territories are almost empty and short of labour, while in the old settled regions there is some degree of rural over-population. There is a broad correlation between the distribution of property and the density of the rural population. The under-populated new regions are dominated by large ownership and large-scale operation. The regions with the higher rural population densities are the provinces of the Hauran, the Jebel Druze, Latakia, and Hama, in the first three of which small ownership is important. The province of Hama is an exception to this correlation, since large estates take up most of the good land in the region. The position of the share-croppers is worse in this province than in other

83

parts of the country; and it is not surprising that the agitation for land reform originates here. (See 'Postscript', p. 226.)

Population pressure is, however, a local condition only, and does not affect the country as a whole. Organized settlement in the north, and settlement in the reclaimed lands of the Ghab valley (in the Hama province), would suffice to relieve it. With a better regional distribution of population, more effort to raise the standard of farming, and social legislation, Syria could employ a larger population on the land at a higher standard of living.

A further point of contrast in the agrarian structure of the new regions and the old is that the new farmers employ wage-paid labour, either as skilled workers in tractor and combine work, or as seasonal labour for cotton-picking. In the old regions share-cropping is still predominant. It might be expected that mechanization would have led to substitution of wage labour for share-cropping: but so far as could be ascertained this has not taken place to any great extent, except for cotton-picking.

The contrast in the agrarian structures of the different regions means that the problems of reform differ greatly. Since published information on social and economic change is so meagre, the changes can be reviewed only on the basis of direct observation—necessarily scanty and relying on information obtained from persons who have themselves initiated the changes, or have been affected by them.

The New Regions

The newly-opened-up regions include the eastern part of the province of Aleppo, the northern part of the Euphrates province, and the province of the Jezira. Geographically speaking, the Jezira (meaning 'the island' or 'the peninsula') is the land lying between the Tigris and the Euphrates. Administratively, the province (*mohafaza*) of the Jezira is a smaller region, covering the north-eastern corner of the country. This province has been the centre of most rapid expansion.

These regions lie in the rainfall zone between the Taurus mountains and the Syrian desert, stretching eastwards from Aleppo up to the frontier of Iraq. Within this zone there is a belt of high rainfall, with an annual rainfall of 50–60 centimetres (20–24 inches) running below the mountains; then the rainfall gradually declines and cultivation becomes gradually more risky until the 20-centimetre (8-inch) margin is reached, south of which cultivation is not profitable.

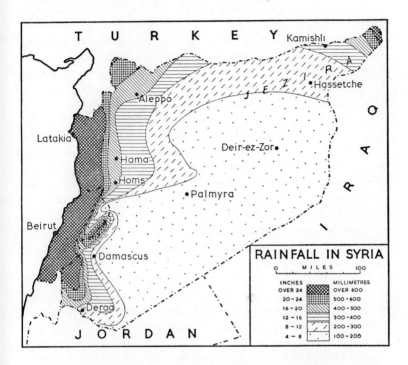

There are no figures to show the rate at which cultivation has been extended, or the extent to which the cultivable land is now cultivated. It seems possible that the limits of expansion for dry farming, in the Jezira province itself, have now been reached.[1] Farmers in Kamishli, who are in the market for land on lease, assert that all the cultivable land is now cultivated. Their contention is borne out by the losses which tractorists incurred in 1951–2 when they pushed cultivation out too far on to the marginal land south of Hassetche, and also by the present tendency on the part of the sheikhs to demand higher

[1] According to the *Statistical Abstract of Syria*, 1950, an area of 444,266 hectares was cultivated (i.e. under crops) in the Jezira in 1948–9. In 1940 an official estimate gave a cropped area of 100,000 hectares. The most rapid expansion took place in 1949–52, but no figures are available for this period.

rents (though rents are still very low by comparison with the more densely settled parts of Syria, amounting to between 10 and 15 per cent of the crop). There is some cultivable land on the Iraqi border, where tribal disputes prevent tractor owners from leasing land, but it is said to be on the border of the rainfall zone and too risky.

This generalization, of course, relates only to dry farming. Irrigation could be extended on the Khabur and on the Euphrates. Official figures show an irrigated area of 40,300 hectares in 1948–9, most of which is on the Khabur, and includes newly irrigated land.

Observation shows that the expansion has been very rapid. East of Aleppo, along the road to Deir-ez-Zor, cultivation now extends on both sides of the road, through a region thinly populated with infrequent clusters of small beehive villages. After the Euphrates is reached, the desert comes up to the road on the south, and the black tents of the Beduin on the one side confront the white marquees of the managers who supervise the disc-harrowing of the fallow land on the other side. There is no settled village population at all in this region, only an occasional petrol station and coffee-house for the lorries on their long haul to the Jezira. As the road goes south along the river, out of the rainfall zone, cultivation ends, and continues only where pumps are used to irrigate the riverain tracts.

North of Deir-ez-Zor and its chugging pumps, the province of Jezira begins when the river is crossed. The road turns at once into a desert track for about 80 miles along the telegraph poles, and then enters the cultivated zone where the road begins again, about 20 miles south of Hassetche. There are still no settled villages, only the new white tents which provide habitation during the harvest and sowing seasons. Police patrols and security officers keep a keen watch for incoming strangers.

Kamishli, the capital of the province, is a mixture of Macedonia and Kansas. The little shops in the *souk* are stuffed with imported tinned food, camel bags and whips, and sequined sandals; the old crafts of rope-making, tanning, and leather work continue beside the smithies repairing big machinery. Ancient Kurdish women in orange and crimson and Beduin in sheepskins sit outside the plate-glass windows of big stores which sell tractors and farm machinery, electrical equipment, refrigerators, washing-machines, baths, and radio sets. There are five or six such shops in a town with a population of some 75,000 (ten years ago it was only 30,000). The town has a new hospital, a new water-supply, and a good new modern hotel with a Lebanese *maître d'hôtel*, Swiss-trained. Its streets are not yet paved.

The little capital is inaccessible. The main line from Baghdad to Aleppo runs through it, carrying some of the region's grain exports, but as the line passes through Turkish territory on the way to Aleppo, traffic is restricted whenever friction arises between Syria and Turkey. Then the road must be used, and the cost of transport is high, for only one road, via Deir-ez-Zor, is open in winter and the journey from Kamishli to Aleppo is 336 miles, most of it on a vile surface, and partly no surface at all. Passengers go by lorry, bus, and car, while the new entrepreneurs use the cheap air service to Aleppo.

The province has changed over from nomadic grazing to highly mechanized grain growing and irrigated cotton cultivation in a short space of time. It is a sparsely populated region; in 1949 its total population as given was 155,643, as compared with 111,300 in 1940. The population is racially mixed, about 50 per cent being Kurdish and 40 per cent Arab. In religion it is predominantly Moslem, with a Christian minority in the towns.

The question arises of whether social and economic change at this pace does not create unrest among the Beduin who are losing their grazing land to cultivation. The region was always unsettled during the mandatory period. The French did not establish their authority there until 1930. They favoured the tribal authorities against the middle-class town population, and so weighted the balance in favour of the nomads against the cultivators. Racial and religious conflicts complicated this situation. There was a demand for autonomy, encouraged by certain of the local French officials,[1] which in 1937 led to a serious revolt of the Kurdish population, supported by the Christians. Though the revolt was put down, unrest continued. It was indeed the main reason why the region could not be developed for cultivation before.

[1] See A. H. Hourani, *Syria and Lebanon* (London, RIIA, 1946), pp. 215-16.

In the last years of the mandate the French authorities, in a last attempt to pacify the region, assigned the ownership of state lands in tribal occupation east of the 'desert line' to the tribal authorities.[1] The tribal sheikhs became the legal owners of very large areas of uncultivated land. These they lease for cultivation to the new tractor farmers, for rents which represent between 10 and 15 per cent of the gross produce; some land has also been sold. As a result the sheikhs have become wealthy, while the tribesmen receive nothing, and lose their rights to graze their herds.

Clearly there is the possibility of social conflict in this situation. The town merchant class is now predominant, and there would seem to be no racial or religious conflicts on the surface. But foreigners are not allowed to enter the Jezira without a special permit, and their entrance and exit are closely watched and strictly controlled. The reason given for this restriction, in Kamishli, was that the Government wishes the social change to proceed as smoothly as possible—which suggests that there is some likelihood of trouble.

Whether or not there is a possibility of unrest among the tribesmen—and there may well be—there was no sign of trouble in 1955. Tribesmen of the Beni Shammar sat sadly in the black tent with green corn on every side, and said that they did not know why they still kept camels.[2] The camels and their attendants have been ousted, and the tribal organization is breaking up. Whether this causes real hardship is difficult to say. Nothing is really known about the effects on the Beduin; the general view was they had moved south across the Iraq frontier into the Sinjar region. The numbers affected are not large, and perhaps there can be an adjustment. The younger generation can find work in the little boom towns, in building and even as tractor and lorry drivers. The Government in 1953 allotted areas of land to tribesmen for individual cultivation, in the district to the east of Hassetche.[3] This measure may suffice to maintain the older generation. It is always

---

[1] See p. 105 below.

[2] Their sheikh was not with them; he is a member of Parliament, and hostile to the Government, and in favour of Syria's adherence to the Baghdad Pact; the single vote for Nuri Said in Syria's last presidential election may perhaps have been cast by him.

[3] See p. 104 below.

sad to see the end of an old technique, and such an exacting one, the basis of such an ancient way of life. But it has been dying for a long time, and only the romantic will regret this dramatic final stage in the long conflict between the nomad and the cultivator.

The Merchant-Tractorists. Nothing certain is known about the distribution of ownership, except that a large proportion of the land is owned by the tribal sheikhs and cultivated by a new class, the merchant-tractorists. The big farmer entrepreneurs of north Syria are not, for the most part, large landowners, but rent land from the tribal sheikhs, at low rents. When the new entrepreneurs undertake irrigation farming and install pumps, they purchase the land. Predominantly they are pioneer risk-taking capitalists investing in machinery and seed; their capital originated in war-time commercial profits, but they now rely largely on bank credit. Credit is provided by the Agricultural Bank lending at 9 per cent, and by the State Bank lending at 5 per cent. Loans are secured on the machinery, since land cannot be offered as security because it is not the property of the borrower. Shortage of credit is the main grievance of this class. Yet in relation to the risks of Jezira farming these rates are not high. Certainly shortage of credit has not hindered expansion, for losses have been incurred because the new farmers pushed out cultivation to the edge of the rainfed zone where even normal rainfall is insufficient. Natural conditions make cultivation risky, and it is unreasonable to expect the banks to share the risks to a greater extent than they already do. The failure of the 1955 harvest would have made most Jezira farmers bankrupt if the banks had not come to their aid.

Most of these entrepreneurs have learnt what they know of agriculture in the last fifteen years, since they were merchants and traders before with no farming background. Now technical experience has been bought the hard way. When they need experts for cotton they know where to hire them—in Egypt—just as they know where to acquire the capacity to run a repair shop—as agents for foreign machinery firms.

It is noteworthy that most of them are self-made men, with no inherited wealth. The families of the largest operators were Christian emigrants from Turkey after the first world war.

Although there are also Moslem farmer-entrepreneurs, it is the Christian minority which has taken the lead. The whole expansion is an interesting example of how capital has been accumulated and invested outside the ranks of the established landowning class, by people who twenty years ago were neither wealthy nor influential.

Three or four of these entrepreneurs now operate on a large scale—large by the standard of any country, and in little Syria enormous. The whole cropped area of this country, it must be remembered, is only 5 million acres, of which less than half is in the north, including rather less than a million in the Jezira province itself. The areas which the largest operators plant are not known with any certainty, for their farming operations are measured not in acreage but in bags of seed sown—an indication of the uncertainty of the return and the flexibility of their investments. Two, however, operate on at least 100,000 hectares (250,000 acres).

The biggest of these entrepreneurs, commonly known as the King of the Jezira, is Pierre Mamarbachi, an Armenian of Aleppo, who was formerly associated with the family grain-exporting firm, Mamarbachi Brothers, but who now operates independently. He is a small quiet elderly man in a dusty air-conditioned office in Aleppo, who has done big things; the irrigation and cotton plantations on the Khabur, the model village settlement at Tell Manajir on the Euphrates, the planting of a million poplars, and tractor-farming on 100,000 hectares—possibly more. At Kaysouma, forty miles east of Aleppo, he has 6,000 hectares (15,000 acres) under wheat and barley, managed by a qualified agronomist, and employs the labour of four villages, newly sprung up clusters of beehives where before there were only two or three houses. The land which was too stony for cultivation has now been cleared and ploughed to a depth of 40 centimetres and produces $1-1\frac{1}{2}$ tons to the hectare, a high yield for Syria.

Labour shortage is a problem, which he meets by building villages, or moving workers in lorries. He pays his workers cash wages and employs them throughout the year, which is better by far than share-cropping. His vast lands in the Jezira are rented from sheikhs, but his irrigated land has been purchased from the state, and sometimes he pays both the sheikh and the Government, to make sure, since no one can say which really owns some of the land. Local gossip, keenly interested and well informed, said that the drought in the spring of 1955 lost him £2 million, for the millions depend on a few inches of rain. He has experimented with rain-making apparatus, but this was a failure, because there was no cloud.

The second biggest operators are the firm of Asfar and Najjar Brothers, with offices in Damascus, Aleppo, and Kamishli. The firm is a family of five brothers, Syrian Orthodox by religion, who emigrated from Diarbekir some twenty-five years ago. They began to cultivate wheat and barley in the Jezira in 1943, and for five years made no profit, because harvests were bad. The good years from 1948 brought high profits and they are now cultivating 100,000 hectares, round Ras el-Ain and in the district of Kamishli. About half of this land has been purchased, the rest being rented from the sheikhs. They also cultivate 3,000 hectares of irrigated land on the Khabur, supplied by pumps. They are constructing a model settlement at Mabrouka, twenty miles west of Ras el-Ain. On their enormous holding they employ permanently only some 500 workers in all, with 700 additional labourers in the cotton harvest season—an indication of how little employment is given by this type of expansion.

The Najjars have found the shortage of labour a great obstacle, and in order to attract skilled workers as settlers they have introduced an original system offering to finance tractor-farmers with loans of machinery on the basis of a five-year share-cropping contract. Under this scheme they offer to the prospective tenant, or to groups of tenants in partnership, 10,000 dunums[1] (2,500 acres) of land and advance capital to the value of £10,000 in the form of combines and tractors, seed and fuel, wages at the rate of £S150 (£15) per month, and the same allowance for the share-cropping tenant himself. The gross output is divided in the proportion of 40 per cent for the Najjar family and 60 per cent for the tenant. The 5 per cent rent is paid to the sheikh by the Najjars, out of their share, while the tenant, out of his share, must repay 20 per cent of the cost of the machinery. At the end of the five years the machinery should become the property of the tenant, and he should then

[1] 1 Syrian dunum = 0·25 acres.

be offered a lease of the land, paying 5 per cent to the sheikh and 5 per cent to the Najjars. Up to the present seventeen such contracts have been made, with small groups working either as partners or as managers with employed labourers who receive a 2 per cent share of the gross produce in addition to their wages. None of these contracts is yet completed, and the 1955 crop failure will delay the payments.

This scheme is an attempt to adapt the customary practice of share-cropping to mechanized farming. From the point of view of the family the expenditure on labour involved is higher than the cost of labour employed directly, but this is more than compensated by the reduction in the cost of supervision and management. This cost item is high, because during the ploughing season tractors work continuously day and night. From the point of view of the tenants the drawback is the difficulty of repaying fixed sums of money when output is so variable. Although the risks may be too great to make this type of settlement both stable and highly profitable, it is a practical attempt to set up farm units which are suited to the technical conditions in the new regions of the north.

The construction of the Mabrouka Settlement, in which the brothers feel great pride, and the contract scheme have given the family a deserved reputation for public spirit, not less commendable because it is welded to private enterprise. It pleases Syrians to see brothers working together, and there is no friction between the family and its Moslem managers and staff. Elie Najjar, the young manager of the Damascus office, represents Kamishli in Parliament as a member of the Democratic Bloc, and urges on the Government the need for devoting more funds to the construction of roads. The parliamentary representation of growing local needs, as distinct from the preservation of traditional wealth, is a new and healthy element in Syrian politics.

There are a few other large operators in the region, among them Abdul-Masih Asfahan, a Syrian Catholic, and Abdul-Aziz el-Nazla. The other tractor-entrepreneurs are small in comparison, planting from 200 to 1,500 bags. In Kamishli alone there are said to be 600 of these smaller farmers, mostly Christian refugees from Turkey. These are the people who buy refrigerators and washing-machines, while the sheikhs buy their annual Cadillac. The smaller farmers run machine-service garages and petrol-stations.

This new class has played an essential part in developing the country, by its willingness to take risks. It does not, as yet, form a stable class, for it does not invest much in land improvement. The irrigation farming is, of course, a permanent improvement in agriculture; but as yet it is on a small scale, compared with dry farming. The variety of the functions undertaken by these new entrepreneurs provides an interesting contrast to the attitude of the landowners in the older regions.

The Old Regions: The Provinces of Homs and Hama

In the old regions of the country the share-cropping system continues unchanged. The proportion of the produce taken by the landowner varies with the density of the agricultural population, being highest near the towns and lowest on the desert rim. When irrigation water is supplied by the land-owner, the proportion taken by the landowner is higher. In central Syria a prevalent share division is 50:50, if the cultivator provides seed, labour, or draught livestock, and the landowner provides only land. If the landowner provides seed, working livestock, and water, as well as land, he takes 75 per cent of the gross produce, and the cultivator takes 25 per cent.

In the Homs–Hama plain region there has been a great improvement in methods of farming, resulting from the irrigation scheme on the Orontes, which has enabled cultivation of cotton. For cotton cultivation landowners generally undertake to supply seed and water, and livestock or tractor work. The proportion of share-croppers working for 25 per cent of the crop has increased: and the proportion of labour employed has increased also. The extent of this change is not known; but local informants estimated that about half the share-croppers in this region work on the 25:75 division. Technical progress has thus reduced the cultivators' share in the gross output of the land, though it may not have reduced their total income, since in the Homs region gross output is certainly higher. In Hama the increase in population in a rather densely settled area, coupled with this change in the customary division, has probably reduced cultivators' incomes.

Conditions of extreme poverty can be seen in the villages on landowners' estates in this region. In the Ghab valley there is a striking contrast between the destitution and disease apparent in the villages on the chief landowner's estate at the bottom of the valley and the prosperity of a peasant village at the head of the valley, Bab el-Takah. In this village the farmers owned holdings of 100, 150, and 200 dunums (25, 37, and 50 acres); they were healthy and well-clothed. Prosperity had come, they said, with the introduction of the cotton crop. To cultivate their lands they jointly hire a tractor from a Hama merchant, giving half the cotton in return for tractor work and seed, an interesting example of enterprise on an informal co-operative basis.

The Hauran and the Jebel Druze. These two regions, among the oldest settled in the country, now have a serious problem of congestion on the land. In the Hauran, a district of black basalt houses and stony fields, the *musha'a* custom of re-allotting land at regular intervals was practised until recently, and may still continue. The villagers live on a narrow subsistence margin. The failure of the 1955 harvest would have been disastrous for them, had the Government not distributed seed. Formerly the surplus labour from these villages went to Haifa to work in the docks; it now goes to Beirut, and to a lesser extent to the Jezira.

Some useful efforts to improve agricultural methods are now beginning. Artesian wells are being dug under the supervision of the FAO Mission. There is a new experimental station at Ezra'a, under the direction of a young Palestinian, working on dates of sowing and on rates of fertilizer application, under the guidance of the FAO Mission. This is the first experimental station for dry farming. There is no tractor ploughing in this region, because the land is too stony and the peasants too poor.

The Jebel Druze villages are also mainly peasant owned, though one of the hereditary ruling families, the Atrash, has large properties. The villages are over-populated, growing figs and olives and grain in tiny terraced fields on the mountainside. The capital, Suweida, has declined in importance and feels the impact of Jezira competition, since it formerly thrived on the grain trade.

The Ghouta of Damascus, intensively cultivated and well irrigated, and also densely populated, has some peasant properties. The greater part of the land is held in medium-sized properties worked by share-croppers, and owned by civil servants and professional and commercial families in Damascus. In recent years they have invested considerably in fruit-trees; some were anxious to emphasize that they were not absentee owners now. A slight improvement in rural living standards has occurred, through the wider opportunities for earning in industry. The only rural welfare services are provided by the health and home training for women carried out in three villages by the Near East Foundation—patient long-term work which every international agency should study. The Foundation has succeeded in training competent young women to teach in their schools and to work with village midwives, that most conservative profession.

In these old regions, with their traditional rural poverty, the economic advance of the country has brought little or no improvement. Their needs are various: in the share-cropping regions the land system does not prevent technical advance, but it does prevent social progress, and reform is certainly needed. In the peasant regions resettlement could relieve the pressure of population. In all regions, rural welfare services and agricultural education are much needed.

Landowners in these old regions reside on their estates to a greater extent than they did in the past. There is great variation in social and economic function among them: some have invested in pump irrigation for cotton, and have shown interest in improving cultivation, while others are absentees with little interest in agriculture. Generally speaking, they are not much interested in long-term improvement. In the Homs–Hama region the big estates have been responsible for the over-cultivation of cotton and excessive use of water, which has lowered the water-table, so that the neighbouring villages are short even of drinking-water.[1]

One landowner, however, has undertaken a large all-round development scheme entirely on his own initiative, combining land reclamation, irrigation, and experimental farming with the settlement of peasant proprietors on reclaimed land. This is the Kurd Hussein Ibish, once world famous as a big-game

---

[1] In the winter of 1955 the village of Selemiya on the border of the rainfed zone was obliged to fetch its drinking-water from Hama, twenty miles away.

hunter and explorer, who took up farming late in life. During the second world war he bought up at a low price—for he was not a rich man—the poor marshlands of the Wadi Awaj, where malaria and Beduin raids on the springs prevented cultivation. On these lands he has now drained and reclaimed 24,000 hectares, partly for irrigation and partly for dry farming, growing cotton, sugar beet, and water melons. The estate at Hijaneh,[1] about twenty-five miles south of Damascus, extends for many miles parallel to the Jordan road. About 6,000 families are now settled there, partly as owners, partly as labourers. About two-thirds of the land Ibish has allotted to the peasants in ownership, simply because he believes this to be right. All profits are reinvested in the land, since he is not interested in anything but the community he has created, where he is judge and absolute ruler.

Not surprisingly, this remarkable man is regarded by Damascus society as an eccentric; his prejudices against electricity, cars, Damascene and Beiruti merchants are more easily intelligible to the English mind. The story is told that when Kuwatli visited Ibish to offer him the premiership he refused, on the ground that it was better to rule in Hijaneh than to be the slave of a parliamentary majority. When the peasants were assembled on this occasion to offer the homage expected by politicians, Ibish introduced the President with the words: 'This is the man who makes you pay taxes'. Counting the world well lost for agriculture, Ibish in character and appearance recalls the English or Scottish landowners of a generation ago, a tall, gaunt old man in tweeds, who would look right in Banbury market or on the Warwickshire County Council.

The old landowner families of the Homs–Hama region are not of this stamp. They use tractors, and have installed canals and pumps to make use of the water provided by the irrigation of the Orontes valley. But they are still *rentiers* in mind and income, who live on the labour of their share-croppers, advancing seed and lending money to the cultivator in return for three-quarters of the gross produce. Their mentality is that of the *grand seigneur*.

---

[1] See 'Postscript', p. 222, for the disastrous effects of the long drought on this estate, expropriated under the 1958 reform.

One who is called the richest man in Syria expressed the views of his class in a long diatribe against the West. The Americans, he said, wrongly believe that social unrest has social causes, whereas in fact the true explanation of social unrest in Syria is the victory of Zionism. In his opinion the whole country, including the Army, is permeated by Communism, and it is the Americans and the Jews who are to blame. This point of view has an element of truth, since the Socialist Party, which is strongest in this landowner's *seigneurie*, is extremely nationalist as well as socialist.

Yet the landowner's argument seemed to carry less conviction when he went on to speak of the imminent danger that the land in the Ghab valley, now under reclamation and adjoining his estates, would be distributed to small farmers, for this would cause a shortage of labour in the region. The settlement of the Ghab lands would, of course, be beneficial to the fellahin, because it would relieve the pressure of population and cause a rise in wages and share-croppers' incomes on the adjacent estates. Thus the old attitude persists; its power is still an obstacle to reform.

CHANGES IN THE LAW OF LAND TENURE

Legal changes carried out in the mandatory period and in recent years have changed the law of land tenure and introduced a conception of ownership based on the French Civil Code. The Ottoman Land Code has never been explicitly abrogated, and its confusing categories of land are still used, but they now have little importance.

The first important change was the introduction of a general system of land survey and registration of title. In 1923 the French authorities granted a concession to M. Duraffourd, to undertake survey and registration as Director of the Bureau de Cadastre. The Law concerning Immovable Property (No. 3339 of 1930) laid down the principles and procedure. Registration was compulsory and survey was efficient. Up to 1943 an area of 3,544,883 hectares had been surveyed and registered.[1] This area covered most of the cultivated land in the older settled parts of the country. No survey or registration was

---

[1] M. Duraffourd died in 1940, but his staff continued the work of the Bureau until the termination of the Mandate.

undertaken in the Jebel Druze or the Hauran, for political reasons, or in the Jezira, which was in a constant state of upheaval, and where not much land was cultivated. In the Euphrates province only small areas were registered.

Registration of title conferred absolute rights of ownership on the individual, and was advantageous in that it introduced greater security. It brought no change in the distribution of property, although the French authorities did grant secure title to peasant cultivators. On the whole, however, the benefits of greater security went to the existing large landowners.

Settlement of title was sometimes, though by no means always, accompanied by the consolidation of the strips into which the peasants' holdings were divided. It was generally accompanied by the cessation of the practice of periodic reallotment of holdings (*musha'a*), a practice which continued in most parts of Syria. Occasionally the registration of *musha'a* land areas was carried out by registering each villager's share in the land as a fraction of the total area. This practice was adopted because the Director of the Survey was impressed by the failure of the Ottoman Government to settle land in divided holdings, and believed that the *musha'a* custom had a real basis in the social life of the country, and should continue if the villagers desired it. However, this practice was not generally followed, and for the most part title was registered in divided holdings, so that registration generally involved the establishment of individual ownership of specific areas of land.

The other important change concerned the legal status of State Domain land. In conformity with the Moslem conception of ownership, the state claimed formal ownership of all land (with the exception of *mulk* and *waqf*). But after 1918 state ownership acquired a new meaning, because the State of Syria had come into the possession of large areas of land which had formerly belonged to the Ottoman Crown estates. These lands had been the personal property of the Sultan Abdul Hamid, and had formerly been administered by a special department in Constantinople, the Sanniya, and had earned a large revenue. After the Young Turk revolution of 1908, ownership of these lands passed to the Ottoman State and thence to the ownership of each of the successor states, in accordance with the Treaty of Lausanne.

Under the system of survey and registration, these lands were registered as the property of the state. Since these lands were held by the state as a juridical person, this form of state property corresponded to a Western conception. A special department, the Directorate of State Domain, was set up to administer them. Laws were passed governing their disposal by sale or lease. These lands were for the most part thinly settled and little cultivated, though they included some good land in the Homs region. Colonization was undertaken, but the work was not completed. The leasing of State Domain was an important source of revenue.[1]

There were, therefore, two categories of state land: the land which was registered in the name of the state, and at the disposal of the Directorate of State Domain; and the land over which the state claimed formal possession according to the Moslem conception. This included all occupied land to which title was not registered, and also all unoccupied and uncultivated land. A law was passed in 1926 confirming the Ottoman right of prescriptive ownership, by which persons who brought uncultivated land into cultivation could acquire ownership if they could prove a period of cultivation. For the occupation to be legal, a licence from the state was necessary, and proof of five years' cultivation entitled the occupier to have the land registered in his name. Thus the old Ottoman prescriptive right was given legal status. However, if such land were already registered as State Domain, no prescriptive right of ownership could be acquired over it, though it could be leased or purchased from the Directorate of State Domain.

Special legislation was passed in 1940 and 1941 assigning unregistered state land east of the 'desert line' to the tribal authorities, granting them registered title through a special emergency procedure (under Legislative Decrees No. 132 of 1940 and No. 141 of 1941).[2] This emergency legislation was largely responsible for the present distribution of ownership in the Jezira.

The main results of the legislation carried out by the French authorities were therefore:

[1] In 1946 the revenue from State Domain amounted to £S14,958,000, while revenue from other sources amounted to £S94,746,000 (Nassib Bulos, *Legal Aspects of Land Tenure in Jordan and Syria* (Beirut, UNRWA, 1953)).
[2] See p. 88.

1. The introduction of absolute freehold individual ownership, under the system of survey and registration. This gave greater security to landowners in the regions where it was carried out, and tended to break up the semi-communal forms of tenure.

2. The introduction of a Western conception of ownership for registered state land.

The Moslem conception of state ownership only retained its validity for unregistered land, which might be land in the occupation of individuals, or land uncultivated and unoccupied.

The Syrian Civil Code of 1949 codified the legislation of the mandatory period. It retains the categories of land used in the Ottoman Land Code, with some modifications, as follows:

1. *Mulk:* absolute freehold, in urban areas only.

2. *Miri:* property of which the title is vested in the state and in regard to which a right of possession may be acquired.

3. *Matruka:* subject to easements: property of which the title is vested in the state, but in regard to which the public or a group enjoy a right by usufruct under administrative law (Public State Domain).

4. *Matruka mahmia* (protected): property owned by the state, government authorities or municipalities (Private State Domain).

5. *Mubah* or *mawat* (deserted or dead): uncultivated land of which the title is vested in the state, but which has not been surveyed or registered.

The *waqf* category was not included, as it is treated by the Code as a 'real right', not a special category.[1] During the mandatory period the French authorities permitted and encouraged the sale of the then extensive *waqf* properties to business enterprises, irrigation concessions, and large landowners. The Civil Code prohibited the creation of family *waqfs*, stating that *waqfs* may not be created except for a charitable purpose. The Husni Zaim administration abolished existing family *waqfs*.

The five categories listed in the Code no longer have much practical importance, since the distinction between *mulk* and

[1] Nassib Bulos, *Legal Aspects of Land Tenure in Jordan and Syria.*

miri is no longer valid. In law, owners who receive registered title are still *miri* holders, i.e. nominally tenants of the state, but in practice they own the land absolutely. The important distinction lies between registered land and unregistered land. Registered land may be either the property of individuals, or of the state. Land registered in the name of the state corresponds to the fourth category, Private State Domain. Public State Domain, the third category, includes land used for public purposes, for example public buildings, market places, and roads. The only element of the Ottoman Code remaining in force was the state's right of ownership over all unregistered land, i.e. the land included in the fifth category, as 'dead' or uncultivated.

So far as this last category was concerned, the Code maintained the provisions of the law of 1926, which entitled persons who had brought *mubah* or *mawat* land into cultivation to have the land registered as their property if they could prove five years' cultivation.

The Syrian Constitution of 1950 laid down the principles on which land reform legislation could be based. It declared that maximum limits of ownership were to be defined when title to property was registered. These maxima, however, were not to be retroactive, i.e. did not relate to properties already registered. (Legislation to enforce a general limitation on large ownership would therefore require an amendment of the Constitution.) The Constitution also affirmed that small and medium ownership was to be encouraged, and that State Domain lands were to be distributed to cultivators without land.

However, after the termination of the Mandate, the system of survey and registration introduced by the French authorities was not continued, allegedly for lack of funds, in reality, it must be presumed, because large landowners were able to acquir properties by extending cultivation over unregistered land. The necessary mechanism for carrying out the provisions of the Constitution therefore did not exist.

ATTEMPT AT REFORM

The first and so far the only attempt to carry out the provisions of the Constitution was made under the Shishakli régime in 1952. The Decree for the Distribution of State Lands

(No. 96 of 30 January 1952) was intended to be a radical social reform. It formed part of the 'programme for workers and peasants', announced in January 1952. Its stated object was to put an end to the illegal occupation of state land. The first provision

declared null and void all possession by feudal lords and other influential persons over unregistered state land, no matter how vast and extensive such land may be, if its area exceeded a limit of 150 hectares per owner in the Jezireh and the Furat [Euphrates] Desert districts and 50 hectares in other parts of Syria.

The decree further declared that only title-deeds to specified areas were to be recognized, and that where landowners held areas of land exceeding the boundaries specified in the title-deeds, these areas were to be ignored, i.e. surrendered. The Directorate of State Domain was authorized, after obtaining the approval of the Council of Ministers, to distribute these lands 'acquired through force and usurpation' to needy peasants in return for small sums payable in instalments. If purchasers failed to cultivate the land, within a period of two years, it would revert to the state.[1]

The law had two defects. First, it was inapplicable, because the area and location of the unregistered state land were unknown. Second, it rested on a confusion as to the legal status of occupiers of unregistered state land. Under the law of 1926, incorporated into the Civil Code, persons who brought unregistered state land into cultivation could acquire registered title by proof of a period of cultivation. However, as the system of registration had been allowed to lapse, there was no legal procedure for establishing ownership, though in practice the right of ownership acquired by cultivation was recognized. Thus the old Ottoman method of acquiring ownership was no longer tied in with the legal system. The tenure held by landowners who had extended cultivation over unregistered state land was not usurped or fraudulent, on the basis of customary law, but neither was it legal, on the basis of the Civil Code. The discontinuance of registration of title broke the link between the old legal system and the new.[2]

---

[1] *First Statement on Achievements of Syria's Government of the New Regime, during three months in office, December 1951–March 1952*, by General Fawzi Selo [Prime Minister] (Damascus, 1952), pp. 50–1.

[2] Nassib Bulos, *Legal Aspects of Land Tenure in Jordan and Syria*.

When the legal defect was recognized, the decree was repealed, and a new decree (No. 135 of 29 October 1952) replaced it. This law abolished the distinction between registered and unregistered state land, and so abolished the last vestige of the Moslem conception of formal ownership. It declared that all *mawat* lands (i.e. dead lands brought into cultivation) were subject to the administration of State Domain, and thus assimilated the status of these lands to the State Domain proper, which the state owned as a juridical person. The law stipulated that no prescriptive title could be acquired over *mawat* lands, despite the fact that they had not been registered in the Registers of Immovable Property or in those of State Domain.

The Decree did not, however, dispossess squatters completely but validated their title to an area not exceeding 200 hectares per person, and a similar area for every member of the family of the recipient. Any area in excess of this figure reverted automatically to the State.

Article 5 of the Decree states that these lands would be sold or leased in accordance with the regulations made by the Council of Ministers. The idea was to sell or lease these lands for a nominal value to landless peasants. It is estimated that as a result of this decree, some five million dunums of land would be added to the State Domain.[1]

But since the area of State Domain land was still unknown, the decree could not be carried out. It was therefore necessary to resume the survey and registration of land. In 1952 a training centre for land surveyors was set up. The former members of M. Duraffourd's staff were recruited, when available, and survey began again in 1953.

According to the figures issued by the Cadastral Survey Office quoted on p. 83 above, the area comprised in the State Domain is some 1½ million hectares. This figure, however, includes only the registered State Domain, and not the *mawat* lands which were brought under the Directorate of State Domain under Decree No. 135 of 1952. Most of the registered State Domain lies in the provinces of Homs and Hama; the total extent of State Domain land, including the *mawat* land, is unknown. Even the area of registered State Domain is not known precisely, since the registers have not been maintained.

[1] ibid.

So long as the Shishakli régime continued it was intended to proceed with the distribution of land under this decree. In January 1953 a decree was issued governing the conditions for distribution of the state land. Persons already cultivating the land and other applicants were to be allowed to purchase the land at a price equivalent to 25 per cent of its real value, and could acquire up to 50 hectares of non-irrigated land and 10 hectares of irrigated land. In the Jezira and Euphrates provinces they could acquire up to 200 hectares of non-irrigated land, and the same area for every member of the family of the recipient.

The only direct action taken under the law has been the distribution of tribally occupied land to its Beduin occupants in the district of Hassetche in the Jezira. According to information received in Kamishli in April 1955, the tribesmen have secured ownership. It should be borne in mind, however, that in this case the state has not distributed land to new owners, but has confirmed the tribesmen's right to hold individual ownership of land formerly occupied collectively. In practice this means that the state gives the tribesmen the right to take an income from the merchant-tractorists who cultivate the land. The usual practice is for the sheikh to take the rent from the tractorist as his own right, and to distribute small gifts among the tribesmen. The practical result of granting registered title is that the tribesmen share the rent among themselves, a useful measure of social security, which protects them against displacement without preventing mechanized cultivation.

An indirect result of the 1952 legislation has been the resumption of survey and registration of title. Progress has been slow, owing to the shortage of qualified staff and funds. In the 1955 budget funds were increased to 1 million Syrian pounds. In the Jezira province aerial survey is being carried out, but here too progress has been slow, and large sums allocated (£S400,000 in 1954 and £S300,000 in 1955) were not spent. The boundaries shown in the air photographs are to be the basis for claims for title registration.

The possible effect on the legal limitation on size of newly registered holdings cannot be foreseen in the absence of figures for the total area of state land. Most of the dry land farmed in big areas by the new entrepreneurs in the Jezira is the property of the tribal authorities who acquired registered title under the emergency decrees of 1940 and 1941, and would therefore not be affected by the limitation on new ownership. The attempt to enforce a limitation on ownership may of course be ineffective. The 200 hectares maximum, plus 200 for every member of the family, would allow a fairly large unit of 2,000 or 3,000 hectares, since families are elastic. The existence of the limitation may simply mean that the entrepreneur who wishes to purchase land to install pumps will register it in the name of remote and elderly relatives.

In principle, it seems unwise to put any obstacle on the size of properties in the regions of rapid expansion.[1] It may check the entrepreneurs' desire to purchase, and so prevent investment, without benefiting new settlers. If the state were able to undertake a positive policy of encouraging settlement in the new regions (or indeed on state land in the whole of the country), the imposition of a fixed acreage maximum would be reasonable. In present conditions, to impose a purely negative restriction on the size of newly registered holdings may penalize the 'developer' and good employer, while exempting the *rentier* landowners in the old regions, killing the plant where it is growing, while leaving the dead wood intact. The real weakness of the new farming is its failure to maintain soil fertility. But limitation of acreage will not remedy this defect.

If it is the object of government policy to prevent new great inequalities in landownership from arising, the best method would be to retain the state land in public ownership, and lease it to farmers in large units for long periods, so that farm sizes could be adjusted to the needs of closer settlement when leases terminate, and leasehold conditions could enforce better cropping practices.[2] Such a policy would fit in with the legislation of the mandatory period governing State Domain land, and with the 1952 law which brings all state land under the administration of the Directorate of State Domain.

[1] The International Bank Mission felt it necessary to recommend a limitation of size for new holdings, though it sensibly recommended 1,000 hectares as a suitable maximum (*The Economic Development of Syria*, pp. 68 and 202).
[2] For an interesting example of the use of this type of tenure in a developing economy see the Australian policy of crown leasehold, described in UN, Dept. of Economic Affairs, *Progress in Land Reform*, pp. 186–9.

LAND REFORM AND DEVELOPMENT

To deal with the problem of inequality in incomes from agriculture without penalizing the developers, the right method would be to reform the system of taxation, with progressive rates according to the size of the property, and allowing rebates for newly installed pumps and tree plantations.

THE POLITICAL PROSPECTS

As the preceding sections have shown, Syria is in the fortunate position of having much land for dry farming and for irrigation in relation to its farm population. There is no need for a general measure for redistribution of ownership. A redistribution policy, on the lines carried out in Egypt, is a necessity in countries which are densely populated and where great inequalities in property allow landowners to exact a monopoly price for the use of land. The object of imposing maximum limits on the size of holdings, in these conditions, is to break up the institutional monopoly by distributing land areas in excess of the legal maximum to small farmers, and thus to secure a wider distribution of income from agriculture.

In Syria, by contrast with Egypt, the differences in the agrarian structures of the different regions make general limitation of the sizes of holdings impracticable. In the Ghouta of Damascus, for example, which is intensively cultivated and irrigated, 100 hectares is a large holding; while in the extensively cultivated Jezira 1,000 hectares is rightly considered a small farm. Nor is general limitation necessary, since over the country as a whole there is no shortage of land, and in the new regions there is no monopoly of landownership. In the north the sheikh landowners cannot exact high rents, because the land is sparsely populated and would not be cultivated by the investing entrepreneurs if rents were not low and competitive. The large incomes of the new merchant-tractorists are not derived from institutional monopoly, but from the profits of risk-taking and investment.

But it is also clear that in the older regions there is a need for reform. In the central regions, large landowners, predominantly of the *rentier* type, hold a monopoly of the good land and use it to take an excessive share of the produce. Technical progress has not benefited the share-cropping villagers. The immediate problem of reform today is the poverty of the peasants in these regions, and also in the southern regions, which are mainly peasant owned but somewhat over-populated. This poverty could be relieved by resettlement, in the northern provinces and in state irrigation schemes, both in the north and in the old regions. Where the landowners' monopoly power is strong, legislation to increase the share-croppers' income could be effective, though it is not likely to achieve a great improvement if no resettlement is undertaken.

Thus Syria needs a reform policy, both for today and for tomorrow. The problem is to combine an immediate policy to relieve rural poverty with a long-term policy to utilize land resources more fully, and to conserve them. The country is developing: there is no need to think in terms of maximum and minimum holdings. Tenure policy can aim at granting holdings that will not only ensure the farmer an adequate living standard, but will also enable him to produce for a growing internal and external market.

Resettlement is the key to both problems.

But large-scale resettlement of population by the state in the dry-farming zones would require heavy investment, both in working capital and public services such as roads. Mechanized farming requires large-scale operation, and the climate is far too risky for small farmers to achieve stability, so that new holdings would have to be large, and organized in group settlements with central services. The mere offer of land, even at a low price, will not attract labour (as is shown by the experiment carried out by the Najjar family, described on p. 91 above). Since the Government cannot even undertake the construction of roads in the Jezira, it is unrealistic to suppose that it could find the capital, or the organizing ability, to undertake settlement in dry farming on these lines. So far as any organized settlement has been undertaken, it is the work of the new entrepreneurs, who have built model villages for their skilled labourers. If it were politically possible to associate the big entrepreneurs with the work of a public settlement authority, their practical abilities might overcome administrative delays and muddles. But the idea that private enterprise should be openly and actively associated with Government is alien to political tradition.

The most that the state can do at present would be to

organize small-farmer settlement in state irrigation schemes, less difficult, because yields per acre are higher and more stable, and intensive cultivation in small units would be easier to organize successfully. The settlement of the state lands under reclamation in the Ghab valley in favour of small farmers would have considerable local importance in weakening the power of the landowners, since the valley lies near the densely populated Hama region, where the conditions of the share-croppers are among the worst in the country.

But agrarian reform in Syria is not so much an abstract necessity in the interests of development as a social necessity which arises from the recent social evolution and economic progress of the country. The demand for reform is now expressed by the Arab Socialist Party (officially the Arab Resurrection Socialist Party). The party can rightly claim to represent the interests of the peasants, since it finds its chief support in the fellahin of the Homs–Hama region, and only to a much lesser extent in the industrial workers of Aleppo and Damascus. Its leader, Akram Hourani, is himself from Hama, a man of the people who has had a stormy career. He first held office in Hinnawi's Government in 1949, and later advised Shishakli in drawing up the programme for workers and peasants (which included the abortive state land law of 1952). Opposition mobilized against him, and before Shishakli's fall, in the autumn of 1952, Hourani was under house arrest in Damascus, from which he eventually escaped to Lebanon, to return in 1954. At the elections in August 1954 the party gained 15 seats, of which 5 represent Hama; 1 seat was gained in Homs in a by-election in November 1955.

The party is generally described by its enemies as Communist, for while it does not subscribe to Communist doctrine, it does represent an uncompromising attitude to Western political influence and its driving force is pan-Arab nationalism. Detached observers regard the party as canalizing a social movement, which in one form or another was bound to appear as the natural outcome of conditions in the Homs–Hama district, and representing demands which the progress of the country should be able to meet. Both these attitudes are right: the party can be regarded as a spontaneous labour movement which may become Communist if its aims cannot be achieved otherwise. Hourani himself makes the impression of an intensely concentrated personality, dynamic and intransigent, and driven by convictions autonomous enough to need no formal dogma. Michel Aflak, another leader, is philosophic and idealistic and an economist. The party procession, celebrating victory in Homs with dancing, singing, and tribal drums, seemed neither socialist nor Communist; but simply Revolt in the Desert, for its flag dates from the first world war.

Whatever its ultimate direction, the party at present represents a well-articulated demand for land reform, at the moment expressed in moderate terms as a demand for improvement in the conditions of share-croppers and farm labourers. The leaders recognize that it is impracticable to attempt reform through limitation of holdings since it would be difficult to enforce different maxima in different parts of the country. In the Jezira, where wages are high, such limitation would be contrary to the interests of labour.

In 1955 the party submitted to Parliament a draft Law for the Protection of the Fellah. This covers both share-croppers and agricultural labourers. For share-croppers it provides that all agreements between landowners and cultivators should be based on a written contract; that eviction of the cultivator should be illegal, except for breach of contract; that all cultivators should be entitled to receive loans from the Agricultural Bank; and that in share-cropping agreements the landowner's share should not exceed one-third of the total crop on irrigated land and one-fourth of the total crop on other land. In the old regions, this would greatly increase the share taken by the fellah, which is generally not more than one-half on dry land and one-quarter on irrigated land. For the agricultural labourers the draft law proposes the extension of the Labour Law of 1946 to cover their conditions, and gives them the right to form trade unions.

Though the changes proposed by the bill are reasonable enough in the conditions of Syria's economy, the bill has no chance of acceptance in the present Parliament. The party's demands and its growing support may none the less encourage the Government to proceed with its own draft law, which proposes special labour legislation for agricultural workers, instead of the more radical proposal for the extension of the

labour law, and for the share-croppers proposes an improvement in security by means of written contracts, without the
essential point, the limitation of the landowner's share, proposed in the Socialist bill. The survival of the parliamentary
system in Syria will depend on whether it can produce a
measure of reform which will give the fellah a degree of protection.

Doubtless the best solution for Syria's problem of reform
would be both legal and economic action. Settlement on irrigated land would relieve population pressure, and weaken
the landlords' monopoly where it is strong. The trade union
policy of the Socialist Party could certainly force up farm
earnings and improve labour conditions. The policies would
reinforce each other, since without some movement to new
land the demand for higher earnings will be difficult to meet,
while resettlement alone will not compel landowners to provide a higher minimum level.

The prospects for a real improvement for the fellahin in
Syria are much greater than they are either in Egypt or in
Iraq, despite the fact that nothing has so far been done. There
is great scope for improvement in farming, as in Egypt there
is not; and there is scope for parliamentary action by a party
which represents the fellahin, while in Iraq and Egypt no
such representation exists.

Whether the social problem can be solved through the
mechanism of parliamentary democracy remains to be seen.
Syrian society is no longer static; it is evolving as a result of
economic change. The rapid upward and outward expansion
resembles that of Western Europe during the nineteenth
century; or perhaps the Middle West would be a better comparison. There has been a similar upsurge of private enterprise,
and a rapid rate of technical change through the investment
of private risk capital. Big profits and big losses have been
made. The state has played little part in economic life. This
nineteenth-century type of expansion has been accompanied
by social changes of a nineteenth-century kind: the rise of new
liberal entrepreneurs, the 'carrier group' for expansion; and
the emergence of a radical labour movement.

The extent of these changes should not be exaggerated;
there is no reason to speak of Westernization or social revolu-

tions. The inhabitants of the Damascus *souk* are recognizably much the same as they were when Isabel Burton visited it nearly a century ago. Tribesmen still camp round Hama, and the Jebel Druze can still get rid of a Government.

None the less, the social changes which accompany economic expansion are perceptible, and the comparison with European social evolution is not misleading. The merchant-tractorists in the north are liberals, objecting to state intervention and to the high level of military expenditure (33 per cent of the ordinary budget), just as Victorian business men objected to these things. In origin, function, and outlook they are quite distinct from the old *rentier* landowners, because they represent the greater part played by capital in the economy of the country, while the rise of the Socialist Party represents the demand of labour for a greater share in the growing national income.

These are the real forces making for reform of the land system, not the old-style politicians or the capable higher civil servants. Syrian Governments still reflect the old established order, old wealth and old power, as they inevitably must while the social changes are still in progress. Institutional reform usually lags behind economic change. To demand that the state should carry out the measures of reform which the economic development of the country requires presupposes a Government detached from the old social structure and exercising functions beyond the needs of the established order. In the meantime individuals have done what governments cannot do. The new entrepreneurs have carried out experiments in settling farmers on the land in the new regions; and one landowner at least has settled farmers in the south—a reflection of the need for reform for the sake of increasing production. At the same time the Socialist Party reflects the need of reform for the sake of social progress. Syria is a fortunate country, not only in having new land and new enterprise, but also in having new men who can realize the social needs of the country.

Syria's nineteenth-century type of development has been accompanied by the emergence of strong 'inner-directed' personalities who break through the crust of tradition in practical ways. The shift to the north has been undertaken by the new entrepreneurs, who undermine the political influence of the old landowners. There is not likely to be a link-up between the liberal Manchester men and the fiery leadership of the labour movement. But the two are not in conflict; for the expansion in production is being carried out on new land by new entrepreneurs who offer higher wages, while the socialist movement springs from the worsening conditions in the old regions, and is directed against the *rentier* landowners.

This nineteenth-century social evolution is taking place in a twentieth-century world. The house is wired for social progress, which might be achieved gradually through the parliamentary system, which Syria for the moment precariously maintains. But the currents which come along the wires are too strong, and may fuse the lights, if they force the landowners to take the side of the West and the socialists to take the side of the East.[1]

---

[1] See 'Postscript', p. 228.

IV

MONEY IN IRAQ[1]

THE BACKGROUND

IRAQ is underdeveloped in the exact literal sense. Its resources are half-utilized; its population is small and poor; its society is primitive and disintegrating; and its environment is only now being brought under control. These conditions are inter-related. The population is small and poor because in the past it could not master its environment, and the environment re-mained uncontrollable because capital was lacking—a low-pressure vicious-circle economy, as compared with Egypt's high tensions.

In every way but one, rural poverty, the economic position is the reverse of that of Egypt, where the environment is tightly controlled, resources are skilfully utilized, population densely settled, and society highly evolved. Though Iraq's resources are underdeveloped, its conditions do not correspond with the 'underdevelopment' model now most frequently postulated by economists. Two things are unusual: the adverse natural conditions of the Tigris–Euphrates valley, and the abundance of capital. Few countries have so much to develop, or so much to develop it with.

The conjunction of these unusual conditions makes Iraq's situation extraordinary. 'Money is not the only thing that is needed', says Professor Arthur Lewis, 'but money is the *sine qua non*.' In this country money is truly a *sine qua non*, because without it the environment could never be brought under control. Yet Iraq's experience is fascinating, because it demon-strates what money can and cannot do.

Briefly, the adverse factors in the environment are these. The waters of the Tigris and the Euphrates do not provide a regular natural renewal of the fertility of the soil, as the Nile does. Until 1956 the danger of flood was always present in south Iraq, major floods occurring once in every two or three

---

[1] This chapter has not been revised; see p. x above.

years on both rivers. The exceptionally severe Tigris floods of 1954 threatened Baghdad itself, and destroyed crops on about one-quarter of the area in the irrigation zone.

Yet at the same time there was a shortage of water, which meant that in most of the irrigation zone only a winter crop could be grown, and there was and still is much underemployment on the land. There are two flood periods, December to March, due to the winter rains, and March till June, when the snow melts in the upper reaches of the rivers; and there could therefore be two crop seasons. But until 1956 there was no storage capacity except in the areas served by the two barrages at Kut and Hindiya, and the water available could not be utilized.

Floods combined with shortage of water are not the only obstacles with which agriculture in south Iraq has to contend. Soil salinity is another.[1] The irrigation zone is a delta of marine origin, and the subsoil is saline. As a result of seepage from the high-level rivers and canals, the water-table is high, and capillary action raises the subsoil water to the surface, where it evaporates, leaving the salt behind. Salinity in high proportion can reduce grain yields and may throw the land out of cultivation. Drainage is the only remedy, and must usually be aided by pumping. Many landowners, however, do not undertake drainage, but simply abandon the ruined land, and shift cultivation to new land by digging new canals.

These obstacles to cultivation have affected the southern half of the country. The methods of farming in this zone are wasteful, and not merely primitive. Elsewhere in the Middle East irrigation is accompanied by an intensification of cultivation, through higher yields, high-value crops, and double cropping. But in south Iraq extensive cultivation is practised on irrigated land, and both land and water are wasted. Long

---

[1] The pump-irrigated lands escape the danger of salinity because the water-table is low, and in some of the flow-irrigated land there is natural drainage (from the Tigris near Baghdad, and farther south where the Tigris drains into the Euphrates). Rather more than half the irrigated land is supplied by flow, the remainder by pumps and other methods. The Haigh Commission estimated that as much as 60 per cent of the flow-irrigated land in south Iraq is affected by salinity (Iraq Govt., Irrigation Development Commission [the Haigh Commission], *Report on the Control of the Rivers of Iraq and the Utilization of their Waters* (Baghdad, 1951), p. 174).

stretches of poor barley, without apparent limits, alternate with long stretches of camel thorn, derelict salt-encrusted land, and expanses of last year's flood water.

The country is sparsely populated. Seen from the air, the region between Baghdad and Basra appears almost empty. The two great rivers wind through an arid featureless plain, with an occasional cluster of mud huts or a small town in the bend of a river. In the north there are vast agoraphobic landscapes of tractor ploughing, with not a house or a tree to be seen for miles.

The last population census, taken in 1947, gave a total of 4,816,185. In 1955 the total was estimated to be 5 million. Nothing certain is known about the rate of increase, though death rates and birth rates are certainly both high.[1] Of this total, between $2\frac{1}{2}$ and 3 million may be estimated as dependent on agriculture.[2] In the last three years the movement to the towns has accelerated, and the lower figure may be nearer the present total.

In relation to this small population, the cultivated area is large. According to the Agricultural Census of 1952–3, the area utilized for agriculture[3] amounted to 13·7 million acres, of which 6·3 million acres were sown with crops and 6·7 million left fallow, the remainder being in orchards, date gardens, vineyards (300,000 acres), and other uses. Assuming that the agricultural population is $2\frac{1}{2}$ million, the area of agricultural land per head is 5 acres, or 2 hectares, somewhat more than in Syria and twenty times as much as in Egypt.

[1] The fact that birth rates and death rates are both high is shown by the fact that half the population is under 20, as Professor Iversen points out (Carl Iversen, *Monetary Policy in Iraq* (Baghdad, National Bank of Iraq, 1954), p. 69; see also Doris G. Addams, 'Current Population Trends in Iraq', *Middle East Journal*, Spring 1956).

[2] The 1947 census gave a rural population of 3,196,304, representing 66·4 per cent of the total population. This number includes an estimated population of 250,000 in nomadic tribes. The Agricultural Census for 1952–3 gave a total of 1·4 million people working on agricultural holdings. This number does not include non-working members of farm families, pastoral farmers or nomadic tribes (*Report on the Agricultural and Livestock Census of Iraq 1952–3*, vol. 1, p. 18). The total population dependent on agriculture, including the non-working members of farm families, should therefore amount to between $2\frac{1}{2}$ and 3 million.

[3] The use of the term 'cultivated land' in Iraq causes confusion, since it may mean the area under crops, or the area under crops and fallow. For this reason the Agricultural Census Report uses the term 'utilized for agriculture', which includes the areas sown in one year and the area in fallow (ibid. table 4).

In addition to the areas which are cultivated now, there are large areas of cultivable land which could be brought under cultivation if water could be stored for irrigation. Estimates of the potentially cultivable area vary, because they depend on what assumptions are made as to capacity for water-storage. The most recent estimate, which is based on the assumption of large storage capacity provided by ten new dams, gives a figure of 5 million acres of additional land.[1] Figures of this kind have a hypnotic effect on official minds. The tendency to regard the extension of cultivation as the main aim of development derives from the engineer's approach which has dominated most thinking about the future of the country. Yet the immediate need is not to add to the area cultivated, but to get better cultivation on the land already in use, particularly in the irrigation zone.

The productive area of 13½ million acres is divided roughly equally between the irrigation zone of the south, in the alluvial plain between the two rivers, and the rainfed zone of the north, where dry farming predominates (see map on p. 123). In both zones land is cropped on the alternate fallow system, half being sown with wheat and barley each year, the other half remaining fallow. In the north this system is necessary because rainfall is insufficient for continuous cropping. The natural conditions in the northern region resemble those of north Syria; yields are low and fluctuating in the plains, while in the hill districts rainfall is higher and cultivation can be more intensive.

Because physical conditions are so adverse, agriculture has been the missing link in the economic development of the country. Surprising as it may seem, in view of the immense antiquity of agriculture in the land of the two rivers, modern Iraq is virtually a new agricultural country. Perhaps as much as three-quarters of the area at present cultivated has been brought under the plough since 1918, and one-third of it since 1945. In Turkish times very little land was cultivated, and the population was very small.[2] Economic life centred not in the

---

[1] Knappen-Tippetts-Abbett-McCarthy Engineers, *Report on the Development of the Tigris and Euphrates River Systems* (New York and Baghdad, Iraq Development Board, 1954; mimeo), commonly known as the KTAM Report.

[2] According to Dr Salih Haider, the population of the three vilayets of Baghdad, Basra, and Mosul around 1880 was 1½ million (*Land Problems of Iraq*).

villages or the country, but in the tribe and the town, as units of political and economic security.

Agriculture developed in dependence on these two bases. In the north grain yields were too unstable for the accumulation of capital in agriculture, and landownership became a function of the town merchant, money-lending to the peasants in the surrounding villages. In the south tribal life continued for many centuries, because nomadic grazing was more secure and profitable than cultivation. Both the city merchant and the tribal organization represented adjustments to an environment which they could not control. Both are extremely ancient adjustments, in which the town and tribe existed in mutual dependence—and mutual hostility.

In the inter-war years agricultural production increased, chiefly in the south. The areas under flow irrigation increased with the construction of the barrages at Hindiya and at Kut. In the north shortage of manpower and horse-power kept the area cultivated small.

Since the second world war expansion has continued, shifting to the north with mechanized cultivation. The following table shows the increase in production in recent years, compared with the pre-war average. It also illustrates the instability of agricultural production. The drought of 1955, which affected the northern zone badly, reduced the harvest to half the 1954 level, as it did in Syria.

TABLE I I

Area and Production of Main Crops in Iraq, 1934–8 and 1950–4

Area
(*000 hectares*)

	Average 1934–8	1950	1951	1952	1953	1954	Average 1950–4	1955*
Wheat	661	950	927	968	1,197	1,390	1,086	1,485
Barley	743	1,000	863	882	1,096	1,122	992	1,194
Total grain	1,404	1,950	1,790	1,850	2,293	2,512	2,078	2,679
Rice	152	217	189	75	95	119	137	60
Cotton	16	32	44	50	21	56	40	—

TABLE 11—*continued*

Area and Production of Main Crops in Iraq, 1934–8 and 1950–4

Production
(*000 metric tons*)

	Average 1934–8	1950	1951	1952	1953	1954	Average 1950–4	1955*
Wheat	478	545	488	500	762	1,160	691	483
Barley	575	851	839	700	1,111	1,239	948	768
Total grain	1,053	1,396	1,327	1,200	1,873	2,399	1,639	1,251
Rice	205	241	190	126	163	180	180	98
Cotton	2	8	6	3	2	7	5	8
Dates	260	305	313	111	350	350	285	—

* Preliminary estimates.

(SOURCES: Iraq Govt., *Statistical Abstracts, 1953* and *1954* and FAO, *Yearbook of Food and Agricultural Statistics.*)

Grain production has increased by 56 per cent over the pre-war level, while the area under grain has increased by 50 per cent. The increase in grain production is nearly as great as it is in Syria, and there has been some improvement in yields. Rice, grown in the primitive provinces of Amara and Diwaniya, remains static. Cotton has been a failure: after a little expansion in the 1950–1 boom it has fallen back to an average level of 5,000 tons.

Most of the new increase in grain production has taken place in the north, in the dry-farming zone. In recent years wheat production has doubled in the provinces of Mosul and Kirkuk, which now produce 70 per cent of the country's wheat. Tractor-farming has spread, though less sensationally than in Syria. According to the Report on the Agricultural Census of 1952–3, there were then 2,091 tractors in the country, but probably a large proportion was not in use. Tractor work is most evident in the north, where it is undertaken by the old-established merchant landowners of Mosul, Arbil, and other northern towns, and not, as in Syria, by new entrepreneurs. But many have taken up tractor-cultivation only to abandon it—because they cannot get spare parts and machine service.

Cotton production has been a failure for two reasons: there s no public authority to combat pests and improve varieties, as there is in Syria; and a 25 per cent export tax on cotton kept prices below the world level, in the interest of the cotton industry (chiefly the Iraq Spinning and Weaving Company). This tax was wisely abolished early in 1956. In Syria governments have not done much to help agriculture, but in Iraq they have actually hindered it. There was no Ministry of Agriculture until 1952, when a ministry was established on the recommendation of the International Bank.

Increased production has not touched the poverty of the fellahin. They live on a bare subsistence margin, in windowless mud huts built up out of the earth. Health conditions are appalling. 'It is not exaggerating to state', says Professor Michael Critchley, 'that the average agricultural worker (*fellah*) is a living pathological specimen, as he is probably a victim of ankylostomiasis, ascariasis, malaria, bilharzia, trachoma, bejel, and possibly of tuberculosis also.'[1] The crude death rate is believed by medical authorities to be about 30 per thousand population. 'An overall average of 300 to 350 per thousand for the country as a whole is probably not far wrong for the infant mortality rate.'[2]

For this misery two things are responsible: the low level of production, itself the result of adverse physical conditions and primitive methods; and the land system. The fellah's income is low because the land produces little, and because the landowner takes most of what it produces.

All past thinking about the development of the country has concentrated on the control of the environment. It has been carried out by consulting engineers, and has followed a tradition established early in this century. Iraq has not lacked technical advice.[3] The methods of control have long been known. The first survey of the irrigation potential was made fifty years ago by Sir William Willcocks, then Director of Reservoirs in Egypt, who was invited by the Turkish Government in 1903 to survey the delta of the Euphrates and the Tigris and to recommend the works needed to bring them

---

[1] A. Michael Critchley, 'The Health of the Industrial Worker in Iraq', reprinted from *British Journal of Industrial Medicine*, vol. 12, 1955, p. 73.

[2] Addams, 'Current Population Trends in Iraq', *Middle East Journal*, Spring 1956.

[3] Contrary to the opinion of the Point Four Mission, which in the spring of 1955 asserted that Iraq had had no technical assistance until they came.

under control. His report, published in 1905,[1] provided the framework for all the surveys which have since been made.[2] Modern Egypt and the irrigation systems of the second millennium B.C. were his guides, and the 'resurrection of Babylonia' his inspiration. Of the schemes which he recommended, only two were carried out, the Hindiya barrage, completed under his supervision in 1913, and the Kut barrage, completed in 1939, the only major work completed between the wars.

Since that time there have been several surveys of particular projects. A general survey was made by the Haigh Commission, which reported in 1951, and followed Willcocks in recommending the two big flood-control schemes, Lake Habbaniya (on which work was interrupted by war in 1913 and again in 1939), and Wadi Tharthar: two new barrages, one on the Euphrates in connexion with the Habbaniya reservoir, and another on the Tigris in connexion with the Wadi Tharthar scheme; and a number of other major irrigation works. In 1952 another general survey was made by the American firm, Knappen, Tippetts, Abbett, and McCarthy, which recommended still more dams, giving financial estimates and estimates of the potential increase in cultivation which could be attained by full utilization of land and water resources.[3] It represents the culmination of the engineer's approach and possibly its *reductio ad absurdum*.

The engineer's approach is two-dimensional, a blue-print in land and water, which money can turn into dams and dykes and drains. Except in so far as they provide labour, the people of Iraq do not enter into it. Because the engineer's approach is proper to the foreign consultant, it has created the belief that water-control is all that development means. When the oil money began to flood the Development Board, the plans for spending it seemed ready-made in the long lists of irrigation projects.

The human resources of the country have never been surveyed. Much more is known about the rivers of Iraq than about its inhabitants. Though the censuses of agriculture and

[1] *The Irrigation of Mesopotamia* (London, Spon, 1911; 2nd ed. 1917). The report was first published in Cairo in 1905.
[2] Even the estimates of cost were of the same order as the actual costs of these schemes today.
[3] KTAM Report.

industry have begun to fill some of the gaps, there has been no long series of investigations into the possibilities of raising living standards comparable to the studies of the land and water potential.

Now that the first big steps towards the control of the environment have been taken, it is time to think in three dimensions. Because the country is not economically or physically unified or integrated, the social structure is extremely heterogeneous. It comprises tribal societies in various stages of disintegration; growing shanty-town agglomerations; many small strange groups unified by craft, religion, and race rather than by economic status; and on the land the sharp class division between the large landowners and the serf fellahin. Between this social complexity and the high-level projects and the big money there is little connexion; the engineer's approach cannot mesh in with the intricacies of real life.

In the past Iraq was poor because its people could not master their environment. Today Iraq is poor because it has more money than it can invest; and the reason why this is so is that the social structure of the country is not adapted to expansion.

Oil Revenues and Development

Since 1951 the revenue accruing to the Government of Iraq from oil royalties has increased rapidly as a result of the increase in oil production. Between 1950 and 1954 oil production rose from 4 million tons per annum to 30 million tons, and oil revenues accruing to the Government increased from £2 million[1] to £67 million. By 1960 the annual revenue from oil is expected to amount to at least £100 million per annum. Revenues have risen more than in proportion to the increase in production, as a result of new agreements reached between the Government and the Iraq Petroleum Company and its associated companies, which gave the Government more favourable terms, in 1952 (retroactive to 1951) at the time of the Persian Oil crisis, and in 1955 (retroactive to 1954) when the Baghdad Pact was agreed.[2]

---

[1] The currency unit is the Iraqi dinar, equivalent to the pound sterling, here used as the more familiar unit.

[2] For the terms of the agreements, and for statistics of oil production and revenues, see UN, Dept. of Economic and Social Affairs, *Economic Developments in the Middle East, 1945 to 1954*, pp. 97–8.

Under a law of 1952, retroactive to 1951, 70 per cent of these revenues is assigned to the Development Board. The Board was first instituted in 1950 to supervise the spending of the loan granted by the International Bank for the construction of the Wadi Tharthar flood-control scheme, and to prepare 'a general economic and financial plan for the development of the resources of Iraq and the raising of the standard of living of its people.' The members of the Board are nominated by the Council of Ministers for a period of five years; they include an American expert and a British expert on irrigation. Later, in 1953, a Ministry of Development was set up; the Minister represents the Board on the Council of Ministers and provides the link with Parliament.

The Board's annual income now amounts to some £50 million per annum. For the first four years of its operations revenue totalled £104 million. Its income in future is likely to rise to £65 million; over the five years 1956–60 it anticipates a total expenditure of £450 million.

These sums are very large in proportion to the economy. No estimate of the national income is at present available,[1] but the significance of £50 million can be judged from comparison with the total state expenditure, which up to 1950 did not exceed £30 million, and the total value of Iraq's exports, which in 1947–50 averaged £16 million.

Whatever criticisms are made of development policy—and these are inevitably many—it is important to keep a sense of perspective from the past. Ploughing back the oil into water represents an immense step forward. Before 1951 oil revenues were small, and the greater part of the income from oil was drained out of the country, consuming its main capital asset. Now a large proportion of this income is directed towards making good that loss, by investment which can lay the foundation for a more productive agriculture and provide the power for industry, against the day when oil revenues come to an end.

The main result of the Board's expenditure, so far, has been the completion of the two big water-control schemes, the Wadi

[1] An estimate made in a UN publication, *National Incomes Per Capita in Selected Countries* (New York, 1949), gave a total national income of £150 million, presumably guessed from cost-of-living figures. As this estimate took no account of income from oil, it is best disregarded.

Tharthar flood-control scheme on the Tigris, and the Habbaniya flood-control and irrigation scheme on the Euphrates,
both inaugurated in April 1956. The Wadi Tharthar scheme
includes a new barrage at Samarra, which will provide water
for a new power station. The Habbaniya scheme includes the
new barrage at Ramadi. These schemes were constructed by
foreign firms.[1] In addition to these two schemes now in opera-

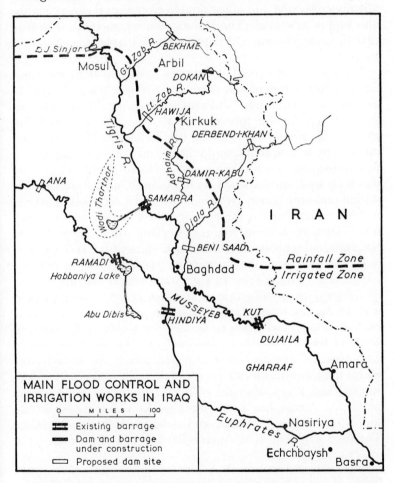

MAIN FLOOD CONTROL AND
IRRIGATION WORKS IN IRAQ

0   M I L E S   100

Existing barrage
Dam and barrage
under construction
Proposed dam site

[1] The contracts for the Wadi Tharthar channel and dyke (awarded to Balfour,
Beatty and Company of London) and the regulator, barrage, and power station
(awarded to the German firm Ed. Zublin A.G.) totalled £16 million, £5 million
more than was anticipated. For the Lake Habbaniya scheme, the barrage contract

tion, the Dokan dam and reservoir scheme on the Lesser Zab is in construction, to be completed in 1958.[1] The sites of these works are shown on the map on p. 123.

Thus money can provide flood-control, more water and more land. The two schemes already completed will protect south Iraq from floods. In addition to providing for flood diversion, the Ramadi barrage will supply additional water to land already cultivated and allow double cropping; it can probably also supply new land. The Dokan dam scheme will, it is estimated, make 780,000 additional acres available for cultivation by 1960.

Money can also build. Contracts have also been awarded for the construction of new roads and bridges, hospitals, water-supplies, and buildings. Unfortunately the Board provides no progress report.[2] But observation shows much activity. The main visible result of the expenditure in Baghdad is new building, chiefly banks, shops, and offices, and the new bridge. The new railway station was not a Development Board project but was built by Iraqi Railways. It has been found unsuitable as a station and now houses two government departments. There is much new housing for the rich and the middle class, and one small housing scheme for the working class; several new hospitals and schools; and a new and efficient bus service.

In the provinces the impression varies. Mosul, a derelict city, had nothing to show in 1955 but a new bridge and a new oil refinery, just coming into production. It is, however, to have a much-needed town-planning scheme, a cotton textile mill, a cement plant, and a sugar factory for which a £3 million contract has recently been awarded to a French firm. Arbil, with most of its population crowded inside the walled city, where the tuberculosis rate is very high, has a new piped water-supply, and a new hospital with a highly esteemed Austrian physician. Amara has a new brick works, a new piped water-supply, three new hospitals, and some working-class housing. The road Baghdad–Kut–Amara–Basra is one of the main pro-

---

was awarded to the French firm S. A. Hersent, at a cost of £1·4 million; other work on the outlet and inlet channels was completed by Balfour, Beatty and Company in 1947–51 at a cost of £2·7 million.

[1] The contract was awarded to the French firm Dumez in 1954, at a cost of £9 million.

[2] No accounts have been published since the financial year 1953–4.

jects of the Board, and on the Amara–Basra section work has begun. The Baghdad–Kut section is impassable after rain, and in 1955 showed nothing new but stranded Cadillacs and Pontiacs. In the Kurdish hills road-building has made progress. Perhaps the best result is the provision of clean drinking-water, from which ninety towns are to benefit.

What money apparently cannot do is increase production. In the preceding section it was shown that agricultural production has increased considerably in recent years; but this increase has been achieved by landowners' private enterprise, chiefly in the north, and cannot be attributed in any degree to development expenditure. Nor, with one or two minor exceptions, has there been any increase in industrial production as a result of the new investment.

Nor can money bring about a general rise in the standard of living, except in so far as clean drinking-water does mean a very real rise for the towns. The effect of development expenditure in Baghdad is to make the contrast between rich and poor more striking. The great increase in imports benefits chiefly the rich, whose consumption of cars, air-conditioning, and luxurious new houses is very conspicuous. The *sarifa* (mud hut) slums are growing fast, without sewage or drinking-water. Very little has been spent on social welfare.

In the larger towns, chiefly Baghdad, Basra, and Kirkuk, the expansion in employment has raised wages. But the supply of unskilled labour is very elastic, because of the low level of earnings on the land. There is much underemployment in the small towns (evidenced by the coffee-house sitters) and in the villages (where men sit round the threshing-floor and the women gather the crops). Consequently the increased demand for labour does not raise wages much, and consumption levels remain low.

Criticism of the results of the expenditure cannot be openly expressed, because the opposition parties have been suppressed and the press controlled since 1954. But there is much dissatisfaction, and a belief that the spending of £100 million ought to show more results. Not all the criticism is justified. There have been no major bungles; in the execution of the projects, technical standards are very high. The big water-control schemes cannot show immediate results, except in so far as they prevent crop destruction. In the provinces there is more improvement than the citizens of Baghdad believe. But it is true that there have been long delays in decision, and it is also true that the money does not percolate downwards. Wealth accumulates and men decay.

Although the failure to undertake economic planning is criticized by economists, the criticism is unrealistic, because when capital is free and no undertaking need show a return, the usual criteria do not apply. To plan means to choose between alternative investments in relation to an anticipated return. Choice is essential, because capital is scarce and must be paid for. But in Iraq capital is not scarce and increases without cost; there is therefore no pressure to select schemes on the basis of their net return. Moreover, investment in irrigation and flood-control does not allow any calculation of the net return in increased productivity. The only calculable effect is the physical possibility of irrigating more land; and so the future development is often envisaged simply as more acres.

When expense is no object, it is much easier to start big schemes than small. 'We like the millions', an Arab ruler told Gerald de Gaury. The same is true of the Development Board. It is said to be easier to get a contract for millions than for thousands. So a £10 million dam can be built while tractors lack spare parts and Dujaila, the pioneer settlement, is undrained. Iraqi planners have yet to learn to do little things.

The result is that too much is invested in the big projects, and not enough in working capital, or in human resources. The country is an economist's cloud-cuckoo land, in a Hayekian gap without a crisis, and building Keynesian pyramids without inflation or multipliers. The crisis is avoided because the big expenditure on deep investment need not show a profit. Inflation is avoided because imports have increased, and because the supply of labour is elastic.

Consequently the result of the expenditure to date resembles, in essentials, the results of planning in the Communist countries of Eastern Europe: concentration on investment in long-term production capacity, at the expense of agriculture and consumer-goods industries. But Iraq is not in the position of a Communist country which must reduce consumption in order to increase productive capacity. It need not concentrate all its capital investment in long-term means of production at the expense of consumption; it can aim at generating an all-round expansion in production, and a rise in its living standard.

At present, the major difficulty is that there is too much of the *sine qua non* in relation to investment opportunities. Where there is so much need for investment in every direction, the choice of priorities might be expected to present great difficulties. The country clearly needs everything: water-control, better farming, clean drinking-water, sewage, drainage, health services, roads, industry, afforestation, education— the list could be prolonged. Yet the problem has not been to decide between different possible uses for the money, but to find uses to which the money could be put. The necessity of choice between alternatives has never arisen, because the annual revenue perpetually exceeds the anticipated and actual expenditure.

The Board has not undertaken any economic planning, though it was set up for this purpose. It has confined itself to financial programming, allocating its total revenues in advance in large sums under different headings. Its main job is to approve proposals put forward by the ministries, obtain the approval of Parliament for specific expenditures, arrange surveys, invite tenders, and then award the contract to a firm, usually foreign. Where the work can be undertaken by an Iraqi authority the Board sanctions the expenditure by the appropriate Ministry or other public authority. It also grants loans to municipal and other public undertakings, for such purposes as drinking-water supply and the Baghdad bus service.

The Board's first expenditure programme, for the six financial years 1951–6, foresaw a total revenue of £155 million[1] over the six years, and allocated this total under six main headings: irrigation, flood-control, and drainage (£53 million); main roads and bridges (£27 million); building (£18 million); land reclamation (£23 million); industrial and mining schemes (£32 million); and administration (£3 million). This was an engineer's programme. The schemes for irrigation, flood-control, and drainage were itemized in detail, listing the Haigh Commission's recommended projects and some others. Road

[1] Iraq Govt., Development Board, *Annual Report, 1953–4* (Baghdad, 1954).

and bridge projects were also listed. The land reclamation and industrial programmes were bulk allocations, with no mention of specific projects.

Unfortunately, no detailed review of the results of this programme is possible. The following table shows the revenue and expenditure of the Development Board for the first four years of the programme.

TABLE 12

Revenue and Expenditure of the Development Board

Provisional figures

(£000)

	1951–2	1952–3	1953–4	1954–5	Total 1951–5
Revenue					
Oil royalties	6,702	22,876	34,823	40,039	104,440
Miscellaneous revenue	765	1,123	454	690	3,032
Total	7,467	23,999	35,277	40,729	107,472
Expenditure					
Administration	100	214	302	277	893
Irrigation	841	2,491	4,795	6,689	14,816
Main roads & bridges	630	1,752	1,917	2,790	7,089
Buildings	788	2,265	2,451	609	6,113
Land reclamation	772	1,035	2,331	1,378	5,518
Industry	—	81	461	2,045	2,587
Total	3,131	7,838	12,257	13,788	37,016
Surplus	4,336	11,161*	23,020	26,941	70,456

* In 1952–3 £5 million were appropriated for the ordinary budget.

(SOURCE: *Quarterly Bulletin of the National Bank of Iraq*, no. 14, April–June 1955.)

From the table it appears that the Board succeeded in spending only one-third of its total revenue during the four-year period. Under each heading, expenditure fell far short of the total allocated. Industry was the weakest section, only half a million pounds being spent during the first three years, against a total anticipated expenditure of £8 million for the period. Even the sum spent on irrigation, far the largest item, fell far short of the anticipated expenditure.

The results are, however, rather less unfavourable than the above figures suggest, as the Board has lent large sums to

municipal and local authorities and public undertakings, totalling £6,276,000 in 1952–3 and £14,113,000 in 1953–4;[1]
later figures are not available, but further loans have certainly
been made. Thus the total direct expenditure does not represent
the total investment resulting from the Board's operations.
None the less, it is certainly true that the Board has not been
able to spend and lend more than two-thirds of its revenue,
perhaps less. No figures are available for the year 1955–6.
At the end of 1955, however, the Board was reputed to hold a
bank deposit of £40 million.

Before the period of this programme had elapsed, a new oil
agreement in 1955 (retroactive to 1954) increased the Board's
revenues, and in April 1955 a new programme was issued,
superseding the six-year programme.[2] It anticipated a total
revenue of £300 million over the five years 1955–9, and allotted
this sum on much the same lines as in the previous programme,
giving irrigation and flood-control £108 million, to include the
Derbend-i-Khan dam scheme at a cost of £16 million. To
meet the criticisms of the first programme, rather larger allocations were made for housing (£9½ million, including £3 million
for working-class housing) and health institutes (£10¾ million).

Revenues again exceed expectations. A year later, in April
1956, another programme was issued,[3] revising the previous
programme upwards, and providing for a total expenditure of
£500 million over the six financial years 1955–60. Under this
programme, irrigation, flood-control, and drainage was
scheduled to receive 30 per cent of the total, or £154 million;
communications £125 million; buildings £96 million; housing
£24 million and summer resorts £2½ million; industry £67
million; agriculture £14 million; and miscellaneous schemes
(ancient buildings, drinking-water, and swamp-filling) £10
million.

The provision for housing is four times the amount allocated
in the previous programme; the Board intends to start a building programme for 10,000 houses in the main towns, and also

---

[1] Iraq Development Board, *Annual Report for the Financial Year 1953–4* (Baghdad,
1954).
[2] *Law No. 43 for the year 1955 for the General Programme of the Development Board
and the Ministry of Development* (Baghdad, 1955).
[3] *Law No. 54 of 1956, amending the Law of General Programme of the Development
Board No. 43 of 1955.*

to construct 'big groups of houses in rural areas'. The building programme includes £5·7 million for hospitals, £8 million for schools and educational institutes, and £2 million for a malaria fighting project. Thus much fuller provision is made for social services. The allocation which seems grossly inadequate is the £14 million for agriculture (including research, livestock improvement, and education)—only 3 per cent of the total, and inadequate both in relation to the irrigation programme, and in relation to the increase in national income which could be achieved.

Engineers' Planning

In his masterly report—rightly described as *A Plan of Action*—Lord Salter describes the Board's policy as engineers' planning.

Water policy . . . is primarily an engineering problem. . . . It starts naturally with such general surveys as those made by the Haigh Commission and by K.T.A.M. These provide the basis of the decisions as to where the great water structures shall be built. The technical surveys also of course indicate what natural potentialities the land possesses for fruitful cultivation with the aid of irrigation and drainage. What they provide in this respect, however necessary and useful, cannot be decisive in the consideration of policy. It is only a starting point for the real, and difficult, task of planning. A dam site may be wisely decided upon on the basis of an engineer's survey. But much more is needed before a prudent policy can be formed as to what irrigation and drainage, or where and when, should be undertaken. For a survey indicates only what land could be developed if there were the settlers, properly equipped with knowledge and all they need for success, to cultivate it. It may provide an engineer's plan to make enough land cultivable to support a population of 20 millions. But the total population of Iraq is in fact only a little over 5 millions. Neither natural increase, nor any probable and permitted immigration, will even double that number for many years to come. The engineer makes a plan for developing the land. But Iraq's task is to develop a nation. The land exists for man, not man for the land.[1]

Lord Salter urges what in effect is a complete change of policy. First, he recommends that no further big dam schemes should be undertaken, since the works now under construction (together with the Derbend-i-Khan dam already decided upon) 'give as much flood protection as is reasonable, provide as

[1] *The Development of Iraq; a Plan of Action* (London, Caxton, for Iraq Development Board, 1955), p. 49.

much new water as can be used, and as much new land as can be settled.' Drainage should take priority over new irrigation works—a recommendation eminently wise.

Instead of more irrigation works, Lord Salter recommends: (1) much greater investment in human resources, through increased expenditure on health and education; (2) greater investment in agriculture, through an active agricultural policy— for 'little, lamentably little, has been done to increase and improve agriculture'. He emphasizes the need for including animal husbandry in plans to increase agricultural output—again a key point, for in livestock-breeding Iraqis are outstanding.

The 1956 programme meets these recommendations by making larger assignments of funds to housing and the social services, though it does very little for agriculture. But will it be possible to act on Lord Salter's main recommendation—to put the standard of living first? The difficulties of spending the money would disappear if that were made the target. But the Development Board is only a group of civil servants. They cannot be responsible for government policy. Engineers can plan without regard to production and consumption, and this is the only kind of planning that can be undertaken under the present political system and with the existing social structure. At bottom, all the Board's problems are the result of new wine in old bottles.

Consider, for example, the launching of new industries. Superficially, the difficulty is administrative. Industrial projects do not lend themselves to the routine procedure of technical survey, tenders, and contracts. The market must be considered; and how can this be surveyed? The Board has decided on a general survey of the industrial potential for multiple development, to be carried out by I. D. Little, the American consultants; and doubtless a good job will be done. But the real obstacle to industrial expansion is the poverty of the bulk of the population. It is sometimes said that there is a shortage of enterprise: but where there is an expanding market, Iraqis can show themselves as enterprising as others.[1]

Or consider the need for improving methods of agriculture,

---

[1] The recent expansion in small brick works, along the Shatt el-Arab and the Tigris in Amara, supplying Basra, Kuwait, and Abadan, is an interesting example; so too, is the mat industry in Echchbaysh.

where so little has been done. Agricultural progress needs the big things, and also many little things, gradually welded into a standard of good farming practice.[1] There are great possibilities —in cotton production, in improving seed varieties for grain, and in breeding livestock. No experimental work has been done on dates of sowing or irrigation, or rates of fertilizer application. But how are supplies and knowledge to be channelled into agriculture? There are no co-operative or local associations of farmers. In the Kurdish peasant villages in Arbil small-scale improvements, such as artesian wells, are beginning, because the administration can deal directly with farmers. Elsewhere it cannot. The great landowners constitute the Parliament, and could make an agricultural policy, if they so desired.

Rural housing is to be improved, according to the 1955 plan, but only in the state land settlements, which comprise about 3,500 families. No funds are allocated for rehousing villagers on large estates. Health services are to be improved—but in the towns only.

If the policy of spending mainly on big capital construction continues, the result will be simply a further increase in employment in building. The main social effect of the development expenditure so far has been an increased rate of migration to the towns, to Baghdad, Basra, and Kirkuk (not Mosul). The population of these towns is increasing very fast, mainly from Amara and Kut, the provinces where the fellahin are most oppressed.

At present the movement to the towns seems to come only from the poorest provinces where there is a strong 'push' factor at work, so that it is possible to obtain labour at low wages, and there is not much increase in consumption.[2] This move-

[1] Professor Iversen, considering development policy from the angle of currency stability, suggests that shallow investment should offset deep investment, and could be increased by providing supplies of agricultural equipment, which could lead to small but widespread improvements in the productivity of labour (*Monetary Policy in Iraq*, pp. 150–3).

[2] Professor Iversen considers that the land system, by keeping labour tied (through the landowner's right to forbid his labourers to leave if they are in debt), is a factor restricting the supply of labour (ibid. p. 147). In Amara where the landowners are extremely powerful, they cannot exercise their authority to prevent movement now, because the usual method of punishing the runaway's family is no longer possible when the family has left. Once the movement acquires real momentum, the landowner cannot reclaim his serfs.

ment is not likely to reduce agricultural production, for land-owners can invest in tractors and combines. One landowner in Arbil expressed the view that the landowners would be forced to use tractors and combines in spite of the difficulties they have so far experienced with spare parts and repairs, because in a few years' time there would be no labour left on the land at all.

That view may be exaggerated, and yet it is certain that the exodus will go on, because the big capital construction works will continue, and so will urban building. For the fel-lahin a big rural exodus is the best thing that could happen. But as a long-term policy Iraq cannot abandon cultivation and live entirely on canned food. A country which is undertaking investment in irrigation on a large scale is indirectly investing in agriculture, and must make some provision for the future of the agricultural population. By the time that perennial irriga-tion allows intensive cultivation, the cultivators may not be there.

This is the setting of the land reform question. It is the land system which is responsible for the great inequality of incomes, the lack of an expanding internal market, the low-wage influx into the slums, and the lack of an agricultural policy. Without land reform, the oil money can do little to raise the standard of living. If land reform were undertaken, the money could be used to equip farmers for better living and better farming. Without it, the big dams will be a succession of Keynesian pyramids, giving employment but not increasing production. The 'resurrection of Babylonia' was an engineer's dream fifty years ago. In the meantime Iraq has acquired what an Iraqi jurist describes as 'the feudalism of Hammurabi'.[1]

From a social standpoint, the serf status of the fellahin is an obvious evil. It is also an economic bottleneck. If Iraq is to develop, it must have a healthy and well-to-do population on the land. Reform is a social and an economic necessity, the key which can unlock the door to a prosperous future.

Reform is also a political necessity, since with the present social structure the development money cannot benefit the people. As Lord Salter points out, the question of who is to

[1] Dr S. A. Nahi, *An Introduction to Feudalism and the Land System in Iraq* (Baghdad, 1955; in Arabic), p. 7.

benefit from the water-control and irrigation projects on which their expenditure has been concentrated is one which directly concerns the Development Board.

The great water schemes, the dams, reservoirs, main irrigation works and main drainage outfalls, etc., are being constructed wholly at the expense of public revenue, derived from the oil royalties, which belong to the whole country not to any one section of it. These water schemes will of course increase the productivity of the land, and therefore its value—to an extent that in time will equal —and indeed ultimately exceed—their cost. It is not unnatural that sections of the community should regard it as unjust that one section, already more privileged than others, should now be further enriched to such an extent at the public expense, and should resent a policy which would have that effect. They may well have an ultimate power which is altogether out of proportion to their present representation in Parliament and their ability to influence legislation by constitutional means. It is this contrast between immediate, and potential, political power that constitutes the danger and the difficulty of the problem.

In these circumstances one tempting course is to outflank the problem instead of attacking it directly. There are large areas of Miri Sirf land, owned by the Government. With the aid of new irrigation and drainage works this land can be made cultivable. Small settlers can be established, without any question of enriching the already rich arising. And in this case, apart from the direct benefit to the new settlers of farming their holdings, either as small owners or as tenants of the State, the existence of such opportunities of new settlement would, perhaps, lead to an improvement of the conditions of work of workers on the great estates. It is along this line, the line of least resistance, that policy has tended to develop.[1]

The line of least resistance evades the real issue. The big water-control schemes will and should benefit the land which is already cultivated. Even if it were politically possible to use all the new irrigation water for small-holder settlements, this policy would not be economic, for, as has already been emphasized, the immediate need is not to extend the area cultivated, but to double-crop the land which now carries only a winter crop. More intensive farming on the land already cultivated would bring a quicker increase in production than the setting up of special settlement schemes.

With the existing tenure system, the new schemes will benefit the landowners, and at no cost. In 1954 a bill was submitted

---

[1] *The Development of Iraq*, pp. 54–5.

to Parliament which empowered the Government to recover by instalments from private landowners the costs of drainage undertaken under the expenditure programme of the Development Board. The bill was passed by the Chamber of Deputies but rejected by the Senate, where the sheikh landowners predominate. Private landowners pay no tax on their property in land, and income tax is not progressive.[1] The new control of Iraq's water and land will thus serve to increase the incomes of a class which now contributes little to development and which is opposed to social progress.

THE LAND SYSTEM

The Origins of Large Landownership

The extraordinary feature of the land system in Iraq is the size of the estates which dominate the irrigation zone. These great holdings are tribal in origin, and have only recently become private property, as a result of the appropriation of tribal land by the tribal sheikhs in the last thirty years.

Up till the end of the Ottoman period, the basis of landownership was the tribal *dirah*, a large area not limited to land actually tilled, but including also non-cultivated land or submerged marsh land, over which the tribe exercised a customary right of occupation. The tribal system, as it then existed, had no legal basis and no protection from the state. In law, the tribal lands were regarded as state land and the tribal occupants as tenants-at-will.

Under the tribal system cultivation was partly communal, partly individual. The method of farming necessitated some communal organization, since single households could not undertake the clearing of land, the building of dams across channels, and the strengthening of the river banks. The head of the clan, the sirkal, managed these functions on behalf of the tribe, organizing canal clearance and irrigation, allotting the seed, and appointing the dates of sowing, harvesting, and threshing. Within the tribal *dirah* the area cultivated was small, and shifted about as canals silted up and the land was impoverished by salt, and so the area cultivated by each peasant shifted also. Individual prescriptive rights to land were known

---

[1] Under the income tax law of 1956, however, income from the rent of agricultural land becomes liable to income tax.

LAND REFORM AND DEVELOPMENT

(*lazma*, *nagsha*, and other customary forms), but these were restricted to a small class in the tribe, in areas permanently cultivated. For the most part there was no individual ownership, since occupancy of a fixed plot of land for a long period was not usual. The cultivators were mobile; cultivation was not their only occupation, and livestock grazing remained the more important alternative.

The function of the sheikh was political; he maintained the tribal militia and kept the *mudhif* (the guest-house and civic and social centre). Revenues to enable him to carry out these duties were collected by the sirkals from the tribesmen; one-third or one-half of the cultivated land was set aside to provide for the sheikh's income. This income accrued to the office of the sheikh, and not to his person. His right to revenue depended on his political functions.

The tribesmen, under this system, were neither individual owners nor labourers; they were cultivators of land communally owned. Dr Salih Haider has well summarized their status as that of 'agricultural labourers in the cultivated part of the tribal *dirah*, as well as partners in it. The latter aspect of their position is still more definite in the uncultivated part of the tribal *dirah*.'[1]

Since the early years of the twentieth century the tribal system has been breaking up, as a result of settlement for permanent cultivation, the opening of markets, greater political security and technical change. When steamship transport came to the Persian Gulf at the end of the nineteenth century markets for Iraqi grain opened, and the sheikhs found it profitable to take more grain from their cultivators, in order to export. In the 1920's pump irrigation gave them a strong motive for acquiring land as their own property. These economic changes were consolidated by the settlement of title to land carried out from 1933 onwards which is described below. The sheikhs have now become legal owners of the *dirah*, the sirkals have become the managers and agents; and the tribesmen have become share-cropping fellahin, with no rights or status.

The fellahin are in law tied to the land; a law of 1933 provided that no labourer could leave the land if he was in debt to the landowner; and as labourers are usually in debt they are

[1] Salih Haider, *Land Problems of Iraq.*

136

in effect serfs. If a labourer deserts the estate, the landowner can punish him by destroying his family's hut and driving them out. Though the cultivator is a share-cropper, he is not properly speaking a tenant, since he has no security or freedom of action.

The land which he cultivates, the crops that he grows, the times of sowing and harvest, all these are decided by the landlord or his agent, who also provides the seed, organizes the marketing and controls the irrigation. The share-cropper therefore differs from the paid labourer only in so far as he does not receive a fixed daily wage; instead his wage is a proportion of the crop and depends therefore mainly on factors beyond his control.[1]

The high level of rents is the main cause of rural poverty, and not the shortage of land. The area cultivated by one family in south Iraq averages 30 donums (20 acres), of which half is cropped and half left fallow. This area should be sufficient to support a family and produce a surplus for sale, even with such an extensive system of farming; but when two-thirds of the produce is taken as rent, it is not sufficient.

The proportion of the crop taken by the landowner varies with the type of cultivation. On flow-irrigated land it is generally three-fifths, and two-thirds if the landowner provides the seed. On pump-irrigated land the landowner takes five-sevenths. In date plantations the share is still higher, as the landowner has made an investment. In the districts where landowners carry on more intensive farming, with a double-cropping system, as in the Gharraf (the region supplied by the Kut barrage), the position of the share-cropper is much better, for though the proportion of the produce taken by the landowner is as high, and sometimes higher, than on single-cropped land, the gross produce is much greater and the cultivator's income is therefore higher also. The condition of the fellahin is worst in the regions where output per acre is low and where the sheikhs are powerful, as in the rice-growing districts of Amara.

The prestige of the sheikhs rests on their former function of leadership in a tribal society which owed the state no allegiance. The foundation of the new kingdom strengthened them, giving them legal ownership of land and representation in Parliament, while it has at the same time weakened them by remov-

[1] H. D. Walston in an unpublished paper on *Land Tenure in the Fertile Crescent*, 1954.

ing the need for tribal wars and tribal rule, through the creation of a national army and a national administration. They thus secured a position of privilege in the state, without obligation to it. Now that their economic function as investors is diminished by the new money, their function is simply to preserve their position in the packed Parliament, and to resist change.

In northern Iraq the land system differs from that of the south. The law of inheritance follows the practice of equal division between heirs, as laid down in the Ottoman Land Code, and this practice tends to break up the larger holdings. In the south tribal custom, reinforced by the *Sharia* law, prescribes inheritance by the eldest son, so that holdings are not subdivided on inheritance, and the large estates are kept intact.

Economic conditions are also different in the north. In the plain regions of the rainfed zone production is highly unstable and there is much variation in yields and between different localities.[1] The large landowners in the Mosul region, predominantly city merchants, have acquired land either by inheritance or by lending to impoverished cultivators, and taking the land when debts cannot be paid. For the most part their wealth has not been accumulated through agriculture: the wool trade, grain-milling, cotton-ginning, and the ownership of urban house property are their main sources of income. New fortunes were made by war profits. The largest fortune in Mosul today has been made in the wool trade.

Even the largest holdings are small by comparison with those in the south. Merchants of Mosul or Arbil say 'I have a few villages', not farms or acres. The largest landowner of Mosul, an enterprising merchant-tractorist, has twenty villages, roughly equivalent to 20,000 donums (12,000 acres), which would not rank as very large in the southern half of the country. The landowners of the Mosul region now undertake more investment than the sheikhs of the south. They have extended the culti-

---

[1] The *Report on the Agricultural and Livestock Census of Iraq, 1952–3*, vol. 1, p. 52, states that in one part of Kufri district, in the Kirkuk province, 'more than forty villages had no crops at all over a period of two years and as there was no food for the animals, they had to be driven away to other parts', while in other districts crop yields were good, amounting to a sixfold and eightfold return on the seed sown.

vated area greatly in recent years by the use of machinery, and have also introduced pump irrigation for cotton on the Tigris. The more enterprising have rented land from the sheikhs of the Shammar, who have recently acquired title to very large areas of state land in the north.[1] The Chief of the Shammar, Ahmed el-Ajeel, is the largest landowner in the province and extremely wealthy; he undertakes tractor-farming on his own account. The lesser sheikhs are grasping and sit in the offices of the Mosul merchant-tractorists, insisting that they should take a grain crop every year instead of leaving the land fallow to recover its fertility.

Rents taken by the landowners are lower in the north, because population is sparse. On irrigated land where pumps are installed the landowner's share amounts to 50 per cent of the gross produce, while in the south it is between 66 and 75 per cent. On dry land rents are low, ranging from one-quarter to one-eighth of the gross produce, or even, in remote districts, to only one-sixteenth. In the Kurd hill villages, where rainfall is higher, the land is held by peasant owners, and the standard of living is higher than in the plains, most noticeably in regard to housing.

The Distribution of Ownership

There are no published figures showing the distribution of landownership. The Directorate-General of Land Settlement (i.e. the department which settles land title) presumably has in its possession the data for classification of properties by size, since properties are registered in the name of their owner. Unfortunately, and for obvious reasons, this classification is not made.

The Agricultural Census of 1952–3 provides a classification of numbers of agricultural holdings in size-groups. For the purposes of the census, a holding is a unit of management, not a unit of property. It is defined as 'a farm or agricultural estate organized as one unit'. This unit

may therefore be very large, extending perhaps to several hundred thousand mesharas,[2] or very small, perhaps as small as two olks

---

[1] See below, p. 160.
[2] The Iraqi unit of area is the meshara or donum, equal to 0·25 hectares and 0·62 acres.

(200 square metres). Some individuals farmed more than one holding as defined above, sometimes in different *Liwas*, but on the other hand, some holdings were jointly held by two or more persons.

This explanation reveals the difficulty in defining the holding. It presumably means that the units of property and management are not the same. This is generally true of the largest estates, which are managed in several large units by the landowner's agents.

Although the census figures cannot be used to show the distribution of ownership, they give an indirect indication of the scale of ownership, in that they show a preponderantly large scale of operation. The census figures relate to a total area in holdings of 25½ million donums or mesharas (6·4 million hectares or 15·8 million acres). Unfortunately the census gives only the number of holdings, and not the area, held in each size-group, so that the proportion of the land held in the large estates is not ascertainable. But the census shows that there are some very large holdings, recording 104 with over 20,000 donums (12,000 acres).

TABLE 13

Distribution of Holdings by Size in Iraq

Donums			Hectares	Acres	Number
Under 4			(under 1)	(under 2½)	24,270
4	and under	20	(1–5)	(2½–12)	25,849
20	,,	,, 100	(5–25)	(12–60)	41,905
100	,,	,, 600	(25–150)	(60–360)	27,555
600	,,	,, 1,000	(150–250)	(360–600)	1,847
1,000	,,	,, 2,000	(250–500)	(600–1,200)	1,702
2,000	,,	,, 5,000	(500–1,250)	(1,200–3,000)	1,221
5,000	,,	,, 10,000	(1,250–2,500)	(3,000–6,000)	424
10,000	,,	,, 20,000	(2,500–5,000)	(6,000–12,000)	168
20,000 and over			(5,000 and over)	(12,000 and over)	104
				Total	125,045

(SOURCE: *Report on the Agricultural and Livestock Census of Iraq, 1952–3*, vol. 1, table 2, p. 16.)

The census indicates the difference in agrarian structure between north and south by showing that the average holding is large in the southern provinces of Amara, Kut, Muntafik,

Diwaniya, and Baghdad, and smaller in the northern provinces, with the exception of Kirkuk.

TABLE 14

Average Size of Holding by Provinces in Iraq

(*in donums (acres)*)

South Iraq			North Iraq		
Amara	6,884	(4,128)	Kirkuk	462	(276)
Kut	1,087	(648)	Arbil	131	(78)
Muntafik	709	(426)	Mosul	128	(76)
Diala	255	(150)	Sulaimaniya	61	(36)
Diwaniya	441	(264)			
Baghdad	407	(240)			
Dulaim	296	(174)			
Kerbela	260	(156)			
Hilla	119	(72)			
Basra	25	(15)			

(SOURCE: ibid. p. 16.)

In the southern provinces, the average is low only in Basra, where date cultivation is carried on in small holdings. In Hilla and Kerbela large holdings predominate, but the average is reduced by the large numbers of small holdings on the Euphrates. Amara, Kut, and Muntafik are provinces with an extreme concentration of ownership, Amara and Muntafik being the provinces where tribal authority is strongest. In the northern provinces the average holding is smaller, and in Mosul and Kirkuk the distribution round the average is close.

The census results do not show the existence of the very large properties exceeding 50,000 donums. Figures compiled from the data in the possession of the Directorate of Land Settlement by Jafar Khayyat,[1] covering privately owned land (i.e. excluding State Domain) in six provinces (Baghdad, Kut, Hilla, Dulaim, Kirkuk, and Arbil) and relating to a total area of 14·3 million donums, show that in these provinces there are thirteen properties between 50,000 and 100,000 donums (30,000 and 60,000 acres) and twenty-one properties between 100,000 and 200,000 donums (60,000 and 120,000 acres).

Two landowners are commonly reputed to own properties

[1] *The Iraqi Village: a Study in its Condition and Reform* (Beirut, 1950; in Arabic).

exceeding 1 million donums. These are the Emir Rabia, commonly called the Second King of Iraq, who owns great areas in Kut province, and has introduced tractors and pumps and carries on intensive farming. The other is Mohan el-Khair Allah, in Muntafik province, who does not introduce modern methods. Five or six others are credited with properties of about half a million donums. These include Naif and Muhsin el-Harian (in Hilla), Abdul-Razzak and his relative Abdul-Abbas el-Mirjan (also in Hilla), and Ballasim and Abdullah el-Hussain (in Kut). In Amara the greater part of the cultivated land of the province is the property of four large owners. These enormous holdings are not highly capitalized and efficiently managed commercial enterprises, like the large estates in Egypt, but cover great expanses of poorly cultivated land and land which has gone out of cultivation, or is uncultivated or uncultivable. Landowners reckon their possessions in pumps or fellahin rather than in donums. As a source of wealth they depend partly on investment in pumps or machinery, partly on the exploitation of the cultivators; they are units of political power.

SETTLEMENT OF TITLE

In determining the present distribution of ownership, the settlement of title to land[1] has been a decisive influence. Registration of title in Iraq is not, as it is in many countries, simply a technical operation conferring greater security and ease of transfer on owners who already hold title-deeds establishing ownership. As in the other countries of the Fertile Crescent, and in any country where communal tenures are breaking up, land registration in Iraq confers legal rights on a customary tenure holder, and thus creates new rights of individual ownership. Usually, though not invariably, these new rights are created at the expense of other customary holders. In Iraq settlement of title has in practice been a process of expropriating occupying cultivators and impropriating the tribal authorities as large landowners. This wholesale alienation of tribal land is a quite recent change, carried out within the last twenty years.

[1] The procedure of granting registered title to land is properly described as land settlement, but to avoid confusion with resettlement on new land, it is here called settlement of title.

It will be recalled that in Ottoman times there had been no general registration. In the northern parts of Iraq, then the vilayet of Mosul, grants of registered title were made round the towns. In remote places the *aghas* or *mukhtars* (village headmen and tax collectors) usually succeeded—contrary to the provisions of the Land Code—in registering the land of the village as their property. Where small owners received the *senet tapu*,[1] they were often defrauded of their title by city notables or forced to sell the land to pay debts. In theory, however, registration was carried out in this part of the country, on the small land area cultivated at that time.

In the south the tribal authorities violently opposed registration, and the provisions of the Land Code, which enforced registration, were not carried out, even in theory. The attempt to enforce registration of title to individual holdings led to conflict, even to actual fighting, between sheikhs and tribesmen, and was therefore abandoned. Two decrees, in 1880 and 1892, abrogated the provisions of the Code enforcing registration in the vilayets of Basra and Baghdad. The land remained in the nominal ownership of the state (i.e. as *miri*, with the state retaining both the *raqaba* and the *tasarruf*,[2] while the tribesmen were regarded as tenants-at-will). Revenue was collected by tribute or taxation, the amount taken varying with the relative strength of the tribe and the Government.[3]

In one province of the south grants of *tapu* title were made, and these have produced a permanent state of confusion. The Governor of the Muntafik province, the head of the Sadun family and sheikh of the powerful Muntafik confederation of tribes, purchased *tapu* ownership of the whole province from the Ottoman Government. These titles have never been recognized, and the title-holders have never been able to collect the revenue from the occupying owners. Recently a new law has been passed to attempt to settle these sixty-year-old claims.[4]

When the new State of Iraq came into existence, the state was in law the largest landowner. This ownership was a legal

[1] See above, p. 68.   [2] See above, p. 67.
[3] Dr Salih Haider gives an interesting example. The chief of the Muntafiq Confederation, virtually independent and ruling vast areas in the late nineteenth century, paid an annual tribute of 70 horses, valued at £7,000, but in Basra, where the revenue officials were more powerful, agricultural produce was subject to high rates of taxation (*Land Problems of Iraq*).
[4] See below, pp. 155–6.

fiction, for the state had no effective rights over the land, except the uncertain power to tax. Only a fraction of the cultivated land was held, somewhat uncertainly, on *tapu* tenure, while the rest was held on no legal tenure at all.

In addition to the state's nominal claim to ownership of all land, the new State of Iraq became the owner of the former Ottoman Crown Estates, the personal property of the Sultan Abdul-Hamid II. These estates had been acquired between 1883 and 1909 by purchase, gift, and reversion of land. They were extensive and included some of the most fertile land in the Tigris and Euphrates valleys.[1] They were administered by a special department, the Dairat-al-Sanniya, under the direct control of the Sultan. After the deposition of the Sultan in 1909 the Sanniya administration was abolished. Much of the land then went out of cultivation, and the canals silted up. Under the Treaty of Lausanne, the lands of the Ottoman Crown became the property of the states succeeding the Ottoman Empire. In Syria a special department, the Directorate of State Domain, was formed to administer these lands,[2] but in Iraq no such department was set up; the lands fell into the possession of private landowners, and in law were on the same footing as other *miri* land.

In the new state, where the large landowners were powerful, strong pressure to introduce a system of land registration came from the sheikh landholders who were installing pump irrigation on the banks of the two rivers. Whereas in the past the tribal authorities had resisted the central Government in its efforts to register land in individual holdings in the names of the cultivators, they now demanded settlement of title as a means of ousting the tribesmen, whose prescriptive rights to graze and cultivate prevented the pump-owner from securing the land supplied by the pump as his own property. It was now the wealthy who wished to use the state against the cultivators,

[1] For information about the Sanniya Estates I am indebted to Miss Albertine Juwaideh, now working on this subject at Oxford. The estates were well managed, improving both irrigation and agriculture. The position of the cultivators was better than that of the ordinary tribesmen, in so far as the officials prevented exactions by the sheikhs. Though the level of share-rent was high, the cultivators were better off by reason of the larger output and interest-free advances of seed. According to Dr Salih Haider (*Land Problems of Iraq*, p. 422), the contribution of the Sanniya Estates to agricultural and social progress in Iraq was considerable, and far exceeded the value of the irrigation works undertaken by the Government.

[2] See above, pp. 98–9.

not the state which aimed at securing the rights of the cultivators against the wealthy.

The conflict between the rival claims of development for the land and security for the cultivators created a difficult problem. Tribal organization was bound to disintegrate, under the pressure of political and economic changes, and could not have been preserved. To attempt to stabilize the customary rights of the tribesmen would have prevented investment. But to meet the full claims of the pump-owners meant ignoring the customary rights of the cultivators and depriving them entirely of security and status. Only a very strong government could have succeeded in reconciling these rival claims. The mandatory Government did not even attempt to do so. Some uncoordinated and spasmodic attempts to settle title were made between 1919 and 1930, including an abortive attempt to settle the Muntafik claims, and the introduction of triennial revenue assessments in Amara. But there was no general policy. In 1929 Sir Ernest Dowson was requested by the Iraq Government to investigate the problem of settlement of title and to make recommendations for its solution.

Dowson's report[1] is a classical exposition with sound recommendations which in essentials was ineffective. In retrospect it is easy to see why it was so. Its first main recommendation was that no attempt should be made to introduce a general settlement of title in freehold ownership, but that grants should be made, after survey, in ten-year leasehold tenancies. In a country with such great agricultural potentialities it was important for the state to retain its right of ownership so that it could resume control of the land at a later stage in the development of the country.

The second main recommendation was that settlement of the rival claims should be made on the principle of 'beneficial occupational use'. To give due weight to the prescriptive claims, Dowson recommended that settlement should be preceded by local investigations of claims in the community itself, and that special land courts should be set up to hear appeals from, or cases referred to by, the settlement authorities. It was here that Dowson's past experience was not a good

[1] Sir Ernest Dowson, *An Inquiry into Land Tenure and Related Questions* (Letchworth, for Iraq Govt., 1932).

guide. As an Indian Civil Servant, he approached the problem of settlement in Iraq as if it could be handled by administrators who were independent of the large landowners. 'Painstaking, experienced and impartial' officers, he believed, would be able to arrive at satisfactory settlements by reconciling the claims of the actual occupiers. To settle title meant deciding between the rival claims of the sheikhs, sirkals, and cultivating tribesmen on the basis of confirming the previous rights. If, that is to say, the sheikh had a claim to one-fifth of the produce from each of a hundred cultivators, he should receive a holding of land equivalent to one-fifth of the total, and each cultivator should receive a holding equivalent to four-fifths of the land he cultivated. The settlement officers were not impartial, and generally acceded to the claim of the sheikh to the whole of the tribal land. As Dowson observed 'Personal influence . . . is commonly the decisive factor at any moment in any particular land dispute: and anyone may find the most convincing claims set aside.'[1]

Where personal influence was so strong, and the authority of the Government so weak, 'beneficial occupational use' was too elastic a principle to be satisfactory. It would have been better to have proposed the allotment of a specific area of land to every adult male cultivator whose right to participate was recognized. This course was suggested to Dowson as the only practicable one, in view of the difficulty of investigating and settling the rival prescriptive claims, but he rejected it on the grounds that 'it savours of a new allotment of land rather than of a recognition of a claim based upon previous use'.[2]

Wisdom after the event is easy. Dowson could not have foreseen that the principle he recommended allowed too much discretion. But because so much nonsense is now talked about evolutionary reform, it is worth recalling that twenty-five years ago, when the land system was still fluid, it would have been possible to grant title to land to a broad section of the fellahin, and so to constitute a class of small farmers, on the basis of rights which custom then recognized.

In the event, both Dowson's main recommendations were set aside. From 1933 onwards land settlement was carried out, under the supervision of British officials, on a systematic basis.

[1] ibid. p. 27.   [2] ibid. p. 53.

Tribal land was alienated, in what are in effect freehold tenures, to the sheikh landholders. This result has not been universal. The principle of subdividing land in proportion to the income received by the sheikh, leaving a portion to him and to the cultivators, has been practised in some parts of the country, as for example on the Middle Euphrates, where the water-wheel owners form a settled peasant class. The effective principle has been that the size of the plot varied inversely with the power of the Government. Where it was powerful, the tribesmen gained a useful share of the total, and where it was not, the land was assigned in enormous holdings to the tribal sheikhs as their individual property.

Registration of title was carried out under the Land Settlement Law of 1932, which gave the Government the right to settle title to land and established the procedure of registration. During the 1930's settlement was carried out chiefly on the pump-irrigated lands. The Law for the Sale of Miri Sirf Land of 1940 greatly accelerated the process of assigning tribal land to large landowners, especially in the flow-irrigated regions.[1]

The Forms of Tenure

The two main forms of tenure for private landowners in Iraq are *tapu* and *lazma*. Large areas are retained in state ownership as *miri sirf*. Small areas are held in the old categories of *mulk*, *waqf*, and *matruka*.

The three main forms were established by the Land Settlement Law of 1932. It laid down that all land not found to be *mulk*, *matruka*, or *waqf* should be classified as *miri*, either granted in *tapu*, or in *lazma*, or retained in state ownership as *miri sirf* (from *emiriye sirfa*, absolute state property). According to the law, both *tapu* and *lazma* are included in the *miri* category, and according to the conceptions of Moslem law are conditional tenures, because the state grants the *tasarruf* or right of usufruct, and retains the *raqaba*, or right of absolute ownership. They should properly be described as *miri tapu* and *miri lazma*, though in ordinary usage they are not so described. In practice, both grant what in English law would be considered absolute ownership, since they confer rights of disposal and

---

[1] Hassan Mohammed Ali, 'Miri Sirf Land Development in Iraq', *International Social Science Bulletin*, vol. 5, no. 4, 1953.

inheritance which are subject only to minor or nominal restrictions.

Tapu corresponded to the old Ottoman tenure, while *lazma* was a new form of tenure instituted in 1932 by the Law of Granting Land on *Lazma* Tenure. *Lazma* had been one of the chief forms of customary tenure recognized in Ottoman times, and the law gave it legal status. The object of instituting the new form was to confer individual ownership while preserving tribal solidarity. The law decreed that *lazma* tenure could be granted by the settlement authorities to any person who had enjoyed the usufruct of land, if he could prove that the land had been cultivated (according to local usage, i.e. allowing for fallow) over a period of fifteen years preceding the date of settlement. Land so granted was heritable and transferable, and could be mortgaged. The transfer of *lazma* land was to be subject to the approval of the Tapu Department of the Ministry of Justice, and permission might be refused if the transfer was likely to cause a breach of the peace, or reduce the holding to an uneconomic size. The object of making transfer subject to official sanction was to prevent the sale of land outside the tribe, and so safeguard tribesmen against the alienation of their land. However, the institution of this new form of tenure has not had this effect. *Lazma* was used chiefly by the pump-owners to acquire ownership of land on which they had installed pumps, and the prescriptive rights of the tribesmen were usually disregarded.

There is now no practical distinction between *tapu* and *lazma* tenure, except as regards the formal requirement of official approval for transfer of *lazma* land. Before 1939 owners of *tapu* and *lazma* land had to pay taxes on their land and water, and *lazma* owners paid at higher rates. In 1939 these payments were abolished, in return for amortization of their capitalized value over a period of ten years, so that this distinction has now been abolished.

The remainder of the land to which title has not been settled remains in the formal ownership of the state—as *miri sirf*. This category includes land actually in the possession of sheikhs or other landowners who in fact enjoy undisturbed rights of possession. These occupiers pay a light tax on their holding. The *miri sirf* lands also include all uncultivated lands which are not registered. In regard to these lands the state's power of dis-

posal is important, because it gives the Government the right
to grant title to land which will become cultivable through the
new irrigation works. Special legislation (described in the next
section) was passed in 1945 and 1951 giving the Government
the right to confer ownership on small farmers.

Figures published by the Agricultural Census show that the
land in holdings was distributed in 1952–3 between the different forms of tenure as follows.

TABLE 15

Types of Land Tenure in Agricultural Holdings in Iraq

	(*ooo donums*)	(*ooo acres*)	(*per cent*)
Tapu	10,109	6,065	39·6
Lazma	6,713	4,028	26·3
Other tenures	1,012	607	4·0
Rented lands	7,702	4,621	30·1
Total	25,536	15,321	100·0

(SOURCE: *Report on the Agricultural and Livestock
Census of Iraq, 1952–3*, vol. 1, table 3, p. 17.)

This classification is, however, confused. Presumably 'rented
land' refers to *miri sirf* tenure, i.e. land rented from the Government. Much of the land classified as 'rented' is in Amara, where
97 per cent of the land in holdings is returned under this heading, and where the land is in law *miri sirf*.

Figures published by the Directorate-General of Land
Settlement relate to a larger area and include uncultivated
land, as follows:

TABLE 16

Land Title in Iraq: Area Settled by 1953

Type of tenure	*ooo donums*	*ooo acres*
Tapu	10,922	6,553
Lazma	10,295	6,177
Miri sirf	39,256	23,553
Other tenures	4,030	2,418
Total	64,503	38,701

(SOURCE: Govt. of Iraq, *Statistical Abstract,
1953*, table 133, p. 98.)

The areas settled in *tapu* and *lazma* tenures, according to these figures, are larger than the areas in agricultural holdings recorded under these tenures, from which it might be inferred that landowners have acquired title for land not yet cultivated, and staked their claims on land which development projects will make cultivable.

It is worth noting that the greater part of the land now held in *tapu* and *lazma* tenure has been settled in the years 1943–53. In 1953 21 million donums were held in these tenures, as compared with 9 million donums in 1943. From 1945 onwards successive Iraqi Governments have stated that their aim is to encourage small ownership by distributing state land to cultivators. During the same period settlement of title has proceeded steadily in the opposite direction.

Though most of the cultivated land has now been settled, the problem of settlement is still acute in the provinces of Amara and Muntafik. In Amara attempts to enforce registration under special legislation have led to a serious social conflict.

The Amara Laws. In Amara, a remote and primitive province in the marshes of the Tigris, the land is still in the formal possession of the state (i.e. is *miri sirf*) and in the actual possession of the sheikhs, whose status in law is that of tenants of the state, in that they pay tax to the Government in respect of the tribal land which they occupy. Their holdings are exceedingly large. According to the Agricultural Census, 'large holdings of 20,000 mesharas [12,000 acres] or more were found in each of the administrative sub-divisions of the Liwa, and among the 29 holdings in this size group, seven holdings were over 50,000 mesharas [30,000 acres].'[1] Three sheikhs and the family of a fourth are believed to hold most of the cultivated land.

The economy is no longer nomadic, though livestock grazing is as important as cultivation. The large numbers of sheep (half a million), goats, camels, horses, cows, and buffaloes show that the transition to permanent cultivation is still in process. Of the total area in holdings of 3·2 million donums (2 million acres), less than one-third is sown with crops, the rest being fallow, uncultivated, and in part uncultivable.[2] Agriculture is partly

---

[1] *Report on the Agricultural and Livestock Census of Iraq, 1952–3*, vol. 1, p. 35.
[2] ibid. p. 36.

anchored to the river banks by pumps, and partly shifts within the cultivable land area. Wheat, barley, and rice are the main crops, irrigated by pump and flow. In the north of the province there is rainfed land, some of which has recently been converted by a large landholder to pump irrigation.

The social structure is still tribal. One of the three big land-holders, for example, the Senator Mohammed el-Araiby, has 6,000 'people' (i.e. fellahin—tribesmen), a family of 200, and 4 wives. Smaller landholders have between 1,500 and 2,000 people and 2 or 3 wives. The social pattern repeats itself at intervals in every reed-hut settlement along the banks of the water-courses. The sheikh welcomes the guest on the mud bank in front of his guest-house, a large two-roomed brick building furnished with carpets from Kashan and Tabriz, embossed plush armchairs, and Coca Cola posters. Near the guest-house is the *mudhif*, the tribesmen's social centre, a conventional arched reed building, with carpets or reed mats and the beaked coffee-pots in the fire on the floor. The women have a house apart, though the rich sheikhs keep their wives in 'palaces' in Baghdad or Amara town. The sheikh's income is held in big round reed baskets, 10 feet across and 4 feet high, which hold rice or grain, carefully packed with mud and watched by his retainers. A lesser sheikh may have 30 such mounds, represent-ing about 50 tons, awaiting shipment by motor launch. The crops are grown by the cultivators, who must deliver two-thirds or even three-quarters of the produce to the sheikh. Wealth may be shown in the furniture of the house and in the sheikh's dress. The wealth of Mohammed el-Araiby is shown in the possession of bedding for 3,000 people, last used on the occasion of the King's visit.

On the surface, Amara seems an idyllic patriarchal world, with its formal manners and its ancient crafts and skills. The great sheikh is a royal figure, in gold and brown *arba'a*; his tribesmen rise as he passes. The groom displays a white Arab mare and the *Abeed* (negroes, formerly slaves) serve coffee. Hospitality is a duty, magnificently performed. The lesser sheikhs are simple rustic persons, who enjoy boar hunting and keep jesters. The fellahin fish from pitch-lined high-prowed canoes among the palm trees.

But there is great poverty. Its main cause is the extortionate share of the crop taken by the sheikhs, and also the low level of output per head, resulting from low yields and the small area of land cultivated. Bilharzia and other parasitic diseases are general, and so is trachoma. Amara town has a leprosy hospital. New schools are being started, but many children cannot attend because they must work. Some sheikhs oppose education, though there is one, a lesser sheikh at Kalat Salih, who has built a school for his people.

This apparently stable society is now being undermined very rapidly from without. The tribal structure has long been disintegrating as a result of the impact of the central Government, which involves the transfer of judicial powers to the courts. Emigration from the province has been in progress since the 1920's and is now much accelerated. The land system was the chief reason why tribesmen migrated in the past, and this 'push' factor has been reinforced by the Amara Law of 1952.

Unrest first appeared openly in 1952 after the enactment of the Amara Law. This laid down a special procedure for settlement of title in the province. The usual procedure in the past, as has already been explained, was to grant the whole tribal area to the sheikh, without regard to the rights of the cultivators. The Amara Law aimed at preventing this result, for it contained provisions which gave the fellah the right to receive a fixed area as his property. But the law was formulated in such a way that the sheikh and his family could claim the whole of the cultivated land. Thus the benefits to the peasants were illusory, and the law created a legal basis for claims which it could not satisfy. After the second coup d'état in Egypt and the announcement of the Egyptian land reform there were riots in Amara town, which were put down by the police with some loss of life.

Though the law was not carried out, its provisions must be explained, since its consequences have been important.

The Law for Granting Lazma Rights in Miri Sirf Land in Amara Liwa (No. 42 of 1952) laid down the principles on which the right of ownership in *lazma* might be acquired by different classes of occupiers. It distinguished three classes of claimants:

1. The primary *multazim.*

2. The secondary *multazim*.
3. The fellah.

The primary *multazim* means the tax-collector in direct contact with the Government, i.e. the sheikh, who may be regarded either as a collector of taxes on behalf of the Government, or as a tenant of the state paying rent. The secondary *multazim* is the sheikh's agent or sirkal, the head of the clan, who collects taxes and rents on behalf of the sheikh.

The law provided that the primary *multazim* could claim half the area of the holding in respect of which he has paid taxes, and in addition 200 donums (120 acres). The secondary *multazim* could claim one-quarter of the area which he leased from the primary *multazim*, provided that this area did not exceed 150 donums (90 acres). The fellahin could claim 15 donums (9 acres) per family.

The law allowed the sheikh and his family to secure most of the land, because it provided that a secondary *multazim* who was a close relative of the sheikh might be regarded as a primary *multazim*, so that the sheikh could nominate members of his family as his lessees or agents, entitled to a half-share in any part of the holding which the sheikh decided. After the sheikh's own share of half the total holding had been deducted and the members of his family had taken half shares in the remainder, there was little left for the cultivators. Further, since the area of the holding contained both cultivated and uncultivated land, the sheikh and his family might claim the whole cultivated area as their property, leaving only the uncultivated and uncultivable to the fellahin.

When efforts were made to carry out the law, the cultivators exercised their right of appeal against the decisions of the settlement officers. The sheikhs retaliated by destroying their houses and turning out their families. The law gave an impetus to the rural exodus which is now proceeding at the rate of ten lorry loads a day for Baghdad. This movement has already weakened the authority of the sheikhs and reduced their incomes. One of the most hated and extortionate, who formerly had 4,000 people, now has only 1,500. Some smaller sheikhs cannot pay their taxes. The fellahin are beginning to mock their masters and think them arbitrary and despotic. A tribesman from Amara, now a house watchman in Baghdad, told his former landowner (now a professor) that he and his four sons could now earn £50 per month between them, and that they could sleep without being kicked awake by the *mamur* to go an errand—an attitude which the ex-landowner fully approved, because he too had found social relations insupportable.

As a result of the unrest in the province, an emergency decree was issued in 1954 which cancelled the law of 1952 and laid down new principles. These principles were embodied in a new law, passed in April 1955, the Law for the Distribution of State Lands in Amara Liwa (No. 53 of 1955). This made two improvements. It provided, first, that the holding for division should include only the cultivated land, including the areas under fallow, and second, that this area should be divided into two equal halves, each half having a river front, canals, and drainage equivalent to the other half. One-half was to be granted to the primary and secondary *multazims*, i.e. the sheikh and his agents, the other half to the fellah household, in units of 7–20 donums (4–12 acres) of flow-irrigated land for rice cultivation and corresponding areas for other types of land. The household receiving land may not sell, bestow, or mortgage the property until a period of ten years after the grant of title. The uncultivated land can be distributed by the settlement officer. The parts suitable for cultivation are to be granted to the fellahin in holdings equivalent to 7–20 donums of flow-irrigated rice land.

At the end of 1955 the survey preparatory to redistribution was being carried out by the settlement officers. One consequence was that the son of the chief sheikh of the province had been thrown into prison, because he claimed more land than his father would allow. Whether in fact the law will be carried out, and whether the fellahin will be satisfied, remains to be seen. 'The police are working day and night', said the *mutasarrif*, in December 1955, 'that is why everything is quiet.'

The Muntafik Law. The Muntafik province lies in the marshes of the Euphrates. Very large landholdings predominate[1]

---

[1] The *Report of the Agricultural and Livestock Census* for 1952–3 (p. 57) shows that there are 12 holdings exceeding 20,000 donums (12,000 acres), and 26 between 10,000 and 20,000 donums (6,000–12,000 acres).

which are in the possession of sheikh landholders. About half the land in holdings is registered in *tapu* tenure, the remainder in *lazma*.

Concerning these *tapu* lands, there is a sixty-year-old conflict between the actual occupiers of the land (sheikhs, sirkals, and tribesmen), and the Sadun family, which claims legal ownership under *tapu* title granted in Ottoman times. During the nineteenth century this family secured the leadership of the three tribes which formed the Muntafik Confederation, and as sheikhs held all the lands tribally occupied, which in law were state land. The head of the Sadun family, then Governor of the province, purchased *tapu* title to these lands from the Ottoman Government, registering the land in the name of the family and its connexions. The family then increased their pressure on the tribesmen cultivators, demanding a fixed rent irrespective of the actual yield, instead of the proportion which they had claimed as sheikhs. The sub-sheikhs and tribesmen revolted and refused to pay, driving the Sadun landowners off their land.[1] Some of the land has since been resold by the Sadun family to townspeople in Baghdad and Basra. The Sadun family and these other owners still claim legal ownership, but have never been able to collect their rents.

During the British occupation the British authorities reached a temporary solution, which recognized the rights of the landowners; they collected the dues as a percentage (7·5 per cent) of the produce, on behalf of the owners, and paid them into the treasury, to be paid to the landowners when a final settlement of their claims could be reached. An attempt at settlement was made in 1929, by a law 'for the settlement of disputes concerning Muntafik land', which led only to an expensive commission of investigation, and reached no settlement. The land has never been surveyed and investigation alone can reveal nothing, since the areas to which the *tapu* claims relate were never defined.

Twenty years later, in 1952, another law was passed, the Law for the Settlement of the Disputes concerning State Land held by Tapu in Muntafik Province. The holders of *tapu* title, under this law, were to be compensated by the Government in

[1] S. M. Salim, 'Economic and Political Organization of Echchbaysh', thesis to be published as *Marsh Dwellers of the Euphrates Delta* (1962).

cash or in state land, and the actual occupants were to receive rights of possession, after they had paid half the compensation due to the *tapu* holders. At present local committees are bogged down by administrative delays in land valuation.

This question has little importance from the social standpoint, since it is chiefly the occupying sheikh landholders who are affected by the Sadun claims. A law which offers compensation for antiquated claims to undefined areas of land is simply an illustration of the dead hand in legislation.

Tenancy Legislation. It is unrealistic to suppose, with the existing political system, that any real improvement in the position of the share-croppers can be made by legislation to control rents. A law for this purpose was in fact passed in 1952, the Law Determining the Share of the Cultivator in the Produce of the Land. This law provides that landowners may not take more than 50 per cent of the produce. It also prohibits the landowner from making special levies on his cultivators, a practice followed by landowners who wish to raise money for some special purpose (to buy a car, for example, or to educate a son abroad). In the northern parts of the country local officials consider that this latter provision has had some effect. The provision prohibiting the landowner from taking more than 50 per cent of the crop has had little effect, because the share customarily taken in these parts of the country is usually less than 50 per cent.

In the irrigated zone, where the share taken by the landowner and his agents amounts to two-thirds, the general view was that the law is not enforced. According to the President of the Miri Sirf Land Development Committee,

this law does not improve the miserable conditions of the peasants, since the application of the law is greatly doubted, and even if applied, the peasant's share of the crop is far from being enough to cover the cost of a reasonable living.[1]

Even in countries where the landowners as a class are less powerful than they are in Iraq, the enforcement of rent regulations for share-croppers is difficult. In south Iraq, where the landowning class has complete domination over the serfs, such regulation seems obviously out of the question.

[1] Hassan Mohammed Ali, *Land Reclamation and Settlement in Iraq* (Baghdad, 1955).

Without an expropriation of the very large landholdings, no legislation can succeed, for the problem of reform is a problem of political power. Iraq needs serf emancipation. Some have believed, or pretended to believe, that evolutionary reform is possible by settling farmers on state land to be developed under the new irrigation schemes. Some reference has already been made above to the 'line of least resistance' policy.[1] The Development Board naturally follows this line, and speaks confidently of the land that will be available for small-holder settlement in the future.[2] But experience so far is not encouraging, as may be seen from the results of the state lands settlement legislation.

THE SETTLEMENT OF STATE LANDS

No legislation which would infringe on the property rights of the large landowners can secure parliamentary approval. The Parliament is composed of the landowners, who secure election by means of their dominance over the cultivators; and this dominance is unquestioned by any internal political force.

It may be [says Lord Salter] that some among the great landowners will accept or welcome some changes on the principle of 'reform that you may preserve'. In the meantime, however, successive Governments have usually felt that new legislation on land tenancy must be kept within the bounds of what will not be actively resisted by landowners.[3]

These bounds are narrow.

At first sight it appears puzzling that any measures at all, however limited and ineffective, should have been enacted by Iraqi Parliaments, for even when political parties were permitted to exist, the small and disunited opposition groups did not influence policy. The explanation is that the landowners are not the only force on which Iraqi Governments can rely; they depend also on the Army, the Palace and, to some extent, on British support, and are therefore to some degree independent of the landowners. The Prime Minister can therefore arrange, if the stability of the Government seems to require

[1] See above, p. 134.
[2] According to the *Annual Report* of the Development Board for 1953–4 (p. 17), the Dokan dam scheme will provide water for 1·3 million donums (780,000 acres) for small farmer settlement.
[3] *The Development of Iraq*, p. 54.

it, for any particular measure to be passed, by techniques which involve a present to the landowners, in the form of state land, or otherwise. Foreign pressures may be effective, up to a point. If an international mission recommends settlement of farmers on state land, as the International Bank did at a time when a loan was wanted, landowners will be fixed and a law can be passed, and even a little action will be taken. If there is fear of 'Communism' among the fellahin, as there was after the Egyptian revolution, a law can be passed to reduce rents and prohibit unusual extortions, though when the danger recedes it need not be enforced. Serious local unrest, as the example of Amara shows, can get a bad law improved, and perhaps enforced. The old Turkish statecraft requires a semblance of beneficent intentions, though it is unable—and unwilling—to undertake any serious measure of reform. Among the bureaucracy the beneficent intentions are genuine; what has been achieved is the work of enlightened civil servants.

Since large areas of land are still held in the possession of the state as *miri sirf*, and as much of this land can be made cultivable by the new irrigation schemes, there would appear to be great scope for the settlement of small farmers without the necessity of a conflict with the large landowners. To the enlightened civil servants, the distribution of state land seems to provide a way round the political structure of the country. Colonization has even been advocated as an indirect and evolutionary way towards a general improvement in the position of the fellahin; it should, according to this argument, cause a shortage of labour on the land and so induce landowners to offer their cultivators better conditions.[1]

To this indirect approach the main objection is that over the past ten years very little has been done. Two laws governing the distribution of state land passed in 1945 and 1951 have had meagre results for the fellahin, while the large landowners have continued to benefit greatly from the assignment of state land under the process of registration of title.

The Miri Sirf Lands Development Law of 1945 (now known as the Dujaila law) laid down the principles for distribution

[1] Norman Burns in 'The Dujailah Land Settlement', *Middle East Journal*, Summer 1951, quotes a statement to this effect by Darwish el-Haidari, now Director of Agriculture in the Development Board.

of the state lands to be opened up by the new Dujaila canal. This law secured the approval of Parliament because the sheikh landowners in the neighbourhood of the canal expected to get the newly watered state lands for themselves. In fact they were able to secure nearly half the new land as their registered property, and permanent water rights, in return for a single payment of £1 5s. per donum, a nominal sum, as the price of their consent to the settlement scheme.[1]

The law laid down the conditions on which ownership might be acquired by small proprietors on the Dujaila lands. Farmers are entitled to acquire ownership of holdings of 100 donums (62 acres) after ten years of occupancy and cultivation, free of rent and other charges, provided that they fulfil the conditions of a contract signed when the holding is allotted to them. When *tapu* title to land has been granted, after ten years, the owner is bound not to sell the land for another ten years, nor may he lease the holding. The qualifications for applicants were local origin and farming experience. A proportion of the holdings was to be allotted to graduates of agricultural schools, retired officials, and ex-service men.

The results of this settlement scheme are described in the following section. It has not been technically successful, nor has the law been carried out in detail, but socially, it is a success. That there is a great demand for ownership was shown by the fact that 50,000 applications for holdings were received by the authorities.

The Miri Sirf Lands Development Law of 1951 was intended to govern the distribution of holdings on all state land which has been or would be developed or reclaimed. It fixed maximum areas of holdings for different regions and different types of farming: 500 donums (300 acres) on high pump-irrigated land, 400 donums (240 acres) on rainfed land, 200 donums (120 acres) for low pump areas, and 20 donums (12 acres) on mountainous land (i.e. land with high rainfall). The lands were to be reclaimed in large areas under the management of an official Committee, which, with the assistance of engineers and other experts, was to direct and finance reclamation and irrigation, employ labour and maintain cultivation for two years, after which time the land was to be entrusted to the

[1] Burns, 'The Dujailah Land Settlement'.

Government (for control of irrigation) and divided into small holdings. Otherwise the law followed the same lines as the Dujaila law: settlers were to be selected by the Committee, from among the local inhabitants, who should have priority. Land could also be assigned to graduates of agricultural schools and recognized religious schools. Holdings were to be distributed free of charge and recipients were prohibited from sub-letting.

The official returns of the Directorate-General of Miri Sirf lands give the following figures for land distributed under this law.

TABLE 17

Distribution of State Land in Iraq in 1952–4

Place and Province	Areas distributed (donums)	No. of holdings	No. of persons living on these lands
Dujaila (Kut)	143,080	1,478	7,390
Shahrazoor (Sulaimaniya)	32,990	497	2,485
Sinjar (Mosul)	1,794,560	6,863	34,315
Hawija (Kirkuk)	45,700	351	1,755
Latafiya (Baghdad)	23,250	465	2,325
Garma	30,000	300	1,500
The Barrage (Kut)	5,200	65	325
Musseyeb River	10,500	175	875
Makhmur (Kirkuk)	13,340	188	940
Lands in other districts	27,960	384	1,920
Total	2,126,580	10,766	53,830

(SOURCE: Iraq Govt., *Statistical Abstract, 1954*, table 110.)

If this total had in fact been distributed to small farmers, the distribution of state land would represent a large and beneficial change in the agrarian structure. However, the figures are misleading. The greater part of the total is accounted for by the 1,800,000 donums, listed as distributed in 6,863 holdings in the Sinjar region of Mosul province. According to information given by the Mosul Chamber of Agriculture, large areas of the best state land in this region have been granted in registered title to the sheikh of the Shammar, Ahmed el-Ajeel, now the largest landowner in the province, and to his sub-sheikhs. This area includes the lands now farmed by Ahmed el-Ajeel on his own account, and also the lands leased by lesser sheikhs to the merchant-tractorists of Mosul. If this information is correct, the main outcome of the 1951 law has simply been a continuation of the usual practice of assigning tribal land to tribal chieftains.

There is, however, an area of about 1 million donums north and south of the Sinjar mountain, which has been surveyed, and found mostly too dry for cultivation and too risky for small farmers. Some settlement is to be undertaken on the better land; and 935 applicants have been selected.[1]

The area which actually has been distributed to small farmers, in settlement schemes which come under the Miri Sirf Land Development Committee, according to a report by Hassan Mohammed Ali, the Committee's President, amounts to only 232,960 donums (140,000 acres), distributed to 3,434 settlers.[2] There are six schemes, Dujaila, Shahrazoor, Hawija, Makhmur, Latafiya, and the Sinjar Scheme in Mosul, in operation, and one, the Greater Musseyeb, which is being re-claimed for settlement in the near future. Of these, only the Dujaila scheme is important in size, accounting for about half the total area and settlers. The remaining schemes are small and, except for the Latafiya scheme, are rather unfavourably situated.

That a few little schemes of this kind can be hailed as a step towards evolutionary reform shows how completely the original conception of settlement of title has been forgotten. Twenty-five years ago Dowson regarded the registration of title as a means of confirming the prescriptive rights of the culti-vators; the problem, as he saw it, was simply to establish a procedure to ascertain their rights. In 1951 new legislation was needed to give the state the right to assign title to small cultivators on state land. The prescriptive rights of the culti-vators have been so regularly overriden that the right to settle on state land is now a privilege. In the space of a generation the landowners' power of possession has become the right of exclusion.

The settlements are, of course, directly beneficial to the farmers who obtain holdings. But the numbers who benefit are too small to affect the position of cultivators in general.

[1] Hassan Mohammed Ali, *Land Reclamation and Settlement in Iraq*, p. 175.
[2] ibid. p. 75.

Even if this type of settlement were to be carried out on a much larger scale, it would not be able to bring about an improvement in the conditions of cultivators on privately owned estates by causing a shortage of labour, because there is so much underemployment on the land. The rural exodus to the towns reduces the numbers of cultivators on private estates to a far greater extent than settlement schemes even on a bigger scale could do, yet there is so far no sign that it causes landowners to improve the conditions of the fellahin, nor is it likely that landowners will make any efforts in this direction, since tractors can be substituted for labour.

The view that the settlement of farmers on state land can be a step in the direction of evolutionary reform is therefore untenable. It would be a step in the right direction, if there were a direction. But the prospect of achieving any general improvement in this way is an illusion, fostered to please the Americans, and which unfortunately deceives Iraqis also. The present political position is as unfavourable to reform as it has ever been, although economic conditions make reform imperative.

Although so little has been achieved in the direction of general reform, the results of the Dujaila scheme have been useful, in themselves and for the lesson which they teach.

THE DUJAILA SCHEME

The Dujaila settlement is the largest and oldest of these schemes, having been started in 1946 as an example and experiment. It lies about 25 miles south-east of Kut, and extends over an expanse of flat and treeless land, about 25 miles long and 15 miles across. Communications inside the settlement are difficult, and the farmers on donkeys and horses are more mobile than experts and officials in cars on the choppy dirt roads which connect the different tracts.

The settlement depends on the Dujaila canal, which receives water from the Tigris upstream of the Kut barrage, completed in 1939. The main canal is 30 miles long, and serves a total area of 400,000 donums (240,000 acres).[1] This area was all State Domain (*miri sirf*) land before. Rather more than half of it, 250,000 donums (150,000 acres), was assigned to the settle-

---

[1] This figure is quoted by Hassan Mohamed Ali in *Social Science Bulletin*, vol. 5, no. 4, 1953.

ment, and the remainder to private landowners, the neighbouring sheikhs. The greater part of the total area is irrigable by flow, and the flow-irrigated land is divided into thirteen separate tracts, each served by a lateral canal. Of these tracts, eight belong to the settlement, and five to the neighbouring sheikhs. These private estates adjoin the settlement on all sides.

The area granted to small holders in the settlement in April 1955 was said to be 180,000 donums (108,000 acres), with 1,800 families on holdings of 100 donums each. This figure is only a rough guess, and does not indicate exactly the area of cultivated land. Between the eight tracts which are cultivated, there are stretches of uncultivated land, some of which has already gone out of cultivation, so that the area of land actually cultivated cannot be estimated exactly.

It proved impossible to ascertain the total cost of the settlement scheme itself. A figure of £600,000 is quoted, but this includes the cost of construction of the main canal and lateral canals for the private land as well as for the settlement. Apart from the heavy expenditure on irrigation, it would appear that not much has been spent on the scheme. There are a few administrative buildings and schools but no machinery or other equipment. School building was partly financed out of the funds of the now defunct co-operative. The farmers build their own mud huts. Each farmer receives an initial credit of £100, repayable in instalments over five years. But apart from this, they receive no equipment. As the settlers pay no rent, none of the cost is recoverable.

The conditions under which settlers were to be granted land were laid down in the first Miri Sirf law of 1945, i.e. the right of ownership of holdings of 100 donums (60 acres) after ten years of occupancy and cultivation, free of rent and other charges, if the conditions of a contract signed when the holding is allotted to them are fulfilled. The contract obliges the farmer to build a house, storage for crops, and small feeder canals, and to buy trees, seed, and livestock. It also obliges him to follow a fixed crop rotation, including cotton and other intensive crops, but this provision has not been enforced.

The law also laid down the qualifications for applicants, such as local origin and farming experience: it provided that a proportion of the holdings should be allotted to graduates of agricultural schools, ex-policemen, and ex-soldiers. This clause is frequently criticized, because it is said to favour absentee ownership. The ex-soldiers and policemen—agricultural graduates apparently did not apply—prefer to live in Kut and other towns and rent the land to cultivators. How far sub-letting is practised, and on what terms, could not be ascertained; but it is said to be a fairly general practice.

Thus the scheme has not been enforced as the law originally intended, for there is little change in methods of farming; and ownership by the cultivator is not general. The farmers enjoy a remarkable degree of independence. The area of land assigned to them—100 donums or 60 acres of which half is cropped—is about twice as large as that usually cultivated by share-croppers on private estates. The owners pay no rent or instalment of purchase price, whereas on private land the cultivator is obliged to pay at least half and more usually two-thirds of produce as share-rent.

In Baghdad, however, rumour says that the scheme is a failure. Certainly there is no attempt on the part of the authorities to conceal the mistakes or defects in the scheme. On the contrary, they tend to exaggerate them. In the course of a visit to Dujaila in the company of the President of the Development Board, the President of the Miri Sirf Land Development Committee, and other members of the Development Board, there was prolonged and lively controversy about the scheme, chiefly in relation to the frustrating experiences of a Unesco team, which had striven for three years to conduct fundamental education on the borders of the settlement. The controversy, however, turned chiefly on the nature of fundamental education and the need for it, rather than on the organization of the scheme itself. As to these main defects, there is little disagreement.

The real cause of the possible failure of the scheme—for it is not by any means a failure yet—is the lack of drainage. The results of this are apparent even to the inexpert eye. As the rough track from Kut enters the settlement, it passes through land heavily encrusted with salt, either abandoned or cultivated only in patches carrying very poor crops. This first impression is misleading, for these sections are by far the worst. One tract out of the eight has been abandoned almost entirely, and two others are badly affected by salinity, but on the remainder, where cultivation has begun more recently, salt has not yet appeared to the same extent, though it must appear 'with mathematical precision', as an FAO expert put it, as cultivation continues. The destruction of the fertility of the soil has already necessitated moving about 300 farmers to other land. Crop yields have fallen from 400 kg. per donum ($12\frac{1}{2}$ cwt per acre) in the past years to 250 kg. per donum ($7\frac{1}{2}$ cwt per acre). Even this low yield is good for Iraq.

The danger of salinity could have been foreseen, since it has long been known that permanent irrigation without drainage is not possible in most of south Iraq,[1] or indeed in any arid region where natural drainage is not adequate. Salinity is not by any means a problem peculiar to the Dujaila lands. (Salt-encrusted land can be seen all along the road from Baghdad to Kut.) On private lands it is countered simply by abandoning the land, but in a settlement intended for permanent cultivation this course cannot be followed. Every visiting expert since 1950—and there have been many—has recommended drainage. Cost was an obstacle before 1951, but now that the Development Board has a large unspent balance there can be no reason for further delay. Not until 1954 did the Board allocate funds for drainage, and then only for one of the eight tracts, where work began in 1955. A sum of £40,000 was granted to drain this one tract of 25,000 donums (15,000 acres); if this sum is sufficient, the cost of reclamation is about £3 per acre, which is not high in comparison with cost of reclaiming waste land in European countries.

Much else has gone wrong at Dujaila, so much else that it is difficult to decide where responsibility lies. There is, for example, no co-operative or marketing organization of any kind, though this is much needed, because the settlement is remote and communications poor. A co-operative society was started in 1950, to which farmers were obliged to belong, and to subscribe £1 5s. towards its capital. The society made a good start, undertaking marketing and purchase of farm equipment and providing credit and machine service. It owned 10 tractors, 5 ploughs, 2 lorries, and a flour mill. It broke down quickly,

---

[1] The Haigh Commission's report in 1951 was emphatic (see above, p. 114). So too was the *Iraq Irrigation Handbook* of 1943, and so was Willcocks, in 1905.

owing to mismanagement, and two members brought an action against the society, which was declared bankrupt (though unnecessarily, since its assets exceeded its liabilities). A little official help might have avoided this failure.

There is no organization to enforce a better system of crop rotation, and not much experiment in new crops. Most of the land is too heavy for cotton, and no cotton is grown. The cotton ginnery which was built to handle the crop now stands idle. Some advance has been made in vegetable cultivation, and trees have been planted. There is a small nursery for trees and seedlings managed by a skilled gardener. Demonstration plots are well managed, under the direction of an FAO expert. Experiments have shown that Egyptian clover (berseem) can increase the yields of the grain crops. Swiss chard is found to give good results even on poor soil. Thus a beginning has been made, though rather late in the day. A date-palm avenue round the central buildings on one of the tracts relieves the aridity of the scene.

Some schools exist, situated in different tracts, but not all children attend school because the distances are so great. There is a health clinic which gives inoculations against bilharzia, which affects most of the inhabitants, and treatment for trachoma, also widespread. But there is no doctor in the settlement, and none nearer than Kut.

One successful venture is a small textile factory, weaving and spinning cheap woollen fabrics. This has been started by Mr Chitra, an Indian expert in rural industries, working for the UN Technical Assistance Board, who has started similar factories in two other settlements. He enjoys official support and can get his plans approved and executed more easily than other foreign experts, who display a natural professional jealousy. There was some argument among members of the Development Board authorities as to the need for industries of this kind in rural settlements. But since agricultural work is highly seasonal, and likely to remain so, a factory giving off-time employment seems needed. In view of the isolation of the settlement, it would be useful if it could become, as Mr Chitra hopes, the nucleus for a community development. Such factories are the more needed, in view of the difficulty which the Development Board has experienced in starting industries.

The weaknesses in organization result from a lack of co-ordination between local needs and the central authorities. The original conception was sound, but there has obviously been no sustained interest at the top level. Several different Ministries—Agriculture, Irrigation, Education, Health—are responsible for different activities, and neglect them, since there is no organization at the settlement itself to co-ordinate their spheres or to urge action on the authorities.

The defects in administration, however, are unimportant compared with the deterioration of the land itself, which will, unless action is taken, render the scheme a failure. To ascertain how much land could be saved by reclamation, a soil survey was undertaken in 1953–5 by the Department of Agriculture, under the direction of Mr Burnell West, an American soil technologist employed by FAO.

The survey reported that agricultural production could be maintained at a satisfactory level only where artificial drainage could be supplied. The salinity derived from two main sources, the receding Persian Gulf, and the salt left in the soil by past ages of irrigation.[1] 'A thorough drainage investigation must be made of the entire project. . . Otherwise the salinity will increase and the land will be forced out of production in a relatively few years.'[2] Some of the salty land could be reclaimed by leaching, a long process of washing out the soil, but other land is too impermeable to be reclaimed, and must be abandoned. The report recommended summer cropping on the reclaimed land, with rice and barley to prevent the salt rising, and advised against the alternate fallow system.[3]

The soil survey report also recommended better farming practices, as follows:

1. A crop-rotation system, to include the use of legume crops to be ploughed under as green manure, and the cultivation of fodder crops, such as clover and lucerne, to enable numbers of livestock to be increased.

---

[1] The report makes an interesting comment which means that the usual view of Iraq's past history needs revision: 'No evidence has been found that the early irrigators supplied any artificial drainage. There is no doubt that the ancients were forced to abandon a large part of the land covered by this project because of excessive salinity' (*Report of the Soil Survey, Dujaila Project*, by Burnell G. West, FAO mission, published by the Ministry of Agriculture, Government of Iraq, 1955, p. 5).
[2] ibid. p. 14.   [3] ibid. pp. 13–16.

2. The use of heavier draught animals or tractors for deep tillage, needed every few years, and for weed control.

3. Experiments to establish the rates of application of water.

4. Weed control, through irrigation before cultivation, to allow weeds to germinate before the land is ploughed.

5. The use of animal manure, and the cultivation of a wood lot or sesbania as a substitute for dung fuel.[1]

These are grass-root recommendations, not the usual arm-chair planning; they begin from what is now done, and suggest practicable improvements. The recommendations would apply to agriculture throughout south Iraq, and ought to be the basis of a general agricultural policy. The most noteworthy is the recommendation to increase the number of livestock by better feeding, for this is the only branch in which farmers at Dujaila, and elsewhere, are really proficient.

Energetic action and expenditure are therefore needed. Dujaila is a test case for the administration. Burnell West, asked whether the project could be saved, said 'I would not give much for the future of the country if it cannot be.'

As an experiment, Dujaila can be regarded as a success. It has taught an essential lesson, that land must be drained before settlement. On the new state land settlements drainage is to be undertaken before the land is settled.

As an example, it is also a success, because it shows that settlement can bring direct benefits to the settlers. In spite of the fall in yields, farmers are doing well, and are far better off than they would be as share-croppers on private estates, where they would cultivate half the area, pay two-thirds of the produce as rent, and have no social services at all. In the first years, when yields were high, some farmers are said to have earned £600 a year, and the average income was £300. Now, with the fall in yields, it is lower, but even so the farm families have enough to eat and a surplus to spend. Those who make money use it to buy a new English rifle, or an extra wife—habits which officials find reprehensible, the equivalent of keeping coal in the bath. But the pattern of life is still tribal, and these are advances in well-being as it is understood by those concerned.

[1] ibid. pp. 17–25.

This improvement in well-being is, after all, the object of the settlements. The American conception of land reform as an 'integrated programme', involving the provision of fully equipped services, tends to give the impression that reform is an elaborate technical procedure, only to be undertaken with everything laid on. Measured by this ideal, the scheme falls short. But in essentials, it is good enough. There is an atmosphere of rather desolate freedom in spite of—indeed because of—the poor organization.

Dujaila shows that land reform is worth doing, even if it is not done with administrative efficiency, simply because redistribution of land can bring immediate improvements in the living standard. Reform need not wait on better farming: the agriculture of south Iraq is so primitive that there is no risk that a decline in production could follow a division of the big estates. There is no need to aim at perfection in equipping the farmers, or in the organization of services. If Iraq has to wait for land reform until the Government can provide schools, experts, health services, and co-operatives, it will wait too long. These good things can come, and will come, once ownership has been redistributed. What is wrong with Dujaila can be put right, but what is wrong with the big estates cannot be remedied except through a general measure of reform, including the redistribution of ownership.

Other Settlement Schemes

On the remaining *miri sirf* land settlement schemes (described in *Land Reclamation and Settlement in Iraq*, by Hassan Mohammed Ali), the Point Four Mission exercises advisory functions, under its agreement with the Iraqi Government. Members of the Mission have surveyed physical and economic conditions, carried out demonstration projects, and prepared cropping plans. They have also recommended the introduction of supervised credit, a system of granting loans to farmers under the supervision of technical advisers who ensure that the loan is spent in furtherance of a plan to improve the farm, drawn up in consultation between the farmers and the supervisor.[1]

---

[1] The system is operated in the United States by the Farmers Home Administration, for farmers who cannot cover their credit needs through the ordinary channels

The most promising scheme appears to be the settlement at Latafiya, which has better conditions than the rest, in that it has fairly good soil (adjacent to the British-owned Latafiya Estates) and is situated only thirty miles from Baghdad, and so could supply the growing demand for fruit and vegetables. It has sufficient water, but requires drainage, as Dujaila does, and so far has only a drainage demonstration project. Fifteen thousand acres have been settled in 30-acre holdings. Forty per cent of the settlers are ex-officials and ex-service men, who generally sub-let their holdings. The rest are tribesmen from the vicinity. Great efforts have been made by the American advisers to improve cropping practices by demonstration, chiefly by the introduction of alfalfa (lucerne). Although the average annual net income per farm (according to a sample inquiry) amounts to £133, a high proportion of the farmers are indebted, mostly to their former landlords. Supervised credit has been introduced, chiefly to buy livestock, and horses and cattle have been distributed. This settlement, though it clearly has weaknesses, appears to have the makings of success, chiefly because it is near Baghdad and so gets more attention from the authorities.

The Hawija scheme, near Kirkuk, is a small settlement included in a much larger area which can be brought under cultivation by more irrigation. Lack of livestock is the chief drawback, and efforts to set up credit co-operatives, under the guidance of an FAO co-operative expert, have so far failed. The adjacent Makhmur scheme is also small, part of the area to be irrigated when the Dokan dam scheme is completed. Both these settlements have fruit-tree nurseries.

The Shahrazoor project, near Halabja in the Kurdish hills, appears to have been least successful. It relies on canal irrigation, natural springs, and rainfall, but though water-supplies are potentially adequate, the canal does not at present supply sufficient water. Two successive years of harvest failure in 1953 and 1954, the result of pest damage, brought the majority of the farmers heavily into debt to merchants. An attempt was made to introduce supervised credit, but although the request for funds was approved by the Agricultural Bank, few settlers

---

and also in connexion with loans for farm purchase. See UN, *Progress in Land Reform*, p. 214.

took the loans, 'the rest having refused to follow the program recommended by the Committee economist, and preferring to use the loans as they see fit'.[1]

A survey of about 1 million donums of state land round Mount Sinjar in the Jezira on the Syrian border reveals conditions resembling those on the marginal lands in the Jezira in Syria. Crop failures occur every four or five years, yields are very low, and livestock insufficient. Much of the land is altogether unsuitable for cultivation, and even on the better land, which retains most of the moisture, rainfall is inadequate for steady yields. Some of the better land is already settled, and tractor-ploughing is used by the sheikh landowners. On the poorer land a number of villages have been settled by Beduin in the course of the last six years (possibly including the tribesmen who have lost grazing land in Syria, cf. p. 88). 'Some of these villages were in a very badly pauperised condition, and the people in one village were on the edge of starvation.'[2] As a result of crop failure, they had insufficient seed to plant for the 1953 harvest, which would have given them a good return. They acknowledged that one difficulty . . . had been that they did not know how to farm.'[3]

The survey recommended settlement on the better land, in units of 150 or 200 donums according to the type of land, with access to public grazing land, and estimated the livestock needed to establish a family. The Miri Sirf Land Development Committee approved these recommendations, and 935 settlers have been granted land in village sites provided with artesian wells to provide drinking-water.

The picture which emerges from the report is on the whole a gloomy one: heavy debt, and a shortage of credit and no effective way of overcoming it as yet; too little livestock, as a result, and consequently a tendency to buy too much food off the farm; bad health and poor organization. Yet in spite of all these disadvantages, it is said, no doubt truly, that the settlers at Latafiya and Hawija are better off than farmers on private estates. The settlements have been established only recently, and with the help of the expert advisers and some determination on the part of the authorities, these defects can probably

[1] Hassan Mohammed Ali, *Land Settlement and Reclamation in Iraq*, p. 121.
[2] ibid. p. 170.   [3] ibid. p. 163.

be overcome in time. It is, however, obvious that a better selection of sites and land would make success more certain and allow model settlements to come into existence instead of these struggling small groups.

What is useful and good in these settlements is that they do provide an experimental field. They can ascertain by experience the crops that can be successfully grown and marketed, and the system of credit (supervised or co-operative) that is most practicable. The function of the Point Four advisers is obviously valuable, because it can keep the needs of the settlers before the authorities, and can thus prevent failure of the schemes. In the Sinjar region the expert survey evidently averted a failure in selecting poor land. If this experience is digested, it should enable the authorities to ascertain the type of farming, size of farm unit, and the equipment and organization suited to the different regions, and so to evolve a pattern which could be the aim of a general reform policy.

THE SOCIAL VACUUM

The real obstacle to reform in Iraq is not a shortage of experts, or money, or administrative inefficiency. Nor is it, in reality, the 'feudal' landowners. The town middle class represents the public opinion of the country in that it is conscious of the need for change; it provides the official class, criticizes development policy, and it is growing very fast. It cannot, however, link up with the fellahin and provide the political force which would recast the social structure of the country. There is no social or political force which can challenge the power of the sheikhs. The educated townspeople do not, at present, constitute this force, though their number, their intelligence, and their importance in administration should qualify them to become it. That the sheikhs of Amara should rule over the civil servants of Baghdad and the merchants of Mosul seems incongruous to the outsider. The townsman himself shares this attitude, regarding the sheikhs with a mildly amused contempt which he is careful not to show in their presence.

Why, then, do the townspeople not play a greater part in the political life of the country? They are not simply leftish intellectuals who aspire to lead the 'mob', as some Middle East experts believe. To lead the growing and rather menacing hordes of slum dwellers is just what they cannot do, and just what ought to be done. On the surface, the reason is that the urban middle class is politically powerless, because the opposition parties are suppressed; but this formal suppression can hardly have been decisive. The real reason lies deeper, in the political nexus which rules the country, and which is extremely difficult to define.

The question of who rules Iraq finds different answers within the country. Some say that three statues, King Feisal, General Maude, and Sadun (i.e. the landowners), are the real Government. Simple people believe that the British rule Iraq by remote control, while the more sophisticated think that it is the Prime Minister who rules the British. There is truth in both views. It would be idle to pretend that IPC is not a political power. On the principle of no taxation without representation, a company which produces at least half the national income must exert some influence. But the conventions of independence must be maintained, in particular the façade of parliamentary sovereignty, to show that Britain does not intervene.

The sheikhs, of course, have power and prestige outside this façade, of which they are the other main support. They are, however, a ruling class only *pro forma*. The real work of administration is carried out by the civil servants, who are opposed to the surviving sheikh tradition. Government policy is never initiated by the sheikhs, but by the Prime Minister, supported on the twofold base of British influence and the large landowners. How any given decision is reached and why the 'Pack of Cards'[1] is from time to time reshuffled remains a mystery. It is a miracle that, in this situation, the Development Board should have been able to reach any decisions at all.

What is wrong is not that the money is misused. Such allegations of corruption as are made reveal very small-scale inducements. On the contrary, as has been shown, Iraq needs the money desperately, and from the technical standpoint it has been well spent. Yet in the atmosphere of Baghdad there is a feeling of corruption, because the Government's only reliable supporters within the country are the privileged class who support it on condition that their wealth and privileges are un-

---

[1] See Desmond Stewart and John Haylock, *New Babylon* (London, Collins, 1956).

touched. 'The whole position', as Kipling wrote of Egypt n 1913, 'is essentially false'.

The strength of the political nexus rests on tradition, and it may not be a necessity, but it is too powerful to be challenged by the Iraqi middle class alone. Urban society is very old and tradition-bound. It is also extremely urbanized in its outlook: prone to despise the fellahin as backward, and knowing little and caring less about their condition. Among effendis distaste for the land is universal. Even for the rich landowner there is no country life. The tribesman's contempt for manual work is shared by the middle class.

Yet this middle class is not negligible. It is, as far as it can be, extremely constructive. Individual civil servants are hard and devoted workers who draft legislation which does not get into the statute book, or undertake systematic social investigations in their spare time. Among the provincial governors (the *mutassarifs*) and the city mayors there is strong public spirit and high competence. Free to some extent from the dead hand of the central Government, these men are in direct touch with the needs of the people of their provinces and cities. They have begun to compete with each other in showing what can be done with the funds assigned to them by the ordinary budget, and now that the 1955 expenditure programme of the Development Board will put bigger funds at their disposal, they may find ways, as one of them has already done, of mobilizing the coffee-house sitters for community development. But no common opinion unites these sincere people, who should be the leaders in a new society, for they are all ultimately dependent on the Government.

The root of the trouble is simply that there is no new economic class to rival the power of the landowners. The outstanding feature of Iraq's economic revolution is that it is disembodied. The ample funds for investment have arisen without any change in the economy or the society. The oil industry is a one-sided 'developer' because it does not, like other mining industries, require an expansion of the transport and power systems: it uses its own transport and power and requires little in the way of public services. It does not employ large numbers of workers, and so does not have much direct effect on the general level of incomes. IPC is a giant, but its impact is almost entirely financial. An industry which is practically extra-territorial provides funds for investment.

Since these funds do not arise from local enterprise and savings, and since the direct impact of oil on the economy is so slight, there is no new class of business men, no liberal Manchester, to challenge the power of the old aristocracy. There are some new industrialists, it is true, but they are few, and apart from one or two large undertakings the new firms are mostly small. It will be long before there are enough of them to change the balance of political power. For many years past efforts have been made to stimulate new industry, through tax and tariff concessions, but so far without much success, because the market is limited by the poverty of the mass of the population. If there were a strong impetus to develop on capitalistic lines, the prospects of political change through fuller representation of the townspeople would be far greater.

As it is, this half-tribal half-urban society faces the task of constructing the physical framework for development and also the social structure for expansion. This task far exceeds the powers of Iraqi society as it is at present constituted. It is not simply a question of a shortage of 'experts', as is often believed, but of much more serious deficiencies.

As the Baghdad civil servants themselves say, there is a social vacuum, a gap between the economic potential and the social structure. It is inaccurate to speak of conflict between the old and the new society, for the old society is collapsing, and if the new society is represented by the urban agglomeration of Baghdad, then it is taking the imprint of the West like wax—the superficial imprint, without the things that the Western world believes to be its best. There is no stable social structure, only familiar incongruities: the sheikhs in Cadillacs, the tribesmen in buses, the *souks* using electric power, and the new bank buildings in the unpaved and undrained streets. It is inaccurate also to say that Iraq is in a state of transition; whatever is happening, it is change without direction or purpose. Hence the economic problem of where to start: hence the difficulty of spending the money.

But change there is, though it is difficult to pin down by any conventional approach. The typical formal history of the country describes the stages by which a segment of the Ottoman Empire became an independent state and duly acquired a proper Constitution and the correct forms of parliamentary government. Little of reality is revealed by this approach, for the documents do not show how the institutions work. The typical economic report is no better: it surveys a statistical desert, filled with unreliable estimates, and recommends more irrigation, flood-control, transport, afforestation and education, and so on. But these approaches overlook the men who are to do these jobs, and the social life of Iraq slips down between the cracks. The social vacuum can be felt, though it cannot be analysed. The outside observer, unsure of any generalization about it, can only take sights from various angles.

First, there is the phenomenon of the foreign experts. They are clearly a symptom of something lacking. Foreign advisers are nothing new in Iraq; but before the war they were fewer, and far more influential. Now their numbers have multiplied till they infest the Development Board and the Ministries. They advise the Government on broad lines of economic policy, as have, for instance, the International Bank Mission,[1] Professor Iversen,[2] and Lord Salter.[3]

Other authorities advise on town planning, forestry, drainage: they are transient, leaving with the swallows, and each is ignorant of the advice of his predecessors. The representatives of foreign firms with contracts, surveying, studying, and actually constructing, are in a different category, since they are employed by their own firms and paid to do a definite job in a definite time; their position is easier, and their work harder. They are obviously indispensable and must continue to play a part, a technical part, for a long time to come, for they meet a real need.

The most interesting are the experts who advise on moral and social questions, the new missionaries whose essential function is to infuse an element of uplift. Some are office-bound, but others, to their credit, are mobile over long distances and visit remote areas. They carry on their campaigns in the Ministries with spirit, and as individualists. The Point Four men advise on the *miri sirf* settlements. At the Latafiya settlement they can

[1] *The Economic Development of Iraq* (Baltimore, Johns Hopkins Press, 1952).
[2] *Monetary Policy in Iraq.*   [3] *The Development of Iraq.*

be found inculcating the virtues of homespun self-help, urging on the baffled manager the need for ensuring that only those cultivators who can pay may be allowed to have the tractor; and insisting that if any farmer wishes to hire the tractor to work land which the experts consider unsuitable he is to be allowed to do so, in order to learn by experience. At Dujaila in 1955 Unesco officials were propagating the principles of fundamental education to the inhabitants of the saline tracts.[1] Up in the north an FAO expert strove to instil the spirit of agricultural co-operation, as it has worked in Nigeria. Mexican girls teach hygiene as in Mexican social centres. Between the settlements darts the UN Technical Assistance expert, not frustrated at all, busily engaged in setting up rural industries on the lines that have worked well in India. The whole civilized world seems to be contributing its mite; but the thought arises that this sort of impetus ought not to come from outside, and that so long as it does it is bound to be frustrated.

All these efforts are in themselves admirable, and should not be decried. But all strive to instil social values which have been proved in other settings, and often the values conflict. They cannot possibly 'take', because the experts themselves are not a permanent or responsible element in the community, and they are not, of course, co-ordinated in any way. Though the old society is crumbling at the edges, it still preserves some of its solidarity, and whatever social obligation is felt is based on the tribe or the clan. The Point Four experts are trying to teach the value of individualist self-help to people whose whole social outlook is opposed to it. The co-operative experts try to teach the value of co-operation in the economic sphere, through conscious organized methods, to people who co-operate unconsciously with great ease. Probably it is impossible for foreign advisers to work with the old society at all, because it is breaking up, and presumably their only direct influence is on the civil servants with whom they come into contact, and who are as frustrated and disunited as themselves.

Insight into the nature of the old society is difficult to gain. It lies not far below the surface, and glimpses of it can be seen even in the most urbanized circles. The important families of Baghdad still retain their tribal surnames and boast of their

[1] The Unesco Mission has since left Dujaila, in despair.

tribal ancestry. In law-suits townspeople often claim the protection of the tribal regulations which impose lesser penalties. At a cocktail party a young society girl may explain the difficulty which one of her friends had to get the blue tattoo marks removed from her nose; and it emerges that the rich families of Mosul, until quite recently, used to give their one-year-olds into the care of the Beduin for four or five years, to avert the vengeance which may come on those who love their children too much. These are the superficial signs of a world still tied to its tribal origins, but they do not show how far its values are still dominant.

There is, however, one study of Iraqi society at the village level which vividly reveals the existence of the social vacuum, Dr Salim's study of Echchbaysh.[1] The community studied, a population of 11,000 living in 1,600 small islands in the great permanent marsh of the Hor el-Hammar,[2] has undergone rapid economic change over the past thirty years, for agriculture has declined with the shrinkage of the cultivated area caused by flooding, and the people have therefore turned over to mat-making as a main occupation, producing, at the rate of a million a year, the reed mats which are used as a roofing and building material for huts and houses throughout Iraq. It has also undergone a political change (because its sheikh was deposed and the sheikhdom abolished by the Iraq authorities in 1924, when the sheikh's *mudhif* was bombed by the RAF and the sheikh exiled). Yet though it is a commercialized market economy, without traditional rule, the social structure of tribal life, and the social values associated with it, are still strong and intact.

Two quite distinct class divisions exist side by side. One is a social gradation, corresponding to the old tribal society, in which the religious men (Sayyids), the sirkals (the chiefs of the nine clans which compose the community), the *mukhtars* (lineage headmen), and the *Ajaweed* (the council of 'good people' or elders of the clan) constitute the class ruling over the ordinary tribesmen, the *Abeed* (negroes, formerly slaves), and the *Subba* (a non-Moslem group of craftsmen, excluded from clan membership). The sirkals, in consultation with the headmen and elders, administer the tribal code, by which rights and

[1] 'Economic and Political Organization of Echchbaysh'. [2] See map, p. 123.

obligations are still enforced on a clan basis. In the *mudhif* etiquette is elaborate and rigid, recognizing the gradations of rank in a complex archaic society.

Side by side with this order, in which heredity determines rank, there exists a new class division on the basis of economic function, which has arisen in the transition from cultivation to mat-weaving. There are now two broad groups on the basis of income level, those who enjoy a comfortable living standard—with brick houses and furniture—which includes the 'rich men', landholders and shopkeepers, and those who live on a low standard, the artisans, employees, and mat-weavers and cultivators. The 'rich men', whose incomes range upwards from £1,000 per annum, are money-lenders, dealers in the mat trade, and owners of motor launches. Their origins are various, four having sprung from the class of 'religious men' and one from the former chiefly clan.

But the new rich have acquired no prestige, and social standing is still in accordance with the hereditary classes, not in accordance with wealth. The rich men and shopkeepers are collectively described as 'Ahl es-Soug', which means literally 'the people of the market', but in fact means 'those who have departed from tribal traditions to acquire wealth'. Prestige in society depends on membership of the *Ajaweed*, and qualifications for membership are character, numerous kinsmen, and knowledge of the tribal law. Wealth confers no standing of any kind.

The men with high reputations in the tribe, the *Ajaweed*, are mostly mat-weavers and cultivators having only the lowest standard of living and frequently in debt, but they are far more influential in the society than any of the rich men. Of the wealthy men, only those whose families belonged to the religious men or the chiefly clan enjoy high social standing, and only because of their ancestry and in spite of their wealth.

'A penniless Sayid, in fact, enjoys very much higher prestige than a rich Sayid.'[1] The prevailing social values are those of a warrior society, 'in which the two dominant themes are courage and generosity. . . . Meanness is the nadir of vice. To be mean implies a want of confidence in one's own ability to gain more plunder.' Dr Salim provides ample evidence for his view

[1] Salim, 'Economic and Political Organization of Echchbaysh', pp. 549 and 589.

that 'Nothing could be more contemptible than thrift, bargaining, or the slightest appearance of attaching value to one's
material possessions.'[1] 'What is the use of money to a man if he
loses his dignity?' is the view of the guest-house, or 'Money
and commerce are the greatest evils which have befallen the
people of Echchbaysh.' Social standing and economic status no
longer correspond.

Tribal tradition is not only strong in maintaining these attitudes to wealth; it also prevents the people from taking up
occupations which would greatly improve their standard of
living, such as vegetable growing, dairy production, and fish-
ing. These are by tradition the occupations of the weaker clans
and therefore despised. There is no communal enterprise;
necessary small dams and drains to save the land from flooding
are not undertaken.

On the whole, this community has gained greatly from the
political change which brought them directly under the control
of the central Government in that conditions are more peace-
ful, there is less extortion of high rents, and schools and dis-
pensaries have been started. What is most significant from the
standpoint of development is that the people, though they have
been able to make their needs known to the authorities, are
unable to get any action. Two small projects, the dredging out
of a short length of the Haffar canal and the construction of a
regulator at Gurmat Hassan, would enable thousands of acres
to be cultivated and also improve communications. These projects are simple and not expensive, and the leaders of the community have requested the local authorities to have them undertaken, and have also attempted to undertake the work
themselves.[2] Even local funds are not lacking; the municipality
has an uninvested surplus capital of £10,000 which could be
used for constructing houses needed by teachers and other
officers, to build bridges, or reclaim land.

This is the social vacuum at the village level. The village is
still a community, but it has no power of development on com-

---

[1] ibid. p. 569.
[2] 'Because of their extreme simplicity, the people of Echchbaysh and other inhabitants of the district cannot find any explanation for the failure to put it into
effect, despite repeated appeals to the Government, other than that the Government, for some reason known only to itself, is deliberately neglecting the project'
(ibid. p. 301). The Gurmat Hassan regulator is now under construction.

munity lines. The poor livelihood, the insecurity of the floods, and the exactions of the money-lenders drive people out to seek work outside as seasonal labourers. Echchbaysh is a microcosm for the whole country; its values are those of the tribe, and its economy is dependent on the 'people of the market', while its real needs are neglected.

Baghdad in the chaos of 'development'—one need not call it progress—reveals the vacuum in urban life. At the last census in 1947 Baghdad's population was 364,000; now it may be twice as large. Sixteen thousand cars a day, canary and crimson and iridescent purple, pass down the seedy two-mile length of Rashid Street. The plate-glass of the car dealers and air con-ditioners and the Bata and Orosdi-Beck stores throws the sur-rounding squalor into higher relief. Shops are bulk-breaking booths stuffed with imports of canned food, Penguins, razor blades, just unpacked from their crates. Cinemas show the most violent films obtainable, including one banned by the film censorship in England; but the bookshops operate under a censorship which bans *War and Peace* and *A Tale of Two Cities*. New roads cut through old slums, leaving their inhabitants living in the rubble on either side. The only public amenity is the bus service, clean and efficient in exotic London red double and single-deckers.

Nightmare new slums are growing. Most of the families come in clans from Amara. Tribes from the marshes bring their buffaloes to live with them. One such new slum is at Sheikh Omar, outside the Bund (the dyke round the city) adjoining the sewage dumps. Here some 40,000 people are living in mud huts, rebuilt after being destroyed in the 1954 floods. With the traditional gentle manners they welcome the guest into the filth. There is much trachoma and dysentery, but no bilharzia or malaria, because the water is too polluted for snails and mosquitoes. The infant mortality rate is 250. A woman has a 50:50 chance of raising a child to the age of ten. There are no social services of any kind; the dispensary which existed before the floods was not put back again. There would be no drinking-water if Professor Michael Critchley, of the Baghdad College of Medicine, had not succeeded in persuading the authorities to put in pipes and taps. Earnings of the poorest average 100 fils (2s.) a day. On the adjacent dumps dogs with rabies dig in the sewage, and the slum-dwellers pack it for re-sale as garden manure.

Opposite the royal palace is a slum enclosed behind a high wall, where families are earning as much as £2 per week, but pay £1 10s. per month for the tiny patch of land on which they build their huts, divided by a warren of narrow alleys. There children die more frequently in their second year, when they begin to crawl in the dust. The higher standard of living is shown in the possession of a wooden bed, a clothes chest, and highly coloured pictures of Queen Elizabeth and General Neguib.

These are the places where the experts do not go. Professor Critchley, revered by the dwellers in the *sarifa*, brings his students, and would like to invite the King to visit his people. It needs no expert advice to see that what Baghdad needs is more housing for the working class and a sewage system. Iraq is in the early throes of its urban revolution, and as yet it has no Chadwick among its civil servants and no Shaftesbury among its aristocracy.

The older generation consciously feels the gap between the old and the new. Superficially criticism focuses on the use of the new money, the failure to use it to meet social needs. But there are deeper issues at stake. An explicit view was put forward by the assistant *mutasarrif* of Mosul. In the past, he said, the rich commanded respect, for they paid the tithe for beneficent purposes as enjoined by religion, and did not antagonize the poor by demonstrating their wealth. Now the whole balance of society was destroyed, and the poor felt envy and spite towards the rich. This cancer in social life could be cut out, he thought, not by going back in time, but by finding a new balance. Mosul feels the strain most, because its labour and capital are draining away to Baghdad and it has lost the position it held in Ottoman times. But all who think seriously about the future of the country share this feeling that the new life has lost standards and solidarity.

The young reject the old outright, but feel the strain of the divided mind no less. The young bureaucrat just back from California with a degree in economics has apparently learnt nothing but contempt for his fellow countrymen, and particularly for those who struggle on as teachers or 'trainees' with the international agencies on the settlements. Behind a smart-alec manner he hides a wretched conviction that 'nothing will be done by this Government'.

The social vacuum is not peculiar to Iraq. But it is more evident there than elsewhere, because of the money. In Syria internal capital and enterprise are playing a leading part in development, and foreign experts are employed on technical work only. In Egypt the Government itself takes the lead, and is some way ahead of opinion. But in Iraq the social obstacles to development are stronger, and the economic potential greater. How the gap will be filled cannot be foreseen. Perhaps the 2,000 Iraqi students now in Britain and America may help to fill it. Perhaps the Development Board, if its scope of action can be made independent of Parliament, will acquire greater courage, and mobilize opinion behind it. Or perhaps, as the more frustrated foreign experts are inclined to say, 'something will crack'.

CONCLUSION

THE DYNAMICS OF CHANGE

It is the international aspects of the social and economic changes proceeding in the Middle East that chiefly interest Westerners. They ask whether land reform and development will weaken or strengthen the influence of Communism; improve the chances of agreement between Israel and the Arab States; find room for the Palestine refugees; and promote stability in the region.

Though this study is concerned with the effect of these changes on the position of the fellahin, and not with their international aspects, such questions as these inevitably do arise, and it therefore seems necessary to explain why there is so little that can usefully be said about them. Many elements are involved in what is called the Middle East crisis, and attempts to find definite answers to questions of this kind usually lead to over-simplification. Perhaps the only thing that can certainly be said is that no long-term social change or process of development is likely to contribute towards the solution of any immediate political conflict.

Consider, for example, the belief that land reform will check the influence of Communism. In the countries surveyed, Communism is a term which has ceased to have a precise meaning. Examples have been quoted to show that it is currently used to describe the views of opposition parties, or elements in the governments; it may refer also to any uncompromising attitude to Western political influence; or to real social unrest (as in Amara and Mosul). How far Communist doctrine or activity is involved in this unrest is of course anybody's guess. Clearly land reform can weaken the influence of Communism in so far as it arises from such unrest, because reform both meets the needs of the fellahin and fills the social vacuum by giving the bureaucracy a social function. It has already been

184

emphasized that the international consensus of opinion in favour of reform is a valuable influence, because it means that the Western Powers are less committed to the support of the big landowners; but this influence can only serve to make the struggle for reform a little easier for those who are concerned with the welfare of their own people—and who will probably be described as Communists by their political opponents.

Certainly greater social equality, and a more stable economy, would provide a social structure more resistant to Soviet influence, more resistant, indeed, to any external influence. But this long-term certainty has no bearing on the present situation.

Or consider the question of reform as it affects relations between Israel and the Arab States. It used to be believed that when the Arab States ceased to be feudal, they would become more 'progressive' and so less hostile to Zionism—a view which now seems strangely old-fashioned. Today the rising middle class, the Egyptian revolutionary leadership, and the Arab socialist party hold stronger nationalist views than the big landowners, who are more concerned with maintaining their own position against these forces than with hostility to Israel. For the poverty of Jordan, most directly affected by the Arab-Israeli conflict, land reform is not a remedy, and its hopes of economic development depend on the possibility of the Jordan valley scheme, which requires a political agreement before it can be undertaken.

It might well be that the strengthening of the Arab social structure which is implied in a land reform policy could eventually create more favourable conditions, but again, this hopeful speculation does not lessen existing tensions.

Or consider the question of the future of the Palestine refugees. The first conclusion which many people in Britain are inclined to draw from an account of the actual and potential development of the Arab countries is that they could absorb the refugees. Egypt clearly cannot, but since Syria and Iraq have small populations and plenty of land, it appears obvious—to those who have not seen the villages—that these countries could find room for more labour, and so offer a way out of the tragic situation in the Jordan valley.

Political considerations altogether apart, the belief that the availability of land in itself represents 'absorptive capacity', i.e. creates employment, is the old bad economics, for it ignores the social structure and the type of farming. The economic obstacle to the absorption of the refugees into agricultural employment is the low standard of living in the villages. No one who has seen an Iraqi village, or a Syrian village on the estate of a big landowner, would believe that there could be opportunities of settling the refugees in such conditions. The Jordan camps are wretched, because their inhabitants have lost homes and land, but their health conditions are better than those of the poor villages in Syria and most villages in Iraq.

With land settlement and more intensive farming, both Syria and Iraq could employ more people at higher standards of living. Yet to argue that these countries should undertake land reform in order to absorb the refugees is to vitiate the real case for it. It represents an attempt to shift the responsibility for the solution of an urgent problem, and is an example of the alibi approach which pervades so much thinking about the region and within it—shifting the responsibility on to somebody else, and shelving the problem when that somebody else has been identified.

These brief references to the Power conflicts suggest, not that the question of land reform is irrelevant, but that its relevance is distorted if it is regarded as a solution for them. It is a way of raising the standard of living and of improving agricultural production, and rather a slow way. It is not likely to pluck irons out of the fire for the West, or to settle issues in the cold war. Power in the region will ultimately belong to those who take the responsibility for rural poverty, and break with the alibi approach, as the Government of Egypt does, but power is a by-product and not the object of reform.

So far as any general conclusion can be drawn from the preceding survey of the three countries, it is simply that the picture of the Arab world as static and medieval is no longer true. Each country is in a state of rapid economic and social change. It is true that Egypt, Syria, and Iraq do not constitute the whole of the Arab world, but they represent its most important components, and they determine, in some degree, what happens in the rest of it. The 'feudal potentate' no longer dominates the social scene. Even though there has been no land reform in Syria and Iraq, the balance of social power is changing. The position of the large landowners is undermined, though not overthrown, by the impact of money and enterprise.

This is one aspect of the general shifting of power positions in the region. Alibi thinking is prevalent, because the changing balance of power gives rise to disparities in the economic and political position of each of the participants. Britain's 'special position', i.e. political dominance, has gone, but British opinion is still largely conditioned by the attitudes appropriate to the time when Britain was the arbitrator between Jews and Arabs, and main owner of the oilfields. The United States, on the other hand, now has immense capital investment in the region, but is as yet unwilling to consider whether this does not imply some responsibility for its development. The Arab States have greater economic power than their political structure enables them to use. Soviet policy can play on these unbalances more easily than Communist doctrine can influence opinion.

In this situation, it is obviously impossible to forecast the possible effects on the Western Power position of the changes that have been described. They constitute new elements which alter the framework within which solutions must be found, without providing any formula for solution, or clearing the problems away.

But must the conclusion remain so indefinite? Do these changes simply increase instability? They are all, in one way or another, steps towards the abolition of poverty, the great need of the region. The possibility of ending poverty does exist. Is it possible that the Western desire for stability could be reconciled with the fulfilment of the region's need? To answer this question, it is necessary to take the theme of the three dynamics a little farther, to see how their operation is likely to affect the region as a whole.

To illustrate the relationship between economic development and social change, the preceding studies have suggested some historical comparisons—the mid-Victorian expansion, the Edwardian surfeit, and the industrial revolution. These comparisons are useful because they remind us that new things can happen, and happen as a process of evolution, in any society, without being a mere reflex of foreign influence. Too often the Arab world is pictured as a more or less inanimate body subject to shock treatment from Zionism or Communism, and reacting by nationalism or xenophobia. This habit of applying labels is a crude attempt to pin down a complex reality into an intelligible pattern; behind it lies the false assumption that these societies have no power of change within themselves. Historical comparisons can correct this tendency to think in terms of physical impact and reaction, and help us to realize that they are living organisms.

Yet the Arab countries do not live in time pockets of the past. They exist in our own time, and in their own place. In a period when the demand for oil is inexhaustible, the Middle East possesses 66 per cent of the world's total proved reserves.[1] No historical parallel will serve to illustrate the paradox of a barren and primitive region which has as high a rate of industrial development as that of the most advanced countries.

The extraordinarily rapid expansion of the oil industry in the last ten years is the result of an enormous investment of foreign capital.[2] American private capital has been invested in the Middle East on a larger scale than anywhere else in the Old World, and it is one of the few regions in which new British capital is invested to an increasing extent. Now that the oil companies aim at expanding production to the maximum before atomic energy becomes a competitor, the rate of expansion is likely to be even higher.[3] Atomic power is not likely to be a significant source of energy for the next ten years, and it may be as much as twenty or twenty-five years before it supplants oil in its main uses.

The West's need for oil gives the Arab oil-producing countries great economic power, which their own economy cannot use, partly by reason of the social structure, and partly because their territories are too small, or too barren, to absorb such investment. In Iraq, through the policy of engineer's planning, oil revenues are used constructively, and even there, as has been shown, money does not do all it might because in-

[1] UN, Dept. of Economic and Social Affairs, *Economic Developments in the Middle East, 1954 to 1955*.
[2] Cumulative gross investment in properties, plant, and equipment, before depreciation, in the oil industry of the Middle East region increased from $1 thousand million in 1945 to $2·2 thousand million in 1954 (ibid.).
[3] P. H. Frankel, 'Has the World Enough Oil?', *Listener*, 12 July 1956.

vestment comes up against the barriers of the social structure. In Kuwait there is also considerable investment, but revenues far exceed opportunities in the sheikhdom, and a large proportion is invested under British guidance in British securities. In Saudi Arabia much of the revenue is wasted in conspicuous consumption, or used for political propaganda and bribery. So long as this situation continues, the region must be unstable, both internally and externally. The money dynamic alone is not sufficient to raise the standard of living, though oil revenues are and will be sufficient for the long-term investments which are needed throughout the Arab world.

The dynamic of private enterprise, though it has done much, also cannot alone provide the basis for stability and higher standards. Natural conditions are too adverse. By reason of the desert environment, the only stable basis for agriculture is more irrigation. For this a strong and enterprising policy on the part of the state is essential; without it, the countries of the Arab world must remain poor and unstable.

The revolutionary dynamic comes from Egypt, the advanced agricultural country without oil revenues to finance the big development schemes which it so urgently needs. To British opinion—or at any rate to that small section of it which takes a sustained interest in Arab affairs—this dynamic appears to be a disturbing factor, stirring up upheavals from Aden to Algeria and from Jordan to Bahrein. Yet the ideals of the Egyptian revolution—the national function of the professional middle class, the new status for the fellahin—fill the social vacuum and meet the needs of the region better than any imported ideology. To bring the Arab world together by giving its social structure greater strength and coherence is certainly an essential condition of development, and also of stability.

None of the three dynamics in isolation from the rest can open the way to the abolition of poverty. Only if they were linked together would the way be open. When the revolutionary drive can use the money originating from oil production and transport to invest in the big schemes needed, and in the human resources, the problem of raising the general standard of living will be soluble. The question is not whether the Arab world will 'go Communist'. It is whether the great reservoir of wealth can be used to mop up the great reservoir of poverty—

of the fellahin, the tribesmen, and the refugees. If the Arab world is to face this problem, and to survive at a higher living standard, after the demand for oil has ceased, the pace of change must be fast, for it must get its economy and its political and social structure on to a new basis within the lifetime of a single generation.

POSTSCRIPT

AGRARIAN REFORM IN THE UNITED ARAB REPUBLIC

FROM the preceding chapters it will be evident that the agricultural and demographic conditions of the two countries composing the former UAR are strongly contrasted. In Egypt all cultivation is dependent on irrigation, and production is intensive, stable, and uniform in methods and cropping. Syria, by contrast, depends mainly on uncertain rainfall, and apart from cotton, grown chiefly as an irrigated crop, production is extensive, with low and variable yields and much regional diversity in farming methods. Egypt is over-populated, while Syria has a shortage of labour in some regions and a surplus in others. Because the backgrounds are so dissimilar, the problems of reform in the two countries were different.

When the Union was dissolved, Egypt's first reform was nearly complete, but in Syria less than half the land to be expropriated had been requisitioned, though the area redistributed was not much less than the Egyptian total officially redistributed. In several respects, the Syrian reform was a development from the Egyptian. Because the Egyptian experience lay behind it, the reform in Syria was a more courageous all-round attack on rural poverty in a more difficult environment, which the reform itself was improving by extending irrigation, introducing new crops, and resettling farmers.

In spite of the contrasts, however, there was an underlying unity in the aims and methods of agrarian reform in the two regions of the Republic. In both the same type of group farming was used, the special co-operative pattern, first evolved in Egypt and then applied in Syria. Much of the interest in comparing the two regions lies in the question of how far a reform on the Egyptian model can be successfully applied in an entirely different setting. This question was raised in Chapter II (p. 64) but was not discussed in detail, since five years ago the success of supervised co-operation was not yet established, and the possibility of its application to the conditions of the Fertile Crescent could not then be envisaged in practical terms.

EGYPT: THE EVOLVING REVOLUTION

Since 1955 land reform has been firmly established as an economic success. Although output per acre in Egypt was the highest in the world, its level has been raised as a direct result of the reform. This achievement has not been easy, and has required a high degree of administrative and technical efficiency. But so far as the redistribution of income is concerned, the results have fallen short of expectations. As a social revolutionary measure, the reform has waned in significance.

Up to 1960, economic success provided the motive power for a new direction in agrarian policy, working towards a gradual remodelling of the agrarian structure for higher productivity through the extension of supervised co-operation. At the same time the rate of redistribution was slowing down, in spite of supplementary legislation to widen the scope of the initial land reform decree, and it was evident that the social dynamic was slackening. In 1961 President Nasser decided to restore the original revolutionary impetus through a new decree reducing the maximum individual landholding. Thus there are now two directions in agrarian policy, complementary to each other: the evolutionary economic trend and the revolutionary revival. Both stem from the later phases in the execution of the Agrarian Reform Law of 1952.

THE COMPLETION OF THE AGRARIAN REFORM OF 1952

The first land reform is complete, in that the large landholdings liable to expropriation under the Agrarian Reform Law of 1952 have now been expropriated and for the most part redistributed. Expropriation and redistribution are, however, still proceeding under legislation supplementary to the 1952 law.

This supplementary legislation related to land held in *waqf* (i.e. land entailed in family succession), land reclaimed by private companies, and state land. Under Law No. 1529 of 1957, private *waqf* land, exempt under the original law, became liable to expropriation in the same way as other properties exceeding the maximum. In consequence, about 150,000 acres were added to the land available for distribution. Under Law No. 84 of 1957, private companies engaged in land reclamation (previously exempt from expropriation for twenty-five years) were compelled to sell 25 per cent of the land reclaimed to the Ministry of Agrarian Reform for resettlement by small farmers; the remainder they were permitted to sell to private owners, in holdings not exceeding 200 acres. This law has been socially beneficial in Aswan, where new land reclamation has added 30,000 acres to the small cultivated area, because it enabled the Ministry of Agrarian Reform in 1960 to purchase 10,000 acres for small farm settlement from the Kom-Ombo Company.[1] State lands were transferred to the Ministry of Agrarian Reform in 1959, also for the purpose of small farm settlement.

The object of this legislation was to obtain more land for redistribution, for as expropriation proceeded it was found that private sales and transfers (legal or illegal) had considerably reduced the area in large properties originally liable to expropriation. With the intention of preventing landowners from exceeding the legal maximum holding by buying land in the names of their children, a 1958 amendment to the 1952 law limited family ownership to 300 acres.

Even with the help of this supplementary legislation, however, it did not prove possible to distribute the 650,000 acres which was expected to be available when the 1952 law was first issued. At the end of 1960, the total area requisitioned was 581,712 acres (including 467,257 requisitioned under the 1952 law, 104,785 under the *waqf* law, and 9,670 from land belonging to foreign owners). The total area redistributed at the same date was 384,076 acres (of which 299,282 came under the 1952 law, 81,594 under the *waqf* law, and 3,200 from former foreign-owned land). Fairly large areas have been retained by the Ministry of Agrarian Reform as 'unsuitable for distribution'.

The area officially redistributed amounts to only about 7 per cent of the total cultivated land area. About 150,000 families, or less than 5 per cent of all farm families, have received land in conditional ownership and have gained considerably in income, security, and social responsibility, but they represent only a small fraction of the farm population.

[1] The largest private company engaged in land reclamation, nationalized in 1961.

Holdings distributed in conditional ownership now range between 2 and 3 acres (not $3\frac{1}{2}$ as in the first stages). The period in which ownership can be acquired by the new conditional owners has been extended from thirty to forty years. In 1961 the payments due from new owners in respect of the purchase price of land were reduced by half, and interest due on such payments was abolished. (See p. 209 below.)

Effects on the Distribution of Property in Land

To assess the social effects of the reform, it is necessary to estimate the extent to which it has promoted greater equality of ownership, both directly, through official expropriation and redistribution, and indirectly, through private sales and transfers. Unfortunately official statistics do not illustrate these changes, because the figures for distribution of agricultural land by size of holdings for 1957 (the most recent year for which such figures are published) do not show the effects of expropriation and redistribution. The large landholdings taken over under the reform are still included in the 'over 200 feddans' size-group, as 'temporarily owned by the Government' (because the land is distributed to small owners in conditional ownership only) and these holdings are therefore not distinguished from others in the same size-group (e.g. the holdings of land reclamation companies). However, it is possible to compare the distribution of agricultural land by size of holdings in 1957 and 1952 to show changes in distribution due to private sales and transfers (though not all such changes can be attributed to the reform, since the normal process of subdivision on inheritance still continues). The table opposite for 1957 may be compared with that for 1952, on p. 24 above.

Comparison of the two tables shows that the number of holdings over 200 feddans has been reduced from 2,000 to 1,000, while their area has decreased by 386,000 feddans, balanced by an increase of 349,000 feddans in the other size-groups, and an unexplained decrease of 37,000 feddans in the total area in holdings. So the area which has changed hands voluntarily is almost as large as the area officially redistributed; and nearly half of it has gone to the small properties under 10 feddans. The comparatively large increase in the area of properties between 50 and 100 feddans is presumably due to transfer from large

TABLE 18

Egypt: Agricultural Land by Size of Holdings, 1957

Size-group (feddans)*		Owners		Area		Average area (feddans)
		(000)	(per cent)	(000 feddans)	(per cent)	
1 and under		2,058	71·3	827	13·9	0·4
Over 1–under	5	660	22·9	1,447	24·3	2·1
Over 5– ,,	10	81	2·8	539	9·1	6·6
Over 10– ,,	20	50	1·7	670	11·3	13·5
Over 20– ,,	30	14	0·5	337	5·7	23·5
Over 30– ,,	50	10	0·4	369	6·2	37·2
Over 50– ,,	100	8	0·3	501	8·4	67·1
Over 100– ,,	200	3	0·1	464	7·8	136·5
Over 200*		1	0·0	791	13·3	543·3
Total		2,885	100·0	5,945	100·0	2·1

* Holdings exceeding 200 feddans are temporarily considered as owned by the Government according to the Law of Agrarian Reform of 1952.

(SOURCE: *Statistical Pocket Year-book, 1958*, p. 42.)

landowners to their children, permitted to the extent of 50 feddans each under Article 4 of the law. Some transfers, particularly in this size-group, have been purely nominal for the purpose of avoiding expropriation, so that the figures exaggerate the extent of the decline in large properties.

By adding the number of families receiving land (150,000) and the area redistributed (384,000 feddans) under official expropriation, to the number and area in the 1–5 feddans size-group in 1957, it is possible to obtain an impression of the direct and indirect effects of the reform on the agrarian structure. Comparison with 1952 would then show an increase of 30 per cent in the number of properties and of 36 per cent in the area in the 1–5 feddans size-group. Farms under 5 feddans (including those officially redistributed in conditional ownership) now represent 44 per cent of the agricultural land area, as compared with 35 per cent in 1952. So the reform has brought about some improvement in the distribution of farm property. But the holdings with less than 1 feddan still represent 70 per cent of the total number of properties and take up only 14 per cent of the total area in holdings. Two million farmers still have less than half an acre, while the number of landless cultivators has probably increased.

More redistribution is certainly needed, and will be carried out under the 1961 Decree for the Amendment of the Agrarian Reform Law, which reduced the maximum individual holding from 200 to 100 feddans (pp. 209–11 below). How much more land will become available for redistribution as a result of this decree is at present uncertain. Assuming that the figures in the preceding table for 1957 give a true picture of the present distribution of landownership, the area liable to expropriation in the 100–200 feddans size-group would not much exceed 100,000 feddans. In fact, however, the figures understate the area in this size-group and also in the size-group exceeding 200 feddans, because some landowners have escaped expropriation or have again acquired properties in excess of the maximum by means of nominal or inter-family transfers. The extent of such evasion is not known. Perhaps through a rigorous enforcement of the new maximum it might be possible to redistribute between 300,000 and 400,000 feddans, and so approximately double the area officially redistributed to date. Even so, the number of new owners would still represent only a small proportion of the total number of farmers with insufficient land. This is of course no argument against carrying redistribution farther; on the contrary, the success of agrarian reform in this direction is a good reason for extending its benefits more widely, particularly as in the direction of rent control the law has not been enforceable.

Rent Control

So far as the incomes of farm tenants are concerned, the reform has lost most of its earlier social and economic significance because rent control is now evaded.[1] The provisions requiring drastic reduction of farm rents to a legal maximum, which in the first stages of the reform were more widespread in their impact than land redistribution, are no longer generally effective. As anticipated (on p. 39 above) rents have risen as land prices rose again and the fear of expropriation receded. In consequence the incomes of tenants (who form a majority of all cultivators) have tended to fall. Efforts have been made to tighten up enforce-

[1] Sayed Marei, *U.A.R. Agriculture Enters a New Age* (Cairo, 1960), p. 52.

ment, but on the smaller properties this proves difficult since competition for land is as intense as before, and tenants acquiesce in breaking the law designed to protect them.

Greater security of tenure for tenant cultivators has, however, been provided by supplementary legislation. The original Agrarian Reform Law provided that all existing tenancy contracts should be extended for another year. This provision has twice been extended by special decree, for a period of three years on each occasion, in respect of half the area leased. New leases are not to be made for less than three years, the contract to be in writing, irrespective of value.[1] By contrast with the situation in 1955, the most general benefit conferred by the reform is no longer the reduction of rents, but this greater degree of security.

New Rural Welfare Measures

Though the income benefits of the reform are now much less widespread than in the early stages, its importance as a turning-point in the history of Egypt is not thereby diminished. It is no longer the only policy in the interests of the fellahin, and is more or less eclipsed by other measures with wider social effects. But without the essential act of commitment, these other measures would never have been undertaken.

To benefit the poorer farmers and offer them some compensation for not receiving land, President Nasser, in 1959, initiated the *Gamoos* Scheme. This enables cultivators without livestock to buy buffaloes in calf on hire purchase, the price being repayable in instalments over seven years. It is a most popular scheme, for the *gamoos* is the backbone of small-scale farming in Egypt.

The Drinking Water Scheme, introduced in 1955, is now nation-wide, providing clean water to the majority of villages; this is, of course, a great advance.

The most striking sign of social change in the countryside since 1955, however, are the Combined Centres, set up in 1955–8 to provide health, educational, social, and agricultural services to the villages. In 1960 there were 250 such centres, each serving on an average 15,000 people. Another 100 are to be built under the Five Year Plan. The total of 350 centres in 1964, together

---

[1] E. Garzouzi, *Old Ills and New Remedies in Egypt* (Cairo, 1957), p. 82.

with the expanded old rural health centres, will then serve about three-quarters of the rural population.[1]

The special principle of their work, which existed in embryonic form in the old rural health centres, is the joint provision of co-ordinated services. Each centre is staffed by a doctor, nurse-midwife, laboratory assistant, and male and female assistant nurses; a headmaster with ten or twelve male and female assistant teachers; and an agricultural adviser, who is also a social worker. In theory all the services are co-ordinated, but in practice it is the health service which draws the others together; for example, the doctor's advice is reinforced by the health-education campaigns in the school, the social worker encourages village projects for latrines and drainage. The small hospital, maternity ward, clinic, and operating theatre form the real centre of each unit.

The health service is of inestimable value, for it has reduced trachoma to a fraction of its former terrible incidence. Bilharzia is intractable, for reinfection follows cure: disinfection of the canals has so far been tried only in the province of Sharkia. Infant mortality is falling sharply in the districts served by the centres. Villagers are becoming health-conscious, instead of accepting disease as inevitable.

The school supplements other schools in the district, and has no special community function, though its curriculum is varied by handicrafts, which produce rugs, pottery, and carvings for sale. But the real educational work is aesthetic. The buildings are simple and beautiful, and now there is one place in the village that is clean.

In agriculture, the centres (financially backed by the Rural Economic Development Scheme introduced in 1957), offer technical advice and demonstrations on the farm plot, and keep breeding livestock at stud. Their work seems particularly useful in improving livestock breeding and encouraging poultry, rabbits, and bee-keeping, all directions in which Egyptian farming is backward. But as the agricultural adviser is also responsible for the numerous social projects, he is over-worked (like the doctor). The idea of widely diffusing shallow investments

---

[1] For further details, see *Report on the Work of the Combined Centres to 1960*, published by the Provisional Council for Local Government (Cairo, 1960), summarized in UN, *Land Reform and Community Development in the United Arab Republic* (New York, 1961).

to help the small farmer add to his income and diet is excellent. It does not, of course, bring about the all-round big improvement in crop yields which is essential to raise farmers' incomes. This is the achievement of the supervised co-operatives. But the centres are happier places.

Agricultural Production

In the evolution of the new agrarian reform policy, the decisive factor has been the need for finding a form of farm organization which can increase agricultural production *in general* at a more rapid rate.

Since the revolution, agricultural production has increased much more rapidly than in the years preceding it. In the race between population growth and agricultural production (pp. 16–19 above), the latter is now drawing slightly ahead. From 1951 to 1958 total population increased by 19 per cent, from 20,872,000 to 24,781,000, while agricultural production in the same period increased by 25 per cent.[1] There has therefore been a slight improvement in food supply per head of total population. The agricultural population is presumably still increasing, though at what rate will not be known until the results of the 1960 Agricultural Census are available; but it can be presumed that the rate of industrialization, though high, has not been high enough to absorb an appreciable proportion of the increase of the agricultural labour force.

The more rapid increase in agricultural production since 1952 is due chiefly to intensification of production (now known as 'vertical expansion'). Higher output per acre cultivated has been achieved through state and private investment in the conversion of basin-irrigated land to perennial irrigation, so increasing the cropped area from 9·3 to 10·3 million acres. Better pesticides (particularly toxaphene for cotton) and heavier use of fertilizers have been other major factors in increasing output per acre. So the scope for intensification has proved greater than was anticipated, for the rate of increase of production has slightly exceeded the Population Commission's estimate of 25 per cent as the maximum possible increase over the 1947–51 average (p. 21 above).

[1] The official quantum index of agricultural production (1935–9 = 100) shows a rise from 105 in 1951 to 131 in 1958.

LAND REFORM AND DEVELOPMENT

Much of the recent technical advance has been concentrated in the supervised co-operatives set up under the agrarian reform, though private landowners have also contributed. If the methods used in these co-operatives—i.e. large-scale operation, unified rotations, and supervised credit—were generally introduced, to level up the output of the farms under 5 feddans which constitute the majority of all properties and take up nearly half the cultivated area, then it should prove possible to achieve a considerable further increase in total output. The compulsory co-operatives have pioneered the way by showing that much more can be done to increase production in an already highly intensive system of farming than was earlier believed possible.

As to 'horizontal expansion' (i.e. the extension of the cultivated area), the vast project of the High Dam is still rightly regarded as a matter of life or death for the Egyptian economy (p. 23 above). Construction began in 1960, with Soviet aid and equipment; Russian engineers are now working under an Egyptian chief engineer, with about 3,000 workers employed on the project. The completion of the first stage, the construction of two coffer dams and the central dam, scheduled for 1964 to represent the culmination of the First Five Year Plan, will provide increasing supplies of water for irrigation. When the main dam reaches a level of 155 metres in 1967, the supply of water will be sufficient to irrigate 1·3 million new acres and convert 700,000 acres to perennial irrigation.[1]

But there still remains the need for faster land reclamation in the interval before the High Dam comes into operation. The scope for adding to the cultivated area with the existing water supply was somewhat overestimated, and the original aim of reclaiming 300,000 new acres by 1956 was not achieved. The total area reclaimed between 1952 and 1959 amounted to 180,000 acres.

In particular the earlier enthusiasm for the Liberation Province (*El Tahrir Mudiria*) was cooled by revelations of wasteful expenditure, and in 1957 its administration was transferred to the Ministry of Agrarian Reform. The project continues to work on the lines described on pp. 49–54 above, except in so

---

[1] See *Aswan*, pamphlet published by Dept. of Information, 1961. Estimates of the addition to the cultivated area vary. The above figures, quoted on p. 22 above from estimates current in 1955, are still in use (cf. 'Agriculture and Industry in the Plan', in Central Bank of Egypt, *Economic Review*, vol. 1, no. 1, 1961, p.30).

far as economies have been made and the social regimentation has been abandoned, though it has left its mark in strikingly high standards of health and cleanliness. Overheads are still high in relation to the area reclaimed. In February 1961 this was 25,000 acres, of which 2,000 were about to be distributed in provisional ownership to 200 families in 10-acre holdings (larger than the average distributed under the reform, because cotton cannot as yet be cultivated). The EARIS project at Abis (p. 22 above) will complete reclamation of 32,000 acres in 1961; in 1960 5,000 acres were distributed to 1,000 families.

To speed up the rate of land reclamation to achieve the total of 585,000 new acres scheduled under the First Five Year Plan, a new system of water economy was introduced in 1960, involving several new controls, chief of which is the lowering of the level of irrigation water to half a metre below the land level, to avoid the habitual wastage in flow irrigation, now entirely eliminated. New reclamation is undertaken by the Ministries of Public Works and Agrarian Reform, the Desert Valley Authority set up in 1957 to reclaim land in the south-western oases, and private companies, including foreign firms working under contract. The biggest new resettlement and reclamation project now being launched is at Kom-Ombo in Aswan province, to provide 34,000 acres for the Nubian families who will be displaced by the flooding of the High Dam reservoir.

The belief in 'changing people' by the outside dynamic personality-swung approach which inspired the early stages of the Tahrir project has now given place to more sober methods of consultation to create confidence, evidenced by the preparations to receive the Nubians at Kom-Ombo. Leaders of the tribal groups to be resettled make fortnightly visits to the Director of Agrarian Reform in Aswan in charge of the scheme, and discuss their problems in detail, so that everything shall be as much like home as possible when the first groups move in 1962 and 1963. Here, as in all new settlements, the organization will be based on the well-tried principle of supervised co-operation.

The Supervised Co-operatives

The economic success of the co-operatives set up under the agrarian reform is attested by the rise in output per acre and the high rate of profit earned. The yield of cotton per feddan has risen by 45 per cent in the supervised co-operatives,[1] from the pre-reform period to 1959, while the average for Egypt increased by 15 per cent in the same period. Figures for other crops are not available, but doubtless are well above the average, though probably not in the same ratio as for cotton.

This rapid increase in output reflects a high rate of reinvestment of profits in farm equipment, pumps, fertilizers, and insecticides. The older and larger co-operatives are now earning large profits; in one region visited, the Shibin el-Kom land reform area in Minufia province, figures were provided showing profits ranging from £E5,000–8,000 per society in 1960–1. Profits are allocated, in broadly similar proportions in all societies, to reserves (40 per cent); dividends (30 per cent); the social fund, which covers sickness and accident insurance and medical care (20 per cent); and refunds to members from sales (10 per cent). The high proportion invested reflects official control, for in the absence of financial supervision members would doubtless invest less and distribute more income in the form of dividends. Thus the co-operatives which began as a system of maintaining and increasing production on the former large estates have now become a method of enforced saving.

Quite recently, the supervised co-operatives have begun to devote more funds to social investment, particularly in village schemes, such as club-houses, in rivalry with the Combined Centres (which do not overlap, as they are usually not started in a land reform village, though they can be used by members of supervised co-operatives in the neighbourhood). Rural rehousing is the next gigantic task to be undertaken.

In the early stages of the reform, the question naturally arose as to whether these compulsory societies were not more like collective or state farms than genuine co-operatives. But now the question seems scarcely relevant, for it is obvious that they combine both collective and co-operative elements in an original pattern. Unlike the collective farms in Eastern Europe, these societies maintain the principle of individual responsibility through distribution of income to the cultivator of the holding,

---

[1] This figure is a weighted average calculated from cotton output and acreage of supervised co-operatives in sixteen districts (*Information and Statistics relating to Agrarian Reform in the Southern Region* (1960)).

and unlike them they are well managed, by capable technicians.

Though the co-operatives began as artificial and compulsory creations, and are still firmly controlled, self-government has been fostered, and a sense of community responsibility has developed. In 1959 President Nasser asked the Minister of Agrarian Reform to relax control of the co-operatives wherever possible.[1] Accordingly official supervision has been removed from two of the most successful societies, Zafaran and Bourgaya (pp. 44–5), and they are now autonomous. Eighty others (out of 326 in existence in 1960) are to become independent in the near future. Incentives are being substituted for compulsion in marketing; members now receive a premium of 10 per cent on the market price of cotton sold through the co-operative.

Their success can be attributed to two factors. One is the organization itself, which reconciles individual incentive and the growth of co-operative spirit with large-scale operation and skilled management.

The other is the quality of the men in charge of the administration. In all agrarian reform policies, a balance must be held between the social and agricultural aspects, for over-emphasis on social claims may lead to a decline in production, while conversely over-emphasis on the need for increasing production may lead to regimentation of the farmers. In an attempt to give due weight to both aspects, the administration of the reform in the early stages was the responsibility of an inter-ministerial body, the Higher Committee for Agrarian Reform, representing several government departments including the Ministries of Agriculture and of Social Affairs; supervising officials in the land reform co-operatives were at first responsible to the latter. But the Higher Committee was slow in reaching decisions, and in 1956 its functions were taken over by the newly created Ministry of Agrarian Reform. During the Union there were separate Ministries of Agriculture and Agrarian Reform in each region, controlled by a single Ministry of Agriculture and Agrarian Reform at the central Government level, a position held till 1961 by Sayed Marei. Through this combination of functions at the top, agrarian reform is now much more closely integrated with

---

[1] In a speech at Edfina estate, 27 July 1959. See G. Saab, 'Rationalization of Agriculture and Land Tenure Problems in Egypt', in American Univ. of Beirut, *Middle East Economic Papers* (1960).

general agricultural policy, a situation which, though desirable from an economic standpoint, might lead to neglect of the social side, if care had not been taken to select and train a new *élite* of land reformers, men with high technical qualifications in agriculture and a strong sense of social responsibility.

This agricultural intelligentsia, a rare asset in the under-developed world, has acquired a socially constructive function in training co-operatives for self-government.

EXPERIMENTS IN AGRARIAN POLICY

The new direction in agrarian policy consists in the application of the principle of supervised co-operation (i.e. co-operation for higher productivity, with supervised credit and official technical guidance) to ordinary villages, where there has been no redistribution of land, and where there is inequality of ownership between large, medium, and small farm proprietors. The approach to the new policy has been experimental, since it was by no means certain that the same system could be made to work in an unreformed structure, where the farmers were not dependent on the Ministry of Agrarian Reform, and might regard the new system as restrictive. Moreover, the organization of the supervised co-operatives had been successful through the concentration of technical and managerial ability in a narrow field; if these resources were more widely extended there might be some loss in efficiency.

Unified Rotation Co-operatives

The first experiment began in 1955, as an attempt to deal with the problem of fragmentation. In every Egyptian village today nearly half the land is in holdings under 5 acres, and the majority of the holdings are less than 1 acre in size; and usually each holding is fragmented into several pieces. This situation is a result of extreme population pressure and the law of inheritance, under which landholdings are divided equally among heirs (equal shares to each son, and half a share to each daughter). The problem of excessively small holdings has proved intractable in many countries, but the effects are far more serious in Egypt than elsewhere, because of the wastage of water and labour entailed by the great number of separate small irrigation systems. It really necessitates a new reform of the agrarian structure, not by further subdivision of the larger farms, but by combination of the smaller farms into more economic units. The consolidation of fragmented holdings into single pieces of land would not accomplish much, since the majority of holdings are uneconomically small. But legislation for this purpose would, of course, rouse insuperable resistance from small owners. On the *tabula rasa* of an expropriated estate, a rational field lay-out could be introduced without difficulty. Elsewhere compulsory consolidation and combination is out of the question, for ownership means security.

In 1955, therefore, an original approach was made through an experiment in a new field lay-out at Nawag (near Tanta in the province of Gharbia). This village was chosen because subdivision and fragmentation there had gone to extreme lengths. The total area of the village is 1,850 feddans, divided into 1,585 properties; of these 668 are less than half a feddan; 678 are between half and 1 feddan, 167 between 1 and 2, 61 between 2 and 10, and only 11 between 10 and 15 feddans.[1] The number of plots was 3,500, each with different drainage and irrigation systems.

The initiative was taken by the Central Ministry of Agriculture and Agrarian Reform, through the agricultural co-operative society (founded in 1932). Members were asked, at a general meeting preceded by a feast, to introduce the new system. This meant an agreement by all the farmers to follow a uniform crop rotation in a new field lay-out, which would divide the land into several large fields, each under one crop, and each including a large number of holdings or pieces of holdings. The farmers were offered big incentives: fertilizers, pesticides, and seed on credit at cost price, loans repayable when the crop was sold. Even so, they would only consent to try out the experiment on 100 feddans. This proved so successful that the following year they agreed to put all the land under the new system.

Each of the several fields is now under one of the main crops (in winter: wheat, berseem, and fallow cultivation in preparation for cotton) and each contains the holdings of several hundred owners. Most of the farmers therefore have all their land under

---

[1] Figures from Ministry of Agrarian Reform, Co-operation Dept., *Nawag: a Pilot Experiment for Solving the Problems of Fragmentation* by Mahmoud Fawzy (Cairo, 1958). See also D. Stewart, *Young Egypt* (1958), pp. 161-2.

one crop in each crop season, and so lack the other crops. They adjust this situation by agreeing to exchange produce or land among themselves. A farmer whose land is under cotton will exchange part of the crop with neighbours or relatives for what is agreed to be an equivalent amount of wheat or berseem. In the following season, he grows wheat, and takes cotton and berseem from others. No standard basis for these adjustments can be found, and farmers are left to sort them out as they choose. At Nawag, I was informed that it worked well because relatives could agree between themselves on the method of exchange. At Minshat Sultan, another village now working on the same basis, the principle was to exchange feddan for feddan; this would clearly not work satisfactorily if land varied in quality, but the villagers asserted that it did not, and that anyway the exchange was reversed in the next crop season, and so was in the long run satisfactory. It should be noted that this system docs *not* mean any change in the distribution of property, and there is no consolidation of fragmented holdings, or combination of farms. The system rests on an agreement to rationalize the rotation, and to exchange produce by voluntary adjustments between the owners.

The increase in productivity has been surprising. Cotton output at Nawag had increased from $3\frac{1}{2}$ cantars per feddan to $7\frac{1}{2}$ cantars per feddan in 1958 (in which year the average for Egypt was $5\cdot2$ cantars per feddan). Maize yields have risen from 8 to 10 ardebs per feddan (average for Egypt 7). Since cotton is the money-spinner, farm incomes have risen quickly, by 30–40 per cent, to about £E50 per feddan. The increase is attributed to much heavier use of fertilizers and the introduction of toxaphene. The co-operative had invested part of its profits (£E800 in 1957) in the purchase of a tractor, which is hired to members at a rate much lower than that charged by local landowners.

Similar results were observed at Minshat Sultan, a much bigger village in Minufia province, with an old co-operative society, which began to follow the Nawag model in 1959 with more confidence because of Nawag's example. In 1960 the cotton yield rose to 6 cantars per feddan, as compared with $3\frac{1}{2}$ cantars in 1959, while the wheat yield rose from 4 to 9 ardebs per feddan. Since the new system began, the co-operative society has purchased three tractors on credit repayable by instalments over five years; these work at a fee of £E1 per feddan for two cultivations in preparation for cotton. The society has a reserve fund of £E3,463, and a social fund of £E144, mainly used for relief grants. Asked for proof of new wealth, members of the Board said that farmers could now afford to buy livestock, and that more people could now go on pilgrimage to Mecca. The latter index of prosperity was also quoted at Nawag.

The Nawag model is now to be introduced in 100 other villages. Several others have already introduced it.

Thus through the application of methods used in the supervised co-operatives to the old agricultural supply and credit societies, a new type of village organization has emerged, in effect a new reform of the agrarian structure. If this method were to be applied generally throughout Egypt, it could obviously achieve a large increase in production per acre.

Its advantages are two. First, economic: it can achieve quickly, without cumbrous or vexatious procedures, a rapid rise in yields and income. Of course the combined rotation does not alone achieve the increase; without higher investment in fertilizers and pesticides, it would achieve much less. The advantage of the co-operative society in the new system is that it provides a channel through which capital can be invested, with a certain return, because the technique of production is so much improved. Its second advantage is that it can diffuse some of the benefits gained by recipients of land under the reform to other small farmers, although of course in the unified rotation co-operatives the benefits are not shared equally between farmers with equal holdings, as is the case in the land reform co-operatives.

Reorganization of the Ordinary Agricultural Co-operative Societies

The new policy finally took shape at the end of 1960 through the decision to make supervised co-operation the method of fulfilling the agricultural targets of the Five Year Plan, by applying the system to the old agricultural co-operative societies. These now number about 3,500, and are mainly concerned with purchase of farm equipment and the supply of credit. Many have long been dormant. They were stimulated to greater activity by the new Co-operative Law of 1956, which extended their privileges, and by the Rural Credit Scheme, introduced in 1957 to expand the provision of credit to co-operatives. But because they are not directly concerned with the organization of production, the old societies were incapable of increasing farm output to any significant extent.

Three reasons were responsible for the decision to reorganize the agricultural co-operative movement. One was the success of the agrarian reform co-operatives in raising yields, and the successful application of the unified rotation to 'unreformed' villages, which showed that the potential was high. The second was the need for increasing agricultural production under the Five Year Plan, which allocates £E192 million to 'horizontal expansion' and £E122 million to 'vertical expansion'. Under the existing structure, production could not increase at a sufficiently high rate. The third reason was that it was considered socially and economically desirable to channel the investment of public funds into agriculture on a new co-operative basis, since capital provided through the banks, or even through the ordinary co-operative societies, would inevitably benefit chiefly the larger farmers. Unless official supervision guarantees repayment of loans, no large credit expansion is practicable on small farms.

The first step in the reorganization was the transfer of the responsibility for the old agricultural societies from the Ministry of Social Affairs and Labour to the Ministry of Agrarian Reform; at the same time the consumers' co-operative societies were transferred to the Ministry of Industry.

The Ministry of Agrarian Reform is to channel state funds allocated to agriculture to the agricultural co-operative societies on the supervised credit system (i.e. granting credit for specific production purposes). Each society will have a production target, and an official of the Ministry will reside in the village to control fulfilment. The constitution of the societies is to be reorganized to give stronger representation to the smaller farmer, hitherto overshadowed by the capital contributed by the larger farmers, whose money will no longer be decisive when credit is supplied from public funds.

THE SECOND LAND REFORM

From being a lever in the overthrow of the former ruling class, the agrarian reform had evolved into a useful instrument for the fulfilment of the Five Year Plan; and in the process the original conception of reform as a broad measure of income redistribution had evaporated. The authentic social impetus had been overlaid by the drive for economic efficiency. This, as the Introduction to this book points out, is a weakness inherent in the modern type of well-managed reform: it fails to give people what they want. The problem is to combine agricultural progress with social change; and in Egypt the balance was shifting too far on to the technical side. In spite of the impressive achievement in rural social services, particularly health, the variety of community development projects, and the increase in output, the fact remained that hopes had been disappointed by the small scale of redistribution and cynicism fostered by the evasion of rent control. If the old spirit could not be restored, there would still be much to show as its achievement; but the Egyptian revolution would lose its role as an original dynamic force.

The President, with unfailing insight into what people want, had from time to time intervened to keep the technocrats in line with this objective, as for example by initiating the *Gamoos* scheme and by suggesting that control of the supervised cooperatives should be relaxed. But the decision to undertake a further measure of land redistribution was held in abeyance until 1961, when it was suddenly announced as part of a new general policy of income redistribution in the interests of both industrial and rural workers.

On 15 July 1961, to mark the ninth anniversary of the revolution, Nasser issued four presidential decrees. The first limited landownership in the Egyptian region to 100 feddans per individual instead of 200 as under the first reform law. The second exempted farmers in both regions of the Republic from paying half the price of the land distributed to them under the agrarian reform, and freed them from payment of interest on the instalments of the purchase price, transferring to the state the obligation of meeting these payments. The third imposed a progressive tax on income from rents of residential property in the Egyptian region; and the fourth introduced a progressive tax on general income in the Syrian region. At the same time 400 industrial concerns were nationalized, and working hours were reduced from eight to seven per day, with the object of increasing the numbers in industrial employment.

LAND REFORM AND DEVELOPMENT

In a speech in Alexandria on 26 July 1961,[1] the President explained the significance of these measures as the continuance of the social revolution begun in 1952, strongly emphasizing the persistence of rural poverty:

> If we really want to feel how we live, we should not be impressed by the lights in Alexandria, Cairo or Damascus. We should rather assess the real needs of our revolutionary advance. We should consider as our major problems those which exist away from the glittering lights. Let us consider how the peasants live in the villages. A fellah is hired by a landowner for four or five months in the year and spends the rest of the year without employment living at a subsistence level. Migratory labourers live on the lowest imaginable pay. I visited Kom-Ombo five years ago and visited a plant there. I saw the labourers at lunch-time eating a loaf of hard sun-baked bread of the kind common in Upper Egypt, and an onion. Is this the life we would approve of? Is it a life that anyone could agree that we should live?

He praised the success of land reform in granting ownership to 1 million people (members of farm families), but also drove home its failures:

> We fixed the annual rent for tenants at the equivalent of seven times the basic land tax, but has this been complied with? Landowners have found ways and means whereby they have succeeded in evading the law, with the result that the rent has never been actually fixed by the landowners in conformity with the provisions of the law.
>
> It was our intention to suppress feudalism, but have we succeeded in doing so? I am personally acquainted with families who have taken advantage of certain loopholes in the clauses of the original law restricting landownership. In several cases, landowners retained possession of 200 feddans and through fictitious bequests and sales continued to own 3,000 feddans and thus considered themselves to be the feudal lords of the locality with the peasants as their serfs. Can we possibly tolerate such a state of affairs under the revolutionary régime? Either the Revolution has to take such measures as will achieve its cherished political and social objectives, or else we should proclaim that the Revolution has finally come to an end. In that event, we should have to admit that, despite our success in the political field, we have utterly failed in performing our social task.

The 1961 Decree for the Amendment of the Agrarian Reform Law in the Southern Region (No. 178 of 1952)[2] provides in

[1] Text issued by Dept. of Information, Cairo, 26 July 1961.
[2] Text published by Dept. of Information, Cairo, 25 July 1961.

POSTSCRIPT

Article 1 that the first article of the old law should be superseded by the words: 'No person shall be allowed to own more than 100 feddans of agricultural land. This shall also apply to barren and desert land. Any contract transferring ownership constituting a violation of this law shall be annulled and shall not be registered.' Article 2 prescribes that

Should ownership exceed this maximum limit as a result of inheritance or by means other than contracts transferring ownership, the owner shall dispose of the excess land within one year from the date of the transfer of ownership, or from the date of the promulgation of this law, whichever period is the longer. Land in excess of the maximum shall be disposed of to small farmers, in accordance with rules to be embodied in an order to be issued by the Agrarian Reform Authority. Land which is not disposed of within the period specified or in accordance with the prescribed conditions is to be expropriated by the Government, through the Agrarian Reform Authority (Article 3) against compensation regulated by the terms laid down in the 1952 law on the basis of the 1952 rate of land tax (Article 4), and payable in 4 per cent interest-bearing State bonds negotiable on the Stock Exchange and redeemable in fifteen years (Article 5).

With the object of preventing further acquisition of large properties, Article 7 provides that 'from the agricultural year 1961–2 no one person, together with his wife and minor children, shall be allowed to acquire through rent, seizure or other means more than 50 feddans in addition to the area which he already owns'. Estate agents are prohibited from managing or leasing land in excess of this limit. Contraventions of the law are punishable by imprisonment and/or fines of not less than £E100 and not more than £E1,000—a more drastic and realistic method of enforcement than that of the first law, which imposed the penalty of imprisonment only, and solely for breaches of Article 1.

The object of the new law is to bring about a greater degree of equality in the distribution of landownership by reducing the maximum holding and tightening up enforcement. At the time of writing the consequences cannot be foreseen, for the extent of evasion of the old law is not known, and the administrative regulations governing the disposal of the excess land are not available. Presumably most of the land affected will be sold privately to individual owners and not expropriated. As the areas to be sold or expropriated will in general be much less than those of the very large estates expropriated under the old law, the organization of supervised co-operatives for purchasers or recipients of land may be difficult, because the lots will be mainly small and also dispersed, so that the scale of production will be too small for central management. If, however, the new owners can be assisted through the old co-operative societies now in process of reorganization on the supervised principle, there will be no need for special assistance, and the more equal distribution of ownership will help to strengthen the position of the small farmers in the newly constituted societies.

What is most significant and encouraging is that the second land reform still adheres plainly and firmly to the principle of individual small ownership, representing what the fellahin want most. The original impetus is still strong, in no way daunted by the partial failure of the first reform to achieve its objects.

Syria: Reform and Resettlement

The agrarian reform in Syria was unusual because it combined the two things rarely found in conjunction—economic efficiency and broad social change. The revolutionary spirit was certainly present in the young co-operative managers content to live in isolated discomfort in the villages, and in the tribesmen thronging the provincial Agrarian Reform Offices. At the same time, the organization was well adapted to the agricultural and human potential, and adequately supplied with funds. The combination of these normally incompatible conditions sprang from the union with Egypt, which empowered the social impetus to reform generated by the Arab Socialist Party (the Ba'ath), and at the same time brought the Egyptian experience to bear in a new and difficult agricultural situation.

The reform was the direct outcome of the foundation of the United Arab Republic, on 1 February 1958, through the efforts of the Arab Socialist Party to save Syria from Communism at the top level. The Agrarian Reform Law, to save Syria from Communism at the ground level, followed on 27 September 1958. It was concerned solely with the expropriation and distribution of land, unlike the Egyptian Agrarian Reform Decree, which also contained provisions regulating rents, conditions of tenancy, and agricultural wages. In Syria, provisions of this kind were included in a separate decree, the Law on Agricultural Relations of 4 September 1958 (Law No. 134 of 1958), which limited the produce share taken by landowners, provided greater security for tenants and share-croppers, set up wage tribunals for farm labourers, and permitted the formation of agricultural trade unions. This decree incorporated the objects of the Law for the Protection of the Fellah, advocated by the Arab Socialist Party from 1955 onwards (see p. 109 above). But the Agrarian Reform Law went much farther than the policy formulated by the Arab Socialists, and much farther than the Egyptian reform itself.

Unfortunately the collaboration of the two revolutionary forces which produced the law was not sustained during its implementation. In 1959 the Arab Socialist Party leaders resigned from their official functions in the Government of the United Arab Republic, including the Minister of Agrarian Reform in the Northern Region, who was a strong protagonist of the law. One explanation commonly given for this withdrawal is the slow progress in carrying out the agrarian reform, but it is also alleged that the desire to disclaim responsibility for its unpopularity played some part in the decision, since both landowners and Communists were vociferous in condemnation. Whatever the motives may have been, the retreat of the left now appears rather short-sighted, for it apparently led to some modification in the original targets for expropriation of irrigated land (see p. 216 below) and at the same time has deprived the Arab Socialists of the credit which they could otherwise have rightly claimed for the positive achievements of the reform, inevitably slow to make themselves felt because of the disastrous harvests of 1958–60.

On paper, the provisions of the law follow those of the Egyptian reform very closely.[1] Large landholdings above a fixed maximum were to be expropriated within five years, and the land was to be distributed to small farmers, in holdings of not more than 8 hectares of irrigated land and 30 hectares of rainfed land, who were to acquire full ownership by payment of annual instalments over a period of forty years. Exemption from expropriation was allowed to companies and co-operative societies engaged in land reclamation, industrial societies using

---

[1] UAR, Agrarian Reform General Organization, *Agrarian Reform Law No. 161 in the Syrian Region* (Cairo, 1958).

land for industrial development, and agricultural and benevo-
lent societies, as under the Egyptian law. The order of priority
to be applied in allotting land to farmers is also similar to the
Egyptian, i.e. (1) tenants, share-croppers, or farm labourers
actually cultivating the land on the requisitioned property;
(2) heads of large families; (3) poorer inhabitants of the villages; (4) non-inhabitants of the village. Recipients of land
were required to become members of a co-operative society,
with functions similar to those defined by the Egyptian law
(p. 42 above).

However, in two important respects the Syrian reform was
more radical than the Egyptian. The maximum individual holdings which can be retained are 80 hectares[1] of irrigated land, or
300 hectares of rain-fed land, or a combination of the two in
similar ratios. Additional holdings for wife and children are
allowed up to a total of 40 hectares of irrigated land, or 100
hectares of rain-fed land, making the landowner-and-family
maximum 120 hectares of irrigated land or 400 hectares of
rain-fed land. The maximum areas of irrigated land, 80 and
120 hectares, correspond to the Egyptian maxima of 200 and
300 feddans; but as output per acre in Egypt is much greater
that the output per acre of irrigated land in Syria, the enforcement of the same acreage limitation meant imposing a lower
income maximum. This real and well-publicized grievance of
the landowners had less justification after the maximum individual holding in Egypt had been reduced from 200 to 100
feddans. In Syria it was wise to fix a low maximum, for otherwise the scope of the law would have been too small; and in
the political conditions of the Union, it was vital that the interests of the have-nots should predominate.

Further, the Syrian law was more drastic because it left no
apparent loopholes for evasion. As explained above, Article 4
of the Egyptian law as originally issued permitted private sales
to small farmers, and this provision, though quickly rescinded,
led to much evasion of the law. No such latitude was allowed in
Syria. To prevent private sales and transfers the law prescribed
that every proprietor of land in excess of the maximum must
notify the Ministry of Agrarian Reform of the area of the land
he owns and farms, within three months of the coming into

---

[1] 1 hectare = 2·471 acres.

effect of the law, and in January of every year. Heavy penalties were imposed for evasion and falsification. Other provisions (e.g. defining children entitled to receive transfers of land, preventing subdivision of large estates on inheritance) were included to prevent evasion through transfers within the family.

The provisions governing the rate of compensation differed from the Egyptian, though whether they are more or less favourable is not known, since data were not available. Under the Egyptian law, the rate of compensation to the landowner was based on the valuation of the land for land tax; and as this valuation was low, the purchase price was much lower than the market price of the land. In Syria no land tax was levied, and therefore a rental basis was used. The compensation payable to the landowner is fixed at ten times the average rent of the land for an agricultural rotation period of three years, or the produce share of the proprietor in the rotation, which is not to exceed the proportion laid down in the Law on Agricultural Relations (No. 134 of 1958). Compensation is to be determined by an inter-ministerial committee, representing the Ministries of Agriculture, Justice, and Public Works. After requisitioning orders have been issued, the landowners must pay to the treasury three-quarters of the average rent fixed under Law No. 134 of 1958, in respect of the land requisitioned, until it is taken over for redistribution by the Ministry of Agrarian Reform.

In scope, the reform would have been wider than the Egyptian. Official estimates put the total area liable to expropriation at $1\frac{1}{2}$ million hectares, or about 30 per cent of the agricultural area, estimating this at some 5 million hectares. In addition, it was intended to distribute $1\frac{1}{2}$ million hectares of State Domain land, making the total available for redistribution 3 million hectares or 60 per cent of the total agricultural area. These figures probably overstate the prospects, since they include some arid land not suitable for redistribution. Even so, the reform seemed likely to be a major operation on the agrarian structure.

So far as irrigated land is concerned, there would appear to have been some modification of the original intentions. According to an official statement by the Director-General of Agrarian Reform in Damascus, in early 1961, the area of irrigated land to be expropriated and redistributed was estimated at 94,000 hectares, or about one-sixth of the total irrigated area of some

590,000 hectares; but earlier estimates put the total at 390,000 hectares, or nearly two-thirds of the total.[1] Perhaps the land-owners' outcry against expropriation may have been responsible for the reduction of the original target. The small proportion of the irrigated land then included in the reform was financially disadvantageous, in that the administration had been obliged to take over a large proportion of the estates with low output (even with no output in some cases) so that many of the newly constituted co-operatives could not cover costs. From a social standpoint, on the other hand, the immediate benefits were greater, since cultivators on the drought-stricken rain-fed land were in urgent need of help, while those on irrigated land were better off.

By 15 January 1961, 596,735 hectares, including 14,273 hectares of irrigated land, had been requisitioned, and an area of 135,675 hectares had been redistributed or prepared for redistribution. In addition, 19,257 hectares of State Domain land had been redistributed, making the total distributed or prepared for redistribution 154,932 hectares. Recipients numbered 7,732 families, including 42,256 people.

The table opposite shows the extent of agrarian reform in the different governorates. In the Jezira governorate, now known as the governorate of Hassetche, enormous areas had been requisitioned, though not as yet distributed. These are the holdings of the merchant-tractorists, described in Chapter III. The largest areas then redistributed were in the governorates of Homs and Aleppo (in 1960 subdivided into two by the creation of the new governorate of Idlib). In the two southern governorates, Deraa and Suweida, there had been little requisitioning, as the land was already mainly in small ownership.

The question which inevitably arose is whether it was wise or practicable to introduce the same type of reform throughout the country. For the reform seemed to impose a rigid pattern closely resembling that developed in Egypt, in conditions utterly dissimilar to those of the Nile Valley. Regional differences in land productivity necessarily require different types of farm settlement, if the grant of land is to lead to an improvement in the rural living standard. In practice, however, the organization of

[1] See FAO Mediterranean Development Project, *U.A.R. Syrian Region, Country Report* (1959), Ch. iii, p. 6.

TABLE 19

Syria: Results of Agrarian Reform

(a) Area of land requisitioned to 15.1.1961 (hectares)

Governorate	Irrigated	Dry-farming	Uncultivated	Total
Damascus	384	8,167	27,976	36,527
Deraa	150	5,334	6,420	11,904
Homs	1,203	82,370	8	83,581
Hama	1,006	40,012	132	41,150
Latakia	823	862	—	1,685
Aleppo and Idlib	1,980	81,183	1,213	84,376
Deir-ez-Zor	3,232	5,838	109	9,179
Hassetche (Jezira)	5,495	320,213	2,625	328,333
Total	14,273	543,979	38,483	596,735

(b) Land Distributed or Prepared for Distribution to 15.1.61

Type	Villages (no.)	Families (no.)	Beneficiaries (no.)	Total area
Requisitioned land	135	6,676	35,839	135,675
State Domain	22	1,056	6,417	19,257
Total	157	7,732	42,256	154,932

(c) Supervised Co-operatives as at July 1960

Governorate	Societies	Villages	Area serviced (hectares)	Membership
Homs	12	13	72,571	1,434
Aleppo and Idlib	36	60	43,521	2,476
Hama	38	45	37,050	3,543
Damascus	9	13	11,224	901
Hassetche (Jezira)	6	14	6,517	568
Deraa	4	6	2,833	49
Latakia	5	7	1,559	453
Deir-ez-Zor	3	3	391	71
Total	113	161	175,666	9,495

(SOURCE: Ministry of Agrarian Reform, Damascus)

the reform was much more flexible than it appeared on paper.
In the first place, administration was decentralized. The general
execution of the law was the responsibility of the Ministry of

Agrarian Reform in Damascus, which issued requisitioning orders, took over the land requisitioned, and allotted credit to the provincial authorities. In the capital of each governorate (*mohafaza*) there was an Agrarian Reform Office, administered by a Director of Agrarian Reform, assisted by the Manager and Sub-Manager of Co-operatives, and several agricultural officers. Each office carried out the distribution of the land on the ex-propriated properties in the governorate and organized the co-operative societies. The Co-operative Manager, in consultation with the Board of each society, was responsible for undertaking schemes for agricultural or social investment. One agricultural officer was responsible for each society (or for a group of two or three) and lived in the village. The Co-operative Manager spent three or four days a week in visiting the societies, so that constant contact was kept between the Agrarian Reform Office and every village where reform was in progress. The farm im-provements introduced varied according to the agricultural con-ditions of the region, as will be seen from the examples given below. The functions of the supervised co-operatives ranged from relief (as in Homs and Damascus governorates) to all-round development (as in Latakia), and resettlement (in the Jezira).

Regional diversity was also taken into account by adjusting the size of holding granted to the productivity of the land. When a requisitioned estate was taken over, the soil was surveyed and graded by qualities (in Cairo) to determine its prospective yields, on the basis of which the area needed for a holding of sufficient size to support a family could be calculated. Holdings were then allocated to the claimants, in such a way as to provide the same minimum income per family member. When there is irrigation, the holding always included irrigated as well as rain-fed land. In regions of low productivity, large holdings were allotted, and conversely: e.g. in Aleppo governorate, where rainfall is low, 20 hectares of rain-fed land were granted, and in Idlib, with higher rainfall, only 10, while irrigated landholdings were 3–4 hectares in the Lower Orontes valley, and only 2–3 in the coastal strip of Latakia. However, the economic minimum standard was difficult to apply where the land was congested, since it left too many people unsatisfied. In Hama some of the holdings granted in the first year had proved to be too small. This region therefore had priority in resettlement. In Aleppo governorate, on the other hand, the rural population density is low, so that there is sufficient land to grant holdings of adequate size to all the former cultivators on the estates, or even to some families from other villages. Thus a logical consequence of granting holdings on the minimum income standard was to provide a demographic lens revealing labour surpluses and deficits. The vast areas expropriated in the Jezira were to be resettled in farm sizes suited to rainfall conditions, which in the north-east are favourable to more intensive cultivation and close settlement, while in the prairies large holdings would have been allocated.

On the economic side, the reform met with enormous obstacles to increased production: the wastage of land and water resources, which aggravates the natural instability of agriculture; and the maldistribution of farm population, which wastes labour in the old regions while the new remain short of manpower. These factors (as emphasized on pp. 106–7 above) were as important in depressing the rural living standard as the land tenure system; and reform could bring little benefit to the cultivators unless it could be combined with long-term policies for improving land use and resettling farm population. But such measures entail heavy public investment in irrigation and soil conservation, and also in transport and other services in the new regions. So long as private enterprise enjoyed its triumph in increasing production, the need for stabilization of agricultural production by such policies could be ignored. But the three years' drought showed how precarious was the rapid expansion of the area under grain, for it had brought the increase in production and exports to an abrupt end, and necessitated large grain imports.

The following table shows the effect of the drought on production. After the harvest failure of 1955, grain output recovered to a new high level in 1956, while in 1957 there was a record harvest of 2 million tons. This bumper year was followed by three consecutive harvest failures in 1958, 1959, and 1960, when grain output fell by half, almost to the level of the 1930's (see Table 9 on p. 72 above). Cotton production has doubled since 1950–4, and being dependent mainly on irrigation has declined comparatively little since 1957.

Economic disaster was therefore the first obstacle encoun-

TABLE 20

Syria: Area and Production of Main Crops

Area
(000 hectares)

	Average 1950–4	1955	1956	1957	1958	1959	1960*
Wheat	1,171	1,463	1,537	1,495	1,461	1,422	1,549
Barley	427	614	636	813	769	727	742
Total grain	1,598	2,077	2,173	2,308	2,230	2,149	2,291
Cotton	159	258	272	258	261	227	212

Production
(000 metric tons)

Wheat	815	438	1,051	1,354	562	632	553
Barley	410	137	463	721	228	218	157
Total grain	1,225	575	1,514	2,075	790	850	710
Cotton (ginned)	51	84	93	107	97	98	104

* Preliminary estimates.

(SOURCES: *Statistical Abstract of the Syrian Region, 1960*; FAO, *Production Yearbook*, and *Monthly Bulletin of Agricultural Statistics*.)

tered. In this respect, the initial situation was entirely different from that of Egypt, where the problem was to maintain and increase production on estates which were already intensively cultivated, with high and stable yields. In Syria the task was more complex, for reform of the structure had to be combined with both agricultural development and the resettlement of farmers, and provide the mechanism by which these policies were carried out.

Necessarily therefore the reform was a large credit operation, providing relief to the destitute farmers in the drought-stricken villages, and investing in farm improvement, irrigation, and rehousing in all regions. Funds were adequate for requirements. Financial resources available up to February 1961 totalled 48 million Syrian liras.[1] This total includes a grant of SL10 million from the Agricultural Credit Bank, at the date that the law was issued, for requisitioning and organization; a loan of SL30 million from the Central Bank of Syria, issued under special decree at the end of 1960, for the purpose of financing the co-operatives; and an allocation for 1960–1 of SL8 million for housing projects, in the Development Budget of 1960–1. Expenditure up to February 1961 totalled SL20 million. By contrast with Egypt, where the agrarian reform was self-financing from an early date, and where the supervised co-operatives are now accumulating profits for investment and social services, the agrararian reform in Syria was not likely to cover its costs for some time to come.

Because regional conditions vary, the only way to gain an impression of the results and prospects in 1961 is to survey briefly some of the villages where reform was in progress, from direct observations. The villages visited were chosen because they represent conditions typical of different rainfall zones and different land use systems.

Three villages on the rainfall margin presented a picture of near or complete destitution, because in these regions the effect of the drought had been most severe. Ghazlanieh (Damascus governorate) lies about 25 km. to the south of the capital. About 1,400 hectares of land had been distributed to 159 families, representing 915 people, or half the population of the village, in holdings averaging 1 hectare of irrigated and 8 hectares of rain-fed land. The grain harvest of 1960 was only 86 tons, and even less in 1958 and 1959. To meet this loss, livestock had been sold or slaughtered: what remained was in poor condition, owned by family groups. The ledger of the co-operative society showed only debit items in the accounts of each member, for seed, fertilizers, and diesel oil. But with funds provided by the Ministry, the co-operative had installed 80 wells and diesel pumps, each to serve the land of four families. It was also promoting the planting of fruit trees, through its own demonstration farm. A new village was being built, on an adjacent hill, complete with school, hospital, and mosque. Here, therefore, the reform had been accompanied by investment of funds on a scale

[1] The official parity rate was fixed in February 1961 at 10 Syrian liras to the £ sterling.

which private enterprise could not afford. The prospects for an increase in farm incomes were good, because underground water is available.

Hijaneh, not far distant, was in a much worse position. This village, like Ghazlanieh, was formerly the property of Hussein Ibish, who canalized the waters of the Wadi Awaj, irrigated large areas, and introduced tractor farming, granting owner-ship to a large proportion of the cultivators (pp. 95–6 above). But the Wadi has now dried up, leaving the land waterless and the villagers destitute. The total area expropriated on this pro-perty was 16,000 hectares, of which 2,500 hectares, the cultivable area, had been distributed to 239 families in 10-hectare holdings. The 1960 grain crop was only 39 tons. Pumps cannot be in-stalled, because the underground water is saline. This was a tragic situation, in which the co-operative could help only by supplying food and equipment for the 1961 harvest.

A third village, El Roda (Homs governorate), on the rainfall margin 30 km. to the east of Homs, was also living on relief. Four hundred hectares had been distributed to 37 families, in 10-hectare holdings. An interesting illustration of the difference in mentality between these poor tribesmen and the fellahin in Egypt was quoted by the co-operative manager, who had ad-vised the villagers to plant barley rather than wheat because it is more reliable in the low rainfall zones. They asked 'Is it an order?', and on learning that it was not, decided to plant wheat instead.

Clearly in these villages there could have been no gain in income through the redistribution of land, because there had so far been no income to redistribute. Prospects for future improve-ment were good in the first village, because the wells provide for new irrigation; in the other two, improvement depended entirely on rainfall. The reform had helped, in that the prospects for 1961 were better than in neighbouring villages where there had as yet been no distribution, since the members of the co-operatives were entitled by right to receive credits for seed and fertilizers. It was not surprising to learn that of the 13 supervised co-operatives then existing in the governorate of Homs, 6 were entirely dependent on credit, while 5, with some irrigated land, could meet running costs.

The contrast with irrigated farming was evident at Misrefe,

15 km. to the north of Homs. This large well-farmed property covered 4,300 hectares, of which 362 were irrigated for cotton. There had as yet been no allocation of holdings, and the co-operative had been formed before the land was distributed (a procedure which may have been fairly common, although it contravened the intentions of the law). Two agricultural officers lived on the property, which had been in part centrally farmed, in part let to tenant cultivators, who were stout and slow-moving, a proof of the benefits of stable farming. The area under irrigation was being extended by adding 50 new pumps to the 150 already installed.

In the governorate of Aleppo redistribution had proceeded rapidly. Here the agricultural potential lies chiefly in increasing livestock production, by introduction of fodder crops and improved breeds. To the east of Aleppo, rainfall is low, averaging 30 centimetres, but is normally sufficient for wheat cultivation. Prospects for higher farm incomes are favourable, because large holdings can be allocated and there is some scope for improving yields and increasing irrigation. The majority of the co-operatives in the governorate were able to cover running costs in 1961.

At Houmeyma, 30 km. to the east of Aleppo, reputedly 'the best village in Syria' (i.e. with the highest income among the agrarian reform villages), 62 families had received holdings averaging 21 hectares, including 3 hectares of irrigated land. Total areas redistributed were 1,030 hectares of rain-fed land, 270 hectares of winter-irrigated land, and 90 hectares of summer-irrigated land. Gross money income per farm family in 1960 averaged SL1,600 (£160), from the sale of the cotton crop only, as the wheat crop was too small to be marketed. Four new pumps had been added to the eleven already installed. The co-operative had a plot of 40 hectares as its 'home farm' for demonstration and profit, growing selected seeds, which were distributed to the members. Lucerne had been introduced—a major advance for soil fertility and fodder for the livestock. As there are good stone farm buildings, this farm became a breeding station for cattle and poultry. A herd of Friesians had been imported, stationed here and at Kitian, to produce milk and also breed cattle for distribution to other co-operatives in the region. All cultivation was by tractor, confiscated from the former owner. At the meeting of the co-operative board, demands for four trucks of stable manure for the cotton and repairs for the diesel pumps were stated in a more forthright manner than would be possible in Egypt. The farmers are recently settled tribesmen, living in a 'beehive village' typical of the region (i.e. with bubble-roofs), each house with its well-carpeted and locked guest room.

In the new governorate of Idlib, the co-operatives were generally able to cover running costs, because rainfall is high (50 cm. average) and there is much irrigated land on the Orontes. The Rouj valley irrigation scheme is complete, supplying 5,000 hectares of land, temporarily occupied, but intended for distribution in 1961 under the agrarian reform. Saadieh, in the hills to the north-west of Idlib, had suffered comparatively little from the drought, because rainfall had been sufficient to grow cotton on unirrigated land. An area of 324 hectares was about to be distributed to 27 families in holdings of 10 to 12 hectares. Apart from improved seeds and more fertilizers, there were no major changes in farming. The village was being rebuilt, beginning with the co-operative office. Prospects for income gains through redistribution were good. Exceptionally large income gains were reported in three irrigated villages, Hergamoos, Taloul, and Asrafia, on the Orontes, unfortunately inaccessible because the roads became impassable as the drought broke.

The most impressive results by far were seen in the coastal strip of Latakia. The mountainous region of this governorate presents an extraordinary picture of soil erosion, in the white subsoils and contorted landscape. The present rate of soil destruction is very rapid and 'threatens to reduce the cultivable land to a tremendous extent within the none too distant future',[1] so that there is urgent need for methods of conservation and stabilization of production. On the coastal strip, cultivation is not sufficiently intensive in relation to climatic conditions, for rainfall is high and irrigation water abundant. According to Dr van Liere, the FAO land reclamation expert, the prospects for citrus cultivation are 'unlimited'.

Farmers' incomes have already risen considerably as a result of the reform, since the landowner formerly took half the gross produce as rent, while the cultivator supplied livestock, labour,

[1] See FAO Mediterranean Development Project, *United Arab Republic, Syrian Region*, Annex to Ch. iv, p. 2.

and seed. Since output per hectare had been maintained, and costs had not risen, the redistribution of ownership had roughly doubled farmers' incomes. (Output per hectare in irrigated farming is about four times as high as on rain-fed land.) The prospects for future increases in income through better farming and soil conservation were also good.

Two villages showed both immediate and prospective income gains: Herisoun, situated in the delta between the Sinn and Surid rivers, which are being canalized to supply it with water, and Asrafia, supplied by a new canal from a small dam on the Sinn, recently completed. (A larger scheme on the Sinn is under construction.) By the use of water for summer irrigation, the cropped area will be doubled, an important change, as the cultivated areas are small. In the first village 324 hectares of irrigated land had been distributed to 138 families, and in the second 204 to 80 families. Both were undertaking afforestation, planting trees from the government nurseries, and both have community-developed projects. Asrafia has a new agricultural centre with two agricultural inspectors and a veterinary surgeon to serve other co-operatives in the district, and a nursery for citrus and other fruit for regional distribution. Herisoun consists at present of three small derelict hamlets: a new village was being rebuilt on a central site, which will include a hospital, school, and community centre. All five co-operatives in the governorate have set up primary schools, which also run evening classes for adults.

From the foregoing, it is apparent that the investments were adjusted to the type of improvement which is feasible in each region, with the general aim of stabilizing and diversifying agricultural production. One advantage of the structure was that it could adjust investment to different optimum scales. Individual farmers could not afford to install pumps, but within the co-operative pumps were provided to serve the needs of small groups. The tractors were used by the village as a unit, while the cattle-breeding stations located in one village could serve a large region. Irrigation and drainage schemes could be carried out in collaboration with the Ministry of Irrigation, to supply catchment areas.

It is also clear that the prospects for a rise in the rural living standard were good in the high rainfall regions, and precarious on the rainfall margin. Possibly these poor regions might be aided by resettlement.

Resettlement of farm population, the other major economic need, was undertaken in conjunction with the reform. Farmers from the congested Hama region were already being moved to the Jezira, where forty new villages were under construction. At the receiving end, the Ministry of Agrarian Reform organized land survey, undertook building, and supplied equipment, while the supervised co-operative provided security for the newcomers. Large-scale investment in roads and railways for these regions was projected under the Five Year Plan (1958–9 to 1963–4).

Another opportunity for resettlement from the Hama region lies in the adjacent Ghab valley (p. 79 above) where part of the area drained and reclaimed is now ready for resettlement, and was to be taken over by the Ministry of Agrarian Reform for this purpose in 1961.

The great long-term project for development and resettlement, intended to play a role in the economy of Syria comparable to that of the High Dam in Egypt, was the construction of a dam and power station near Raqqa on the Euphrates. This scheme is to irrigate 800,000 hectares (thus more than doubling the present irrigated area) and produce 600,000 kilowatts of power. Its total cost is estimated at £144 million (of which it is hoped that half will be covered by foreign loans), and it is expected to take ten years to complete. Although the Euphrates project was included in the original ten-year plan for Syria, drawn up in 1958, it seemed probable that lack of foreign capital would prevent its realization, since Soviet aid was requested and refused. Construction was not assured until June 1961, when the Federal Republic of Germany agreed to provide a loan of £45 million, available in instalments over seven years beginning in 1963. Whether this scheme will be implemented is now uncertain.

In the villages it was evident that large expenditure on social services and projects was being undertaken. In several places the village was being entirely rebuilt, af urther point of contrast with Egypt, where rehousing, though just as necessary, was not even contemplated until the supervised co-operatives began to accumulate profits. Probably the explanation is that in Syria it was important to provide an immediate increase in rural employment, particularly in the villages most affected by drought. But even where economic conditions are comparatively good, social investment is needed, because the villages are isolated and their inhabitants are peripheral. So the supervised co-operatives were all-round organizations, linking up all government services at the village level, through credit, technical aid, and social welfare. Such a general provision was not necessary under the Egyptian reform, because government services in irrigation and research were already highly developed; there was some provision of credit for co-operative societies, and some rural health service, however inadequate. But in Syria under the régime of free enterprise nothing was done. Thus giving the cultivator a new economic status meant equipping the villages with a new social framework, not through paper-born community development schemes, but by growth from the ground up.

Social Centres

In community development on the basis of rural social services a beginning had been made through the creation of social centres, resembling the combined centres in Egypt. A pilot social centre has been working at Nashabia (in 1961 moved to new buildings at Haran el-Awamid), and three other centres have been constructed in Suweida, at Charia in the Ghab valley (governorate of Hama), and in the governorate of Idlib. The intention then was to construct one in every governorate, though far more will be needed eventually. The services of these centres would have been most valuable in the southern governorates of Deraa and Suweida, where the reform had little scope. One problem for this type of organization is that villages in Syria are few and far between; consequently the staff of the Centres must go to the villagers, whereas in Egypt the villagers come to them.

Ordinary Agricultural Co-operatives

Owing to the predominance of large properties in land there were previously few agricultural co-operatives of the ordinary type. In 1957 there were only 53 societies with 2,278 members. A few, however, have been successful, through concentrating on specialized products, such as the fruit-growers' society at Daratieh, in the governorate of Homs. Since the union with Egypt, a Unified Co-operatives Law, resembling the Egyptian law of 1956, has been introduced in both regions of the republic, and these more favourable conditions in Syria have led to an increase in the number of societies to 117 (of which 93 are agricultural) with a total membership of 6,320.

Credit facilities for ordinary co-operative societies have been improved, through the revision of the statutes of the Agricultural Bank in 1958, by which the Bank was authorized to give priority to agricultural and other co-operatives in the supply of credit and to issue loans on crops. A Rural Credit Scheme, like that of Egypt, was introduced in 1959, to be applied in places not serviced by supervised co-operatives. But the exceptional demand for credit arising from the drought has so far been an obstacle to wide extension of the scheme, and in 1961 it was working only in the governorate of Idlib.

Whether the reform could have been an economic success in the near future depended on the unforeseeable factor of rainfall. But that the policies followed were in line with Syria's long-term economic necessities is quite certain. On the social side, its success was beyond doubt.

In 1955 it seemed unlikely that Syria's rural social problems could be solved through the mechanism of parliamentary democracy, and far more probable that the opposing political forces would be polarized on the side of the West and the East in a conflict which might destroy the country and bring no genuine reform. But the union with Egypt laid the foundation for a type of reform well suited to the conditions of the country.

Without the Union, no reform could have been durable. Egyptian experience had contributed confidence and agricultural expertise. Trained Syrian staff were not available for the agricultural advisory work of the co-operatives, because at present there is no university faculty in agriculture, though two are being instituted, in the universities of Damascus and Aleppo. Generally, the directors of the provincial Agrarian Reform

Offices were Syrian, while the co-operative managers were Egyptian; capable young men with degrees in agriculture, and trained in a special course on the organization of supervised co-operatives laid on by the Ministry of Agrarian Reform in Cairo. In Aleppo, however, the agricultural capital, and the governorate where reform had been most vigorous, the Director of Agrarian Reform was an Egyptian, with twenty years' practical experience in farming. The reform, in his view, had come 'only just in time'. The co-operative manager was a Jordanian, the accountants Syrians, working, as they rightly claimed, for Arab unity. Union was strength on the side of the have-nots.

Through the suspension of the reform, the interests of the fellahin of Syria have suffered a tragic setback. As things have turned out, it now seems that their needs would have been better served by a more rapid enforcement of the law, with less emphasis on the organization of farm improvements. But that the reform came to an end was not due to any mistakes in its principles or administration. It was defeated because it was more in line with the long-term social and economic needs of the country than with the aims of the opposed political forces: too radical for the landowners (as any reform would have been), too moderate and empirical for the Arab Socialists (now again divided among themselves), it encountered hostility from both sides. At the time of writing it seems certain that the expropriation of the estates which were not yet distributed will be rescinded, and that there will be no further redistribution; the most that can be hoped is that the farmers who had already received land will succeed in retaining it.[1]

---

[1] On 18 February 1962 the Constituent Assembly approved a bill amending the agrarian reform law by raising the maximum holding from 80 to 200 hectares for irrigated land and from 300 to 600 hectares for rainfed land. Within these limits landowners can select the land they wish to retain, cleared of landholders who have acquired ownership under the law of 1958 (*The Times*, 19 February 1962).

BIBLIOGRAPHY

Addams, Doris G. 'Current Population Trends in Iraq', *Middle East Journal*, Spring 1956.

Ayrout, H. C. *Fellahs d'Égypte*. 6th ed. Cairo, Éditions du Sphynx, 1952.

Bulos, Nassib. *Legal Aspects of Land Tenure in Jordan and Syria*. Beirut, UNRWA, 1953.

Burns, Norman. 'The Dujailah Land Settlement', *Middle East Journal*, Summer 1951.

Critchley, A. Michael. 'The Health of the Industrial Worker in Iraq', reprinted from *British Journal of Industrial Medicine*, vol. 12, 1955.

Egypt, Higher Committee for Agrarian Reform. *Replies to the United Nations Questionnaires relating to Egyptian Agrarian Reform Measures*. Cairo, 1955.

—— Permanent Council of Public Services, Economics Sub-Committee of the National Population Commission. *The Population Problem in Egypt*. Cairo, 1955.

Egyptian-American Rural Improvement Service. *Land Reclamation and Resettlement*. March 1955 (pamphlet).

Darling, Sir Malcolm. 'Land Reform in Italy and Egypt', *Year Book of Agricultural Co-operation*, 1956.

Dowson, Sir Ernest. *An Inquiry into Land Tenure and Related Questions; Proposals for the Initiation of Reform*. Letchworth, for Iraq Government, 1932.

Ghonemy, Mohamed Riad. *Resource Use and Income in Egyptian Agriculture before and after Land Reform, with particular reference to Economic Development*. N. Carolina State College, unpublished D. Phil. thesis, 1953.

Haider, Salih. *Land Problems of Iraq*. London University unpublished Ph.D. thesis, 1942.

Hakim, George. 'Land Tenure Reform', *Middle East Economic Papers*, 1954 (published by the Economic Research Institute, American University of Beirut).

Hassan, Mohammed Ali. 'Miri Sirf Land Development in Iraq', *International Social Science Bulletin*, vol. 5, no. 4, 1953.

—— *Land Reclamation and Settlement in Iraq*. Baghdad, 1955.

International Bank for Reconstruction and Development. *The Economic Development of Iraq*. Baltimore, Johns Hopkins Press, 1952.

—— *The Economic Development of Syria*. Baltimore, Johns Hopkins Press, 1955.

BIBLIOGRAPHY

Iraq, Directorate-General of Agriculture, Soils and Agricultural Chemistry. *Report of the Soil Survey and Soil Classification, Dujaila Project, August 1955,* by Burnell West, Soil Technologist, Food and Agriculture Organization. Baghdad, 1955.

—— Irrigation Development Commission (President F. F. Haigh). *Report on the Control of the Rivers of Iraq and the Utilization of their Waters.* Baghdad, 1951.

—— Principal Bureau of Statistics. *Report on the Agricultural and Livestock Census of Iraq,* 1952–3. Vol. 1. Baghdad, 1954.

Iversen, Carl. *Monetary Policy in Iraq.* Baghdad, National Bank of Iraq, 1954.

Khayyat, Jafar. *The Iraqi Village; a Study in its Condition and Reform.* Beirut, 1950 (in Arabic).

Knappen-Tippetts-Abbett-McCarthy Engineers. *Report on the Development of the Tigris and Euphrates River Systems.* New York and Baghdad, Iraq Development Board, 1954; mimeo.

Lewis, Norman. 'The Frontier of Settlement in Syria, 1800–1950', *International Affairs,* January 1955.

Marei, Sayed. *Two Years of Agrarian Reform.* Cairo, Higher Committee for Agrarian Reform, 1954.

Nahi, S. A. *An Introduction to Feudalism and the Land System in Iraq.* Baghdad, 1955 (in Arabic).

Salim, S. M. *Marsh Dwellers of the Euphrates Delta.* London, Athlone Press, 1962.

Salter, J. A., 1st Baron. *The Development of Iraq; a Plan of Action.* London, Caxton, for Iraq Development Board, 1955.

Stewart, Desmond and John Haylock. *New Babylon.* London, Collins, 1956.

UN, Dept. of Economic and Social Affairs. *Economic Developments in the Middle East, 1945 to 1954.* New York, 1955. (Supplement to World Economic Report, 1943–4.)

—— ———— *1954 to 1955.* New York, 1956.

—— Dept. of Economic Affairs. *Progress in Land Reform; Analysis of Replies by Governments to a United Nations Questionnaire.* New York, 1954.

Walston, H. D. *Land Tenure in the Fertile Crescent.* Unpublished, 1954.

Warriner, Doreen. *Land and Poverty in the Middle East.* London, RIIA, 1948.

Weulersse, Jacques. *Paysans de Syrie et du Proche Orient.* Paris, Gallimard, 1946. (*Le Paysan et la Terre.*)

ADDENDUM

FAO Mediterranean Development Project. *U.A.R. Syrian Region, Country Report.* Rome, 1959.

Marei, Sayed. *U.A.R. Agriculture Enters a New Age.* Cairo, 1960.

BIBLIOGRAPHY

UAR. *Information and Statistics relating to Agrarian Reform in the Southern Region.* Cairo, 1960.

U.N. *Land Reform and Community Development in the United Arab Republic.* New York, 1962.

INDEX

INDEX

Jebel Druze, 55, 81 ff., 98, 216, 227; land development in, 94–5
Jezira province: dust bowl danger, 63, 77; expropriation in, 216–17; grain yield, 57, 90; land development, 57, 71, 74–9, 81, 84–93, 94, 107; land survey and registration, 98 f.; merchant-tractorists, 89–93, 111; rents, 85–6, 106; resettlement in, 219, 226; size of holdings, 56, 82 f., 102, 104, 106
Johnson, V. Webster, 4
Jumblatt, Kemal, 62
Juwaideh, Albertine, 144 n.

Kaliuba province, 29
Kamishli, 85 ff., 91 f., 104
Kassem, Ahmed, 80
Kaysouma, 90
Kena province, 29, 45
Kerbela province, 141
Khabur irrigation system, 79, 86, 90; river, 72, 86, 90, 91
Khaldun, Ibn, 56, 61
Khayyat, Jafar, 141
Kirkuk province, 118, 138 n., 141; town, 125, 132, 170
Knappen, Tippetts, Abbett & McCarthy, 120, 130
Kom-Ombo: company, 193 n.; Nubian resettlement project, 201
Kufri district, 138 n.
Kurds: landowners, 62, 139; population in Jezira, 87; villages, 132; women, 86
Kut barrage, 114, 117, 120, 137, 172; province, 132, 140 ff.
Kuwaik river irrigation system, 79
Kuwait, 131 n., 189

Land reform, 2; American conception of, 4–6, 8; definitions, 3–5; and development, 2–3; and experts, 9; 'integrated approach', 8–9, 169; in relation to Power conflicts, 184–7; see also under Egypt, Iraq, and Syria
Latafiya settlement, 161, 170 f., 176–7
Latakia port, 81 n.; province, 72, 79, 82 f.;—land reform in, 224–5
Lazma land tenure, 147–50
Lebanon, 55, 62, 81 n., 108; socialist party in, 62
Lewis, Prof. J. A., 11 n., 113
Lewis, Norman, 57, 76
Liberation canal, 53; province, see Tahrir province
Little, I. D., 131

Mabrouka settlement, 91–2
Mahir, Ali, 12 f.
Makhmur settlement, 160 f., 170
Mamarbachi Brothers, 90
Mamarbachi, Pierre, 90–1
Mansura, 26
Marei, Sayed, 34, 196, 203
Matruka land, 66 f., 100
Mawat (mubah) land, 66 f., 100 ff.
Mexico, land reform, 3, 9, 177
Mezerib irrigation scheme, 79
Minia province, 41, 44
Minshat Sultan, 206
Minufia province, 202, 206
Miri (state) land, 66–70, 100; Miri Sirf law (1940), 147; (1945), see Dujaila law; (1951), 157–61; Miri Sirf Land Development Committee, 156, 161, 164, 171; see also Iraq: State land; Syria: State land
Misrefe, 222–3
Mosul province, 116 n., 118, 138–9, 141, 160, 184; town, 56, 124, 161, 172, 178, 182
Mulk land, 66 f., 100
Muntafik laws, 154, 155–6; province, 140 ff., 145, 150
Musseyeb river scheme, 160 f.

Nahi, Dr S. A., 133
Najjar, Elie, 92
Najjar family, 107; see also Asfar and Najjar Brothers
Nasser, Gamal Abdel, 10, 23 n., 197, 203, 209–10
Nawag, 205–6
Near East Foundation, 95
Nile Delta, 10, 15, 44 f., 49, 53; river, 11, 16, 19 f., 22 f., 46, 48 f., 113
Nomads and cultivators, struggle between, 56, 75–6, 86 ff.
Nuri Said, 88 n.

Oil, 188–90; see also Iraq; Iraq Petroleum Co.
Orontes river, 72, 79, 93, 96, 224
Ottoman Crown Estates, 98, 144
Ottoman Empire: and agriculture, 75, 116; land system, landownership, 58, 66–8, 75, 135–6, 148, 155
Ottoman Land Code, 61–2, 66–70, 97, 101, 138, 143

Palestine, 58
Point Four, see under United States
Poverty, abolition of, 187, 189–90

INDEX

PRINTED IN GREAT BRITAIN
AT THE BROADWATER PRESS, WELWYN GARDEN CITY
HERTFORDSHIRE